HERB GARDENING

*

EATING YOUR WAY TO HEALTH

by Ruth Bircher
edited and translated by
Claire Loewenfeld

HERB GARDENING

Why and How
to
Grow Herbs

CLAIRE LOEWENFELD
Founder of Chiltern Herb Farms

Illustrated by John Gay

FABER AND FABER
3 Queen Square
London

First published in 1964
by Faber and Faber Limited
3 Queen Square London WC1
First published in this edition 1970
Reprinted 1971 and 1973
Printed in Great Britain by
Whitstable Litho Straker Brothers Ltd

ISBN 0 571 09475 9 (Faber Paper Covered Editions)
ISBN 0 571 06024 2 (hard bound edition)

CONTENTS

Contents

Contents

ILLUSTRATIONS

(Between pages 128–9)

Photographs by JOHN GAY

FOREWORD

The growing of herbs was once common practice in English gardening. There were herb gardens from the time of the early monasteries, when herbs were used for treatment in the monastic hospitals, and down through the ages in manor and cottage gardens until about one hundred years ago. Since then, however, the tradition, experience and memory of it all have been lost, partly because herbs were no longer used in daily life and partly because the practice of growing one's own food and flavourings decreased.

Gardens became smaller and were used for recreation rather than for supplies. There were only four herbs about which people knew—parsley, mint, sage and thyme, and even these herbs were often overlooked in favour of substitutes.

All this has changed recently. There is at present a much greater interest in herb gardening as well as in using herbs. So many foods have lost flavour during producing and processing. There is therefore, a growing tendency to use natural flavourings more than ever before and thus the herb garden or the herb corner has become much more important. There is no reason why the present-day smaller garden should not contain many more herbs than it usually does. Herbs make such modest claims on soil and space as well as on the time of the gardener.

However, with the lost tradition, experience in growing and in using herbs has diminished and this book aims to fill that gap. It has, in fact, been written in answer to the many questions we have been asked. We ourselves grow healthy crops of aromatic herbs at Chiltern Herb Farms on a southern slope of one of the highest ridges, and all our visitors who question us about growing methods are equally interested in information on *how to use the herbs* which they have in

Foreword

their gardens. Here follow the answers all based on my own experience, won during years of growing herbs in my own garden, as well as on a large scale. I have also taken into account reports on herbs grown in other countries.

Here I should like to express my thanks for the help I have received from Philippa Back and Eric Reid, Manager of Chiltern Herb Farms. Philippa Back was not only my co-lecturer, but has also lectured on herbs on her own, often answering similar questions to those dealt with in the book. Her untiring assistance in the preparation of this book has been a valuable contribution for which I am very grateful.

Mr. Reid has practical experience of many years' standing in growing herbs organically in our exposed conditions. This has enabled him to check the sections on growing from an experienced herb gardener's point of view. I should like to thank him for his careful and rewarding work.

The book is meant for the herb gardener—as its title implies—but I trust that it will be of equal value to everyone else interested in herbs. From the garden lover to the gourmet, everyone, I hope, will be encouraged to grow herbs more efficiently and use them more imaginatively.

Claire Loewenfeld

Buckland Common,
Near Tring, Herts.

PART I

About Herbs in General

1

WHY HERBS?

The increased use of herbs during recent years is more than just a quaint revival of Elizabethan customs. It cannot be explained by the special interest which garden lovers take in the beauty, scent and flavour of herbs—even the gourmets who want to have herbs for exquisite flavouring cannot be the only ones concerned in this restoration to favour of herbs that had been so long neglected. The most acceptable explanation can perhaps be found in the loss of natural quality and flavour of food in general, caused by industrial preprocessing and prepacking. Important substances are lost and food has become dull. The broiler chicken, the battery hens' eggs, the hormone-fed meat, the frozen vegetables, fish and meat need some extra help if they are to be palatable; without such assistance, people are bound to tire of them in the long run.

All this was first observed in America where mechanization, and the accompanying temptation to use more additives, had an earlier start. It soon became noticeable that salt and pepper alone were unable to make dishes attractive enough. And as it is not everyone's choice to flavour food with strong spices all the time, people turned to the natural flavours of culinary herbs, the old stand-by of French cuisine and, in fact, of all the continental countries and the East. Thus from the extreme West, in fact from California, came new ways of growing, drying and using herbs, while the Continent and the East provided the tradition and the recipes.

The new need was quickly understood in this country and resulted in the growing of herbs for drying in a new way, so that they retain their green colour and flavour and are incomparably better than the old dusty, grey, imported herbs and powders. Precious condensed substances in the herbs offered to us by nature were often lost by careless handling and wrong storage, and many a dish was spoilt. With the help of the new green-dried herbs the cook does not have to rely on the short season of fresh herbs, but can use them all the year round, without missing their flavour and fragrance during winter. Thus it is for the first time really worth while growing herbs. Recipes and menus can be tried out with new herbs; and once they are enjoyed, they can be continued throughout the whole year. Herbs can now be dried so that they retain their value or, if this is too difficult to carry out at home, they can be bought well dried and well packed.

English mint and lavender have always been world renowned; this is partly due to the humidity in the air and partly due to the long hours of daylight during summer in this country, which allow plants to grow into better specimens and at the same time produce more volatile oil, and therefore more fragrance and aroma. The daylight is responsible for this, rather than the sun; sun is rarely needed for the growing of leaves and herbs, and therefore this country scores.

The increasing interference with natural food substances through artificial aids to cultivation, industrialization and mechanization in preserving is not only taking out valuable nutrients and adding harmful substances; it is also diminishing flavour to quite an unexpected degree. Herbs will help to restore some of the value and certainly add a great deal of flavour and enjoyment to our daily menu. The general interest in herbs—I mean that gourmets are not the only ones to seek them out—shows that people are becoming more and more aware of this need.

The development has also been speeded up by new interest in foreign ways of cooking, stimulated by much-increased foreign travel and the many new cookery books in bookshops concentrating on foreign dishes, often suggesting use of many herbs. The traditional herb use on the Continent has mingled with the traditions of America. According to the geographical origin of the recipes and suggestions, they are sometimes based on Spanish, Italian, sometimes on German, Dutch, Hungarian and Russian traditions. Many of the American suggestions, culinary as well as medicinal, were acquired by early pioneers who had to deal with lack of food and illnesses in lonely places and fell back on the experience of their homelands or sometimes adopted the Indian lore and practice.

In this country the culinary notions which came from the Romans via the monasteries to the still-rooms of Elizabethan times, and down the years to us, can be compared with many of the continental ideas, but became gradually less and less current, because of the early Industrial Revolution in this country which encouraged synthesizing many natural products and flavourings because of the early start gained by mechanization in preserving. Only now the wish for natural flavourings is coming back and is connected with the disadvantages which have meanwhile been experienced with processed food, and the hazards which have sprung up as a result of chemical methods.

The extent to which a packeted soup can be improved by the addition of some herbs and a little cream is difficult to believe, and frozen packed vegetables are more enjoyable, if mint, for instance, is added to peas or summer savory to frozen beans. There are an infinite number of recipes which benefit by various herbs and from bouquets of selected herbs which have been so finely adjusted from various herbs and to the type of dish that it will make all the difference. We all know that fennel improves many fish dishes, that basil goes well with tomatoes, but this is only a beginning.

It is not only the palate which benefits from the use of herbs—there is above all a benefit to health. There are specific substances in herbs which, if taken daily, add greatly to healthy functioning of the body; for instance mineral salts, volatile oils or the bitter principles. The herb is still a mysterious concentrated plant which invites a certain amount of guess-work. It does though seem reasonable that this little medicine chest of active substances should be used whole, rather than be analysed as to its chemical parts, taken to pieces, extracted or synthesized. Important principles, and also the value of the interaction of the various principles, may be lost otherwise. Little research has been done as yet, which is perhaps just as well; it may be better in this case to leave nature alone.

In other countries more research has been put into the active principles which are to some extent responsible for certain of the experienced results. Here follow some descriptions of the substances and their effects; further research will throw more light on these mysterious happenings and interactions.

Why Herbs?

The Volatile Oils The most important constituents of herbs are volatile oils. They are elusive, but on the other hand they are responsible for the scent of herbs and have many-sided effects on the increased production of mucus, bile and other important secretions. They help to increase the blood circulation in the skin, help with the elimination of water, and therefore have an effect on the kidneys; they increase perspiration and increase the white blood corpuscles: such effects are often responsible for the herb's healing properties. They also have a quality which is bactericidal and disinfectant. They are the substances most easily lost and all the precautions suggested in the chapter on preserving herbs (p. 44) are dictated by the need for preserving these elusive, but most important substances.

The Mineral Salts A number of salts contained in the herbs, among which are potassium and calcium, are of special importance for the body. Potassium has a diuretic effect and calcium is important for the building up of bones, for a well-ordered functioning of the nervous system, and for increasing resistance to infection. Silicic acid, one of the minerals, can be found in many plants, but there are some, such as horsetail, which are particularly rich in it. Silicic acid has been found to strengthen the tissue, and particularly that of the lungs, and has at times added to resistance to disease. It has also been reported to have an excellent influence on inflammation of gums, the mouth, or the skin in general. Organic acids such as malic acid, citrus acid, oxalic acid, can also be found in herbs. They are, of course in larger concentration, available in fruit or vegetables; their main effect is laxative.

Mucilage Mucilage found in plants has the quality of dissolving in water and producing a slimy mass which is mainly laxative. The intestines, for instance, retain the water, and the mucilage contained in the food allows the content to be moved; in fact it lubricates the intestines. It also has a protective effect on mucous membranes and the surface of wounds, so that inflamed parts can heal safely under the protection of mucilage. Herbs containing mucilage are therefore useful in the case of inflammation of the mouth, nose, throat and intestinal tract. The surprising effect of *Verbascum* may be explained by

18

the content of mucilage in the flowers, but there must be more to it, because the healing power in the case of bronchial coughs is also connected with the colouring substances.

Glycosides They are substances consisting of one part which is sugar and one part which is without sugar. Some of the glycosides which are not yet fully known cause the febrifuge effect of lime flower and the anti-inflammatory effect of chamomile. These flowers should never be boiled for any length of time because the glycosides are damaged during cooking.

Saponines They are also Glycosides—they lather slightly in water and are therefore used for washing; their name comes from the Latin name *sapo*, soap. Only small quantities can be absorbed in the digestive tract. They have a cleaning diuretic and expectorant influence and are contained in many plants.

Bitter Principles They are not a simple chemical group because they consist of alkaloids, glycosides, tannins and so on. Their common quality is that they taste bitter. They improve the secretion of mucus in the mouth and the juices of the stomach. They are also said to be able to increase the number of red and white corpuscles and are supposed to help the circulation; also with digestive troubles, with the function of the liver, spleen, and difficulties of the secretions. They are also helpful in cramp and cholic.

Tannins The tannins have a wide effect on many parts of mucous membrane by exerting a certain influence on the tissues. They are also antibiotic; they have an effect on the inflammation of intestines and of all organs lined with mucous membrane.

These are short explanations of some of the functions of the many active principles contained in herbs. They may not in this country be scientifically proved, but modern research in other countries has taken them up, worked on them, and provided these explanations. Even if they are not yet the full explanations, they are at least an attempt to throw some light on the mysterious constituents of the herb and provide some explanation of the principles on which their great value is based.

Why Herbs?

Until we know more, we can all experiment with the beneficent herbs, and I think that no one will be less than satisfied with the results, or anything but thankful for the rewards of growing herbs at home.

2

USING HERBS

The traditions of using herbs have been passed on from one civilization to another, from one generation to another. That which was done by the Indians—with whom many of the present-day culinary herbs originated—by the Egyptians, the Greeks and, above all, the Romans, has been repeated throughout the centuries. There is one uninterrupted line of uses, which shows hardly any break. Some of the herb traditions in this country go back to the Druids, but most of them were reintroduced by the monasteries after the Dark Ages had destroyed the traditions established by the Romans, who planted and developed them for their occupation army in this country. They knew enough about the value of herbs to claim that their armies needed no doctors if they had sufficient herbs. The monks then developed a high degree of skill in dealing with the vines and herbs, and while the wine tradition has been preserved and developed, the herb tradition was lost. The qualities in both flavour and aroma which have to be preserved in exactly the same way in glass bottles, in the case of herbs were lost by careless handling and wrong storage.

Yet the tradition as a whole has been retained, and it should not be too difficult to find the thin red line running through centuries of herb tradition, and to discard those suggestions which originated in unfounded belief. The empirical knowledge of the past has been mingled with superstitions, belief in magic, folk-lore and astrology. This is the reason for finding in old, as well as more modern herb books, so many (often contradictory) suggestions for using a herb, that it is practically impossible either to use them all or even to make a choice. Only by comparing the repeated suggestions of many different countries one with another, using a great deal of experience, is it possible to rescue those practical suggestions proved to be helpful, and disentangle them from suggestions which are caused by deviations. This book attempts to do just this.

Herbs in Food Most important is, of course, the use of culinary herbs for food; nature wisely provided us with a palate and put enjoyment of food before digestion and absorption, for they depend on it. The absorption of food is, in fact, closely connected with its enjoyment. Pre-digestion starts in the mouth and the flow of saliva is caused by sensory enjoyment: the taste and smell of culinary herbs obviously help, and the green colour and sometimes the lovely shape appeal to our eyes and therefore also play an important part. Well-prepared, nicely arranged food full of fragrance helps the action of digestive work inside the body. The powers latent in the senses will have to be considered seriously; they can be dangerous foes or mighty allies in the business of first enjoying, and then absorbing healthy food.

Herbs and Pepper Culinary herbs have additional important uses; for instance they can replace certain spices or condiments, beloved and needed by some people, but often not good for them or not allowed to them. For instance, basil, summer savory, thyme, marjoram and nasturtium can help to replace pepper, difficult for people with certain digestive troubles; e.g. ulcers, and the lining of the digestive tract, are often affected by too much use of pepper. Most hot spices have their disadvantages, and after years of usage there eventually comes a time when the body gets on better without them and benefits by the use of herbs instead.

Herbs and Salt The clever use of herbs can also help to reduce intake of, or even replace salt. Surplus weight, often caused by the retention of fluids in the tissue, is sometimes put down to taking too much salt; also for heart and kidneys salt can be troublesome; and therefore a saltless diet with the use of many herbs is of great assistance. There are certain herbs, such as lovage, celery, summer savory, thyme and marjoram, which, in the right combinations, can replace salt almost completely or help to reduce salt intake.

Herbs and Sugar It has recently been found that sweet cicely, lemon balm and angelica are three herbs able to reduce the use of sugar in cooking and in sweets. They will lessen the amount of sugar needed with tart fruit and sweets, such as fruit pies or flans made of rhubarb, gooseberry, red currant, black currant, plums and tart apples. All these will benefit from the flavour of the herbs, which takes away the tartness and will make it possible to use less sugar—sometimes up to half the quantity. White sugar has been held responsible for a number of difficulties; it is considered to be a calcium robber and upsets the calcium balance in the body; it is bad for the teeth of children, for the diabetic or near-diabetic, and is certainly feared by the figure-watchers.

Herbs for Lemon Juice versus Vinegar The more subtle flavour of herbs is usually overpowered when used together with malt vinegar which blunts the palate and makes it insensitive to the more delicate flavours of herbs; lemon juice is infinitely preferable for a number of reasons, and it is a condiment highly appreciated by some people as salad dressing, or as a preserving addition to food. It is, therefore, a great pity that the flavour of herbs is so much weakened if they are used in connection with vinegar. Also, connoisseurs of wine do not like food cooked or dressed with vinegar while serving good wine at the table, as vinegar spoils the palate for the appreciation of wine, and the same applies to most foods when vinegar is used in the cooking.

Moreover, vinegar can become a habit-forming food. The more it is used the more it is wanted, as the flavour has to be increased as time goes on for the blunted palate to note or enjoy it. People, in fact whole families, have been known to take it with everything, even with a boiled egg, or constantly need pickles for the sake of the vinegar they crave.

Though wine vinegar is far less a culprit, lemon juice is far better, more subtle and healthier, and combines well with herbs in all dressings and in cooking; it often enhances the herbs—as, for instance, in herb butter.

Herbs for Teas The culinary traditions are difficult to keep separated from some of the medicinal suggestions, because many old culinary traditions such as using dill or fennel with oily fish, or mugwort with fat meat or poultry, makes it difficult to sort out whether they have been originally based on the help they offer to digestion or on the flavour which is by now associated with these dishes in many countries.

The herb teas or tisanes can be of immense help in daily life if they are well grown and dried, that is if their original aroma and colour is retained and they are, therefore, tempting enough. Instead of using lots of little pills and drugs, these teas could become once more what they have been in the past and what they are still in a number of countries today; as strong competitors to coffee or tea they can make us feel more relaxed and less tired and can be used as 'pick-me-ups', as in the case of peppermint; or as a relaxing, comforting drink. The lovely scent and flavour of melissa tea will not only relax and give a comfortable feeling when drunk in the morning and evening, but make a tired brainworker feel fresh without causing the over-stimulation and consequent tiredness which may easily follow coffee. Peppermint will also settle the liver and gall-bladder and still the slight discomfort after too large a meal. Chamomile will settle an upset stomach and also soothe an upset digestion. The honey-scented lime flower will allow a good rest and is a pleasant alternative to an aspirin for a chill just started. The muscatel flavour of elder flower will do the same or will provide a summer drink for children. There are many more of these teas which are not supposed to be used as herbal treatment, but as healthy and helpful additions to the daily diet. Altogether herbs provide many more uses for minor ailments or temporary discomfort, even for exhilaration with or without alcohol. There is, in fact, help and comfort for many situations in life in herbs, many of them clearly described with each herb or found in the Chart for Using Herbs, p. 235.

Herbs in Potpourri There are still more uses for the herbs, the cosmetic ones above all, which are also mentioned with the herb and on the Chart, but there is a pleasure waiting for the herb gardener in making a potpourri for the winter which will perfume and freshen the air in his living-room. There are many different ways of making potpourri. If there is any drying accommodation to be arranged for the herbs anyway, it is great fun to use some of the dried herbs for potpourri and dry carefully some flower petals from the garden to go with them. Flower petals must be dried slowly at a low temperature, otherwise all the drying suggestions on p. 44 are applicable. Here, of course, it is of great importance to retain the full colour and scent. Nowadays, flowers often have less scent than the old-fashioned ones used to have, and in this case it is important to rely on herbs, dried orange peel and a few spices to make the potpourri really scented.

The dry method of making potpourri seems by far the best; no salts or fixatives are suggested. Flowers and herbs should be dried in the suggested way, lemon and orange peel and spices crushed or ground, and these ingredients placed in layers into a bowl with a well-fitting lid. A glass or perspex bowl makes it possible to have the full enjoyment of the colours, but it is advisable to put such a bowl into a dark cupboard while it is not in use. It is best to open the lid and let the scent permeate a room, while it is being used; when going to bed or leaving the room it is best to close the lid well and to put the potpourri in a dark cupboard. This potpourri is certainly one of the most enjoyable memories of the summer herb garden. Bay leaves, angelica leaves, rosemary, tarragon, chamomile, lime flowers, lemon thyme, lemon verbena, eau-de-Cologne mint, verbascum flowers, elder flowers, in fact all leaves or flowers, the colour and scent of which can be retained as much as possible, are best for such a potpourri.

After knowing why to grow and how to use the herbs, the herb gardener can set about making his herb garden or start thinking of an indoor herb garden or a window-box.

3

MAKING A HERB GARDEN

There is no special skill needed to be a herb gardener—in fact anyone interested in herbs, whether from the gourmet or general gardening point of view—can grow herbs well. They are easy to accommodate, easy to grow, and the detailed instructions given in this book can make all the difference between success and failure due to unknown circumstances.

It is best to start with a few herbs for which one really has a constant use, than to plan a herb garden which suffers from too much enthusiasm. Experience has also shown that the fewer suggestions are made as to the position and the layout of the herb garden the better, because only experience will teach what is the best for each household and for the needs of each herb gardener, which may vary and—above all—increase with experience. There is, however, one basic law which must be followed, and that is that the herbs must be prevented from wandering, encroaching and straggling all over the herb garden; a decision has to be made also as to how many perennials and how many annuals are going to be grown. Sometimes annuals can fill the gaps left by young perennials until these have become larger. Sometimes they are better sown in rows away from the perennial herbs. Then the perennials can be treated like a border or a square herb garden. The annual herbs, sown in rows, finish by autumn, and a new decision can be made as to which to start, and where, when spring returns.

As many of the culinary herbs in the herb garden may need to be near the kitchen, it is advisable to start it near the kitchen and in an accessible place. Therefore, stone, brick or gravel paths should lead to it and stone divisions between the herbs are also helpful. For the beginner a small herb border of about 10 ft. × 4 ft. is adequate. This could be backed by a wall or hedge or a fence with a path in front. Mint is better in a border by itself as it spreads so much; and it is important, wherever it is grown, to have slate or wooden divisions to make quite sure that it is not going to encroach on all other plants. If the border faces south and slightly slopes it is all the better. Beds facing north should be avoided if possible. The low-growing herbs should be in front, as with every border.

It is probably best to start with some of the eighteen most well-known herbs for which more details are given, and only after having mastered these should the still very interesting and useful but less commonly known herbs be started. Also, many enlivening drinks and soothing teas can be added later.

It makes things simpler, as already said, if only perennials are grown in a large bed. Useful edging herbs are chives, thymes, sage, marjoram, parsley (if it is sufficiently looked after) and hyssop. Hedge plants are lavender, hyssop and rosemary. The annuals must not be forgotten, unless they are found to make too much work, but chervil and summer savory are very useful and marigold, borage and nasturtium are lovely plants to enliven the herb garden, or even as simple rows. A well-planned herb garden will show a great deal of colour for a considerable part of the year.

To progress from the small border and the annual row to a really elaborately planned herb garden needs experience that cannot be found in books, but has to be lived. However, even with very little experience and a good basic plan (a square with two diagonal stone paths meeting at a round stone circle in the centre) a frame is provided into which one or two plants of each variety are set, filling the four divisions. It is the basic idea of the cloister of a monastery, and if surrounded either by parts of a building or by a boundary rows of tall plants, such as angelica or rosemary, with bay trees at certain key positions, it will become naturally attractive and show the herbs to their best advantage. Herbs which are likely to become very tall should be placed at the back and those which are likely to remain low towards the front along the paths. Some of the small creeping herbs, e.g. thyme or lemon thyme can be set into the stones forming the centre, particularly if it is made of crazy paving.

Shelter from wind can be most beneficial for the herb garden.

Making a Herb Garden

Many of the taller herbs need it badly; and the scented air in a sheltered enclosure, the darting of bees and butterflies busy working on the flowers, complete this rural and idyllic picture. Though for some herbs this sheltered life is the only one—those which show traces of their Mediterranean origin, such as basil, rosemary, etc.—the author has noticed that with some of the herbs grown on exposed ridges of the Chilterns the adverse conditions to which they are exposed seem to provide more volatile oils, in fact, more aroma and scent, particularly with herbs grown on a southern slope.

At certain times of the year the herb garden will be a scented garden, and blind visitors are often welcomed to a really well-stocked herb garden.

Herb planting in multiples, concrete blocks and units, which come in a variety of sizes and shapes, offer an inexpensive way of creating a raised bed for small herb gardens. They allow good drainage, keep plants neatly separated and make it easy to organize diverse plants into a design. Garden and lemon thyme, marjoram, rosemary and sage in dry sunny spots, and peppermint, spearmint, parsley, tarragon and chives in moist shade, create a miniature formal herb garden within an existing bed and provide suitable, but varying, positions.

The soil for the herb garden needs a certain amount of preparation, though most herbs will grow on any soil; but if one wants to succeed from the beginning, it is best to start with certain preparations. Drainage is most important, for very many herbs do not like to stand in stagnant water or have 'wet feet'. If necessary the ground should be drained by pipes or by a layer of clinkers; the soil should be well prepared, and if lime is required, it should be applied after digging or rotovating. This should, if possible, be done not later than September or October so that the summer warmth in the soil is still sufficient to assist in the quick decomposition of turned-in material. It should be allowed to stand there all winter, if possible, and in the spring a light application of compost or rotted manure should be dug or rotovated into the surface of the soil, not deeper than four inches.

Following summer hoeing, the area occupied by perennial plants should be pricked over during the autumn and early winter, perennial weeds removed to the compost heap, and compost spread on the surface of the soil.

4

GROWING HERBS ORGANICALLY

Herbs need very little from the soil and actually take very little from it. In most cases it is sufficient to let the herbs grow on virgin or cultivated soil, as their demands are so few. A little layer of compost used on the herb garden will supply all that is necessary to make one feel certain that nothing interferes with the progress of these most complicated and concentrated plants.

If chemically prepared fertilizers are used in horticulture they are generally intended to force the growth of crops. The supporters of organic methods claim that this kind of forcing weakens the plant and its resistance and leads to the use of poisonous sprays and insecticides. The herbs are equipped not only to protect themselves against pests and disease—they have a natural resistance against disease—but, in fact, they often protect other plants from both. Furthermore, herbs do not need a rich soil and—unless constantly cut for using and drying—over-feeding can produce leggy plants with large foliage and less concentrated flavour and aroma. We know too little about the effects of chemical fertilizers on the structure of the herb, which produces its own volatile oils, minerals and other active substances, to be able to judge the hazards or chemical additions. The volatile oil provides the scent and the aroma, and as we know that chemicals can influence the scent and colour of flowers it is not advisable, particularly if herbs are grown for a household, to run any risk, particularly as many herbs are used in salads without any cooking. Experience gathered during long years of herb-growing on a small scale, and later on a large scale, has produced the most serious warnings to refrain from adding artificials: they are just not needed for herbs.

The earthworm is one of the most essential inhabitants of the soil, providing soil drainage and aeration by its burrows; it helps not only to convert the soil but to convert material into humus as it passes through its digestive system. It is therefore desirable to build up a large population of earthworms and in order to do this they must be supplied with food in the form of compost—a compost which has not been rotted down to such a degree that it has practically turned to soil, but one which provides raw material to lighten the soil in which the worms can feed and breathe.

The object of composting is to assist and quicken the process of rotting of organic material, and provide a finished product of either:

(*a*) a soil-like material rich in humus which will pass through a fine screen and provide plant food quickly—this is only necessary for use in potting mixtures and in cases where there is a need for compost which will give quick results.

(*b*) a material which has partially rotted down and which is to be spread in the autumn and left on the surface of the soil for cultivation the following spring; it can also be used for mulching in the summer months.

This compost should consist of material which, if twisted between the hands, will break easily; and which, when cultivated by surface hoeing in the spring after exposure to the winter weather, and either digging or rotovating, will not interfere with sowing. The first type of compost is good for winter indoor gardening, also for window-boxes of flat dwellers.

Composting can be divided into composting materials without animal manures, composting materials with animal manures, composting animal manures. When composting, much better results can be obtained if certain plants can be introduced into the heaps which have the same effect as animal manures. Nettle is one of the best activators; plant and roots and the leaves of Russian comfrey are also ideal, having a carbon-nitrogen ratio similar to that of farmyard manure. Yarrow, chamomile and all other herb plants have a beneficial effect, and help to quicken the process of fermentation.

It is therefore advisable not only to use the herbs which are mentioned here, but in fact all herb refuse obtained in the garden, or when drying, for the compost heap; also, naturally, all the kitchen waste, particularly in a household where cooking with herbs is a frequent feature. Any organic material can be used, but refuse of a woody nature should first be crushed, and used as a base mixed in with materials such as grass mowings. Bulky materials form a solid mass of rotting vegetation lacking in oxygen and quickly becoming sour and greasy.

The site of the heap should first be dug over in order to allow quick entry of earthworms into the heap. The base, which should be six feet wide, should be made up of a bulky material, such as twigs, in order to help the aeration of the heap. Best results are obtained if the heap is built up quickly to a height of six feet (1·80 m.) with straight sides and a slightly domed top to allow surplus rain to run off. In order to heat up quickly, the contents of the heap must be moist, and in the first stage of decomposition supplied with adequate oxygen; it must also contain either a small percentage of soil or ripe compost from a previous heap. If the refuse to be composted can be thoroughly mixed before stacking, the finished compost will be more uniform in nature. The heap will heat up quickly or slowly, according to the nature of the contents; the quicker the heating, the earlier it should be turned and restacked.

There are a number of publications on compost-making which can be looked up, but it should be said here that the advantages of applying a compost to the soil are the following:

1 it encourages worm population
2 it encourages fungi and bacterial growth
3 it lightens the soil, which is most important for herbs
4 it assists draining in heavy soils
5 it retains moisture in light soils
6 it gives up heat to the soil
7 it provides material for the production of humus
8 it provides a good seed bed, encouraging seed germination
9 it prevents the surface from drying out and forming a crust
10 it favours the release of carbon-dioxide.

Sawdust and shavings also make good compost, but require a much longer time to decompose. They should be mixed with lawn mowings or comfrey leaves; in the latter case lime should also be added.

For those readers who have neither the garden space, nor the time and material to follow these suggestions for making compost heaps, small wooden compost bins can be bought or made quite simply, with which organic refuse—kitchen waste, refuse from herb growing and herb drying, carefully mixed with lawn mowings or parts of them —can be collected and, when decomposed, be transferred to the soil, preferably in autumn.

These are short descriptions of how to make compost—but they are two-way suggestions; the herbs help the compost and the compost helps the herb; for no other garden therefore is compost making and organic gardening of such importance as for the herb garden. Herb growing is intensive cultivation; with a small area and not many plants, very little compost is needed.

5

WINTER IN THE HERB GARDEN

Winter is the hibernation period for the herbs and therefore the largest herb garden can look empty then because most of the herbs disappear from above the ground. The perennial herbs, though often increasing in their roots, still show very little above ground. Each year it is a surprise to herb growers that it is almost the end of June before most of the herbs are visible and recognizable above the ground. The hibernation really lasts a long time, with the exception of a few herbs which disappear late and return early. The most remarkable of this kind is sweet cicely, which can usually be found until November, then so disappears that one hardly knows where it has grown; but starts growing again with fern-like shoots in February, and is one of the earliest herbs to provide large foliage and very early flowers.

The other herb which will never leave the herb grower and offers some lovely fresh luscious green, even during winter, is salad burnet; many herb gardeners grow it mainly for the purpose of having some fresh herbs during winter. It is hardy and not affected by frost or snow, and has this surprising fresh green colour, which is usually not found with evergreens.

When all the herbs have been harvested it is time to think of winter protection for some herbs which may not be able to stand winter in bleak or exposed climes without it. More details will be found with each herb.

Basil, for instance, will die down at the beginning of winter and should go into the indoor garden earlier than any other herbs, while *Salad Burnet*, on the other hand, will stand severe winters and brighten up each spring without any winter protection.

Winter in the Herb Garden

Bay Leaves should have protection. *Bay Leaves* can easily be taken indoors provided they are grown in tubs. If, however, they are left outside and they do get brown from a severe winter they should not be removed from the herb garden but quite a length of time should be allowed for them to shed their brown leaves and grow green leaves again.

Bergamot will die down and only leaves dried for tea will remind one of that lovely plant.

Borage also vanishes completely but seeds in a window-box or seedlings may survive the winter if planted indoors.

Chervil, however, if sown in autumn in the right kind of position will survive the winter beautifully and enjoy winter, autumn and spring more than the hotter summer. In the south of England it will grow outdoors through the winter and can be harvested in spring, but also used during winter.

Chive plants will die after a few touches of frost, and until spring there is nothing possible except putting a cloche over them, indoor growing, or using green-dried chives.

Dill will die out and will have to be planted each spring like newly seeded annuals or sown into an indoor pot or box.

The evergreen *Juniper* will look as lovely in winter as in summer. The black berries will only be available in late autumn and the green shoots remain useful for the purposes mentioned throughout the winter.

Lovage will also die down and can easily overcome even very harsh winters, but in marshy soils there is a danger of frost; and under such conditions it would be better to cover *Lovage* roots.

Marjoram, Rosemary, Tarragon, Thyme and *Winter Savory* all need protection in winter. Leaf-mould is the best mulch for these plants, or a leaf or light straw covering could be placed around the plants on the ground and on the plants as the cold weather approaches. These plants should not only be protected, but uncovered carefully in spring in an exposed or cold area; the protection should come off gradually and remain off during fine sunny spring days, but plants should be covered again at night. If grown indoors they should be cut back to a third of their size before taking them indoors.

Mints disappear completely when frosts come, and therefore can only thereafter be grown indoors and should be done with the careful precautions given in their chapter on p. 150.

Mugwort is a very hardy plant which disappears during winter but requires no protecting of roots.

Rose Hips are one of the latest occupiers of the herb garden, if they are grown there. They cannot be harvested before the frost has touched the berries, but there is no need to think about them during winter.

The *Rose Geranium* plants cannot be left out during winter; they should only be set out in the garden after all signs of frost have passed and the soil is well warmed. The roots should be stored when the cold weather approaches and new plants which are started from cuttings should be wintered indoors.

An eye must be kept on *Sage*. The plants should be mulched with old compost, manure or old soot and this should help the plants through the winter.

Summer Savory can also be planted in boxes or pots in August and then can be grown indoors, but the plant must be carefully transplanted, or seeds sown straight into indoor boxes.

Winter Savory may be killed if the soil is too damp or too rich. Normally, if well clipped before winter starts, or cut back, it will start shooting in spring and begin new growth; it will also survive well indoors.

Valerian is another late occupier of the herb garden, as only in late autumn of the second year are the roots dug.

Lemon Verbena will die down during the winter if not brought indoors and it will then have to be planted outdoors in spring. The roots of *Lemon Verbena* if left should be covered with leaf-mould or some other kind of protection of the roots, but as an indoor plant it will survive the winter well.

Winter in the Herb Garden

The harvest during winter from outdoors and the indoor herb garden is necessarily limited. This is the time to enjoy to the full the green-dried herbs, either dried at home from the summer harvest or, if well dried commercially, available all the year round. It is also the time during which thoughts should be given to the new year; plans should be made for alterations and room allocated to new herbs: how many herbs, where and when they should be planted, should, in fact, be planned before the spring activities start.

6

HERBS ABOUT THE HOUSE
Indoor Herb Garden and Window-boxes

1 INDOOR HERB GARDEN

Once herbs have become a regular addition to daily or festive cooking it becomes increasingly difficult to use herbs during a limited season only. Flavour of familiar dishes will never be the same, and the ambition of every cook must necessarily be directed towards an all-the-year-round availability of herbs.

There are four possibilities for this: domestic drying, freezing, buying commercially green-dried herbs or bringing plants indoors in autumn for ensuring fresh herbs or sprigs during winter.

Everyone who knows anything about indoor growing will find it easy to grow herbs indoors. Practically all herbs, may be so grown, either in earthenware pots or in rectangular flat boxes. The growth, of course, will be stunted, and the cutting done at any one time must be judicious. The ideal conditions for growing herbs indoors are the same as for most house plants: an even temperature, moderately cool moist air around the plants, and moisture for the root system; good sunlight for most of the day and fresh air is also important. Sudden draughts or temperature changes are fatal.

If there is not such a possibility in the house, suitable conditions may have to be improvised in greenhouses, conservatories, patios or glass-covered places where at least a temperature around 60° can be maintained. There are reports of American herb growers who use basements with a humidifier and fluorescent tubes for lighting. The kitchen—the traditional place for indoor herbs—is the least suitable place: the temperature changes too quickly and the cooking fumes clog the pores of the leaves. Though some small-leaved herbs do

37

quite well on the kitchen window-sill—for others a better place should be found, to keep the herbs bright and alive and in no danger of suffocating.

Plants should be brought indoors by stages over a period of time. Transplanted from the garden into individual pots, they should be kept outdoors during daylight hours and brought in at night. Thus their hours outdoors will diminish automatically as the days grow shorter. Most of the plants should be acclimatized to their new environment before the first frost. For most herbs middle or late September is the time to pot them. The mints can be potted at the same time, but should be left outside until after the first frost.

Containers Four-inch pots are satisfactory for most herbs, other than large plants. A few herbs, tarragon, lemon balm, chives and the mints may fit better into a five-inch pot. Some, such as rosemary, will do better when young if somewhat pot-bound. While dill normally grows to a height of three feet out of doors, and fennel may grow to a foot or two higher, as house plants they readily adapt themselves and become dwarfed. If plants have begun in small pots they should be transplanted into larger containers when the hair-like filaments of their roots begin to grow through the drainage holes in the pot's base; the larger container must be big enough to accommodate mature roots.

A planting box for herbs is handy for use when kept close to the back door: a wooden box 18 × 36 in. (45 × 90 cm.) about 12 in. (30 cm.) deep, e.g. planted with chives, parsley, tarragon, rosemary and mint; when plants grow too tall the tender tops can be picked, dried and stored. The seeds of parsley can be sown directly into the box every February; seeds of chervil and basil can also be sown directly into the containers. Mint is best planted in a 3-lb. pail plunged into the box to keep it from spreading. If creeping herbs like the mints are grown in pails, pots or boxes, their runners will not take over, as they soon do when unconfined. Rosemary, tarragon, sage, thyme and marjoram make handsome permanent pot plants and a bay tree in a tub is decorative near the indoor garden.

The indoor containers can be placed on stands, for instance on ndoor glass shelves attached to the sides of the window-frame on brackets, located so that the window may be opened on mild days; or on a branching stand, such as is frequently used for pots of ivy or ferns.

Soil Plants grown in window-boxes or indoor gardens exhaust the soil faster and it is advisable to provide richer soil than in the garden; a good mixture of fibrous loam, peat, leaf-mould, well-rotted compost or stable manure and some coarse sand, thoroughly mixed, is suggested. Any additional plant food, useful for indoor growing, should be organic if possible. The soil should be changed at least once a year. Sufficient depth of earth in the container, 12 in. (30 cm.), is best, but a minimum of 9 in. (25 cm.) is essential.

Drainage and Watering is most important for herbs grown in containers. 'Wet feet' bring sudden death to indoor herb plants. If the air is reasonably moist and the pots are set in containers of pebbles the plants should not be watered more than once a week or every ten days during winter. The soil in the pots should be barely moist. Sprinkling or spraying from the top can be useful for foliage, because they breathe through their leaves, but the sun should not strike them while they are wet. Water should not be straight out of the tap, but should be standing for some time, possibly in the sun. The pots could be soaked every week or ten days by allowing them to take up water from the bottom. If the plants' leaves seem crumbly and dry the air may be too dry, or the sun or any artificial light may be too close to the foliage.

Planting When planting, the hole or holes in the container should be covered with a few pieces of broken crock, concave side down, or some stones. Over these crocks one or two inches of rough fibrous material, such as leaf-mould or peat or a thin layer of gravel, should go, and only then the prepared mixture of compost, etc., adding one inch at a time, firming down each layer; but the soil should only be filled to 1 in. (2½ cm.) below the top. Seedlings should be put in firmly and then be watered well.

Harvest The leaves can be cut continually and the tops be pinched back; a leaf here and there to balance the growth must suffice, otherwise the plant will compensate for loss of foliage by attempting to send roots down too deep. They should be cut back for drying before flowering, only tarragon should be cut in August.

2 WINDOW-BOXES FOR FLAT DWELLERS

The success depends on where a window-box is situated, in which direction it faces, on sun and shelter (not too windy for some herbs) and on a successful drainage. Boxes with a false bottom arranged for drainage or with a thick layer of stones or pebbles in the bottom to allow excess moisture to lie below the soil, or with holes covered by crocks, provide good drainage; it is also suggested setting herb pots in painted tin trays of the size of the window-sill, filled with a layer of about 3-in. pebbles, in which water is kept which cannot reach the pots. This also helps to keep the air moist by evaporation. Top spraying should only be done after the sun has gone and no frost is expected. A little lime should be added to most London window-boxes, but not for sorrel. Bonemeal and dried blood can be sprinkled or watered in as top dressing. The soil should be changed at least once a year and kept fresh and oxygenated. It should also be stirred, but the roots must not be disturbed. Most of these suggestions also apply to indoor growing.

Some perennials can be kept for many years, if kept dwarfed by close-cutting. Any tall herbs should be staked; climbers, such as nasturtium, can be helped with strings or wire.

A herb corner on a balcony can be started by having a few flower-pots or boxes with herbs which are not too difficult to grow. Sowing in boxes is good for chervil, summer savory, borage, sweet marjoram, and pots of sage, thyme and tarragon complete the balcony herb garden. In fact, some herbs such as basil, scented geraniums, lemon verbena may do better indoors or on sheltered window-boxes and balconies than outdoors.

7

HARVESTING HERBS

Herbs can be picked for daily use whenever there are reasonably-sized leaves visible above ground. For some herbs an exact time or size from which, onwards, these can be picked is given with the individual herb. For some herbs of which only parts such as flowers, flowering shoots or roots are used, definite months during which only these can be harvested are described with the herb in question.

From February almost to November there are usually some herbs which can be picked freshly, according to which herbs are grown—and during the months from June to October fresh leaves or sprigs are available from most herbs, and the best possible use should be made of them.

There is, however, a peak time in the life of each herb during which it should be cut for preserving—either by drying, the age-old natural way of preserving herbs—or by the new way of freezing with which we have no long experience yet. Drying has been infinitely improved lately by new knowledge and methods of how to retain the important constituents; and the result is the 'green-dried' herb, preserved by a process which avoids loss of volatile oils and other active substances, thus retaining the aroma, colour and scent.

In order to achieve such results, the herbs have to be picked at the right moment, when their volatile oil content is at its highest; this, with leafy herbs, is usually before they go into flower. It lasts, in fact, from the time when flower buds begin to form until they are half-open, though there are exceptions, such as parsley and chives, which can be cut at any time, and sage and russian tarragon (for instance) which can develop strong and unpleasant flavours unless harvested at an earlier moment. The oil content during the day is at its highest before the sun becomes too hot, after the dew has dried, and there-

41

fore it is best to cut the herbs in the morning as soon as the dew has dried on the foliage.

The effect of the active substances will diminish greatly if the plants or part of the plants are collected immediately after dew or rain, and are still wet.

The content of volatile oil with certain leafy herbs increases up to the flowering period, but then diminishes again.

Individual herbs have been given individual directions for harvesting, but there are general directions which apply to all of them.

Annual herbs may be cut within about four inches of the ground, but perennial herbs should not be cut back more than about one-third. Most of the leafy herbs can be cut two or three times during the summer, depending on the weather. The perennial herbs should really not be cut after the end of September because the new growth will not harden before the cold weather comes. The plants should be cut possibly with a stainless-steel knife, or in some cases with a hook, and should be collected in a flat-bottomed basket, garden truck or box, but never in a sack or a bag. Crushing and bruising can happen so easily and a heap of herbs can heat up so quickly that it is important that all this should be avoided.

After the herbs have been cut they must be sorted out, and weeds and grass that may be mixed with them removed beforehand. Those leaves which are really encrusted with mud should also be discarded, but loose dirt may be gently washed off with clear cool, but not cold, water. They should be shaken to get rid of excess moisture or the moisture should drip off the trays on which they should be put in a flat layer.

It is important that they should not be handled and stay too long in the water because some of the important nutrients and minerals may dissolve into the water. It is therefore also important to take the chill off the water, as the shock of cold water may diminish the content of nutrients.

Any deterioration before drying makes the dried herb useless and therefore they should never be collected unless they can be washed if necessary, spread out and dried immediately afterwards. No more should be collected at any one time than the capacity of the available drying space will take.

Harvesting Herbs

Altogether, the whole purpose of handling herbs when collecting is to avoid damage by bruising or anything else which could deplete the volatile oil. Bruising not only discolours but allows the volatile oils to escape; it is, in fact, the greatest enemy of the green-dried herb.

When flowers are used, they can only be harvested when they are fully open, and have to be collected whenever they open. Flowers are not washed at all but are handled very carefully, not pressed, not heaped. They should not be overripe, wilting or discolouring, as then the volatile oil may already be diminished. Whole and unblemished flowers are necessary for drying or crystallizing or using for any other purpose. Seed herbs, such as dill and fennel, have the seeds gathered when the heads turn brown; the heads can be tested for cutting by tapping the stems each day after they begin to turn brown—if the seeds fall when tapped they are ready to cut. The umbels should be removed with the little stem attached and the heads can be collected in a box to prevent seeds from falling to the ground, or hung upside-down to dry and the seeds should drop on to paper or in to muslin bags tied over the flower heads to catch the seeds. The difficulty in collecting seeds at the right moment lies in the fact that when they are really mature they drop down and are lost.

Berries are collected when the fruit is ripe and the colour at its richest, before they become soft or darken. Too much handling is a great disadvantage and should be avoided under all circumstances.

The roots are harvested in late autumn when the leaves have already started to discolour. They have to be well washed and brushed before drying.

Much depends on the time of the day, the right time in the cycle of the plant, the speed with which the herbs can be collected, washed, freed from the excess moisture and dried. From the moment they are collected they should be prevented from being exposed to sun or light and they should be in the drying place at the earliest possible moment.

8

PRESERVING HERBS
Drying, Storing, Freezing

1 DRYING

It has been suggested that no special skill is necessary for growing herbs, but, without doubt, some skill is essential to have them successfully green-dried, retaining aroma and flavour. Dried herbs should look and taste like fresh herbs when being used reconstituted in a dish.

It is the intention when drying to extract the natural content of water from the parts of the plant through warmth and ventilation while retaining the original natural colour of the fresh plant. It is not the temperature alone which will produce the drying process, for the circulation of air is just as important. The water content and the humidity of the plant when extracted must be carried away by ventilation; this should happen as quickly and as strongly as possible so that the temperature can again have an effect on the herbs. It is therefore necessary to produce a suitable temperature, as good a ventilation as possible, and the process should take place in the dark to avoid any influence of sun or light on the herbs.

There is hardly any other preserving method which is so cluttered up with directions which, if not allowed for, will necessarily cause damage and produce unsuitable results. The old-fashioned idea of domestic drying was to tie the herbs up in bunches, hang them in a well-ventilated place such as a porch or an attic, and let them dry. This drying process was, of necessity, slow and this and the influence of light or sun on the herbs led to discoloration. There is also a suggestion to put paper bags round the plant, but this slows the drying process still more. The air cannot circulate around the plants; and slowing the process of course means more discoloration.

The principle is that the plants should be dried as quickly as possible—all delay is damaging—but at the same time as carefully as possible. Too much heat, too high a degree of warmth, which might be helpful for quick drying, is as damaging to colour and aroma as it is too slow drying, which exposes the plant to the drying process for so much longer.

The perfect drying method needs special equipment and is therefore not possible for domestic drying but there are a few basic conditions under which drying can be carried out relatively successfully in a household.

Herbs must never dry in the sun as sun extracts or evaporates the volatile oils; in fact, once the herbs have been cut and severed from their roots the loss of volatile oil begins as explained in 'Harvesting'; and there can only be one aim therefore,—to shorten the time between cutting and the beginning of drying. During this period the herbs should be washed if necessary but never left in heaps, and certainly not in the sun, because they will heat up and deteriorate. They have, in fact, to be put as quickly as possible on to some frames which are the size of the drying cupboard, oven, airing cupboard or wherever the herbs are supposed to be dried. Whilst handling, bruising must be avoided.

Equal importance should be given to temperature and air circulation. It is just as important not to have too high a temperature as to have good ventilation. The temperature should be kept between 70° and 90° and never go beyond 100°. The drying should take place in a darkened room, to which not only no sun, but also no light has access. The best domestic suggestions are an airing cupboard, a cooling oven, a plate-warming compartment, the lower, less warm oven of an Aga or a Rayburn—all these should have the door ajar—or near a boiler, in a darkened greenhouse or clean shed with an electric heater and possibly a fan, or a home-built drying cupboard.

The trays should consist of a wooden frame covered with a light porous material. The idea of wire mesh should be discarded as contact with metal is damaging to the herbs, but a tight piece of muslin or any strengthened nylon net material is suitable. The more porous the material the better the ventilation. The herbs should be evenly and thinly spread out on the surface of the tray; they should then be allowed to go into the drying space but the frames may perhaps have to have, or stand on, little feet in order to allow the air to circulate from below and above. The door of the oven or airing cupboard should be kept ajar for the air to circulate, and if it is possible to have a small electric fan which can be put either near or into the drying space this would be of great assistance. There must also be a possibility for the moisture to escape. The herbs should still be on their stalks when put on to these trays and even when the leaves start to become dry the stalks will help to keep the herbs on the frame.

It is not possible to foretell the time each plant needs for drying until the exact conditions, such as temperature, ventilation and size of drying space are known. This has to be found out by experience but there are certain signs when a herb is dry.

Leaves should be brittle and make a noise when being touched, but they should not be so dry that they almost become powder when touched or removed from their stalks. The stems, if they should be used together with the leaves, should no longer bend but must break, or the leaves can be rubbed off the stems, when they are still bending. The flowers should not feel sticky; fruit should also make a noise when passing through the hands and roots should not be soft inside, but should be brittle all through.

It is important that the places in which herbs are dried be extremely clean; they should have ideally a smooth surface, on which no dust can settle unseen.

A special domestic drying cupboard was suggested during the war to dry fruit and vegetables, and this can be used for herbs. It consists of a vertical cupboard 1 ft. (30 cm.) square, to suit the size of a small heater, but it can also be made larger. The sides each consist of hardboard supported by two upright posts 1 in. (2½ cm.) and from 2 ft. 6 in. to 3 ft. 6 in. long (75 cm.–1 m.) long, depending on the type of heater. Six horizontal cross bars of 1 in. × ¼ in. lath are fitted on the inside of the side walls as supports for the trays. A sheet of hardboard forms the back which is braced by wood laths. For the door, another piece of hardboard suitably strengthened is fixed in some convenient way. The dryer trays are made of wooden frames (covered with nylon net) and provided with an edge to allow them to slide easily into the dryer. It is better to make the posts too long so that they can be shortened after the effect of the particular heater used is known, as it has been observed that the governing factor is that the lowest tray should not be overheated. The heater suggested here is a ½-unit electrical greenhouse heater and the height of the first tray should be 1 ft. (30 cm.) from the floor. Experiments can be made with the new type of heater blowing warm air, which can be blown on to the trays provided the heat can be kept low enough.

The herbs are then loaded into the dryer on the trays and the heat turned on. It may be found desirable during the drying to change round the lower and upper trays so that the drying may be evenly carried out. Slow-drying herbs can be continued when partly dried as soon as the dryer is again filled, but there should be no break; the herbs should dry continuously until ready and should be rubbed, sieved and stored immediately.

There are some herbs which can be dried almost better in a cooling oven and parsley and lovage for instance show quite good results, though parsley is the herb which can stand the highest temperature. All experiments with the cooling oven are better carried out with a thermometer so that the temperature can be checked. It should never go above 90° and drying too quickly because of a higher temperature usually results in a loss of colour except with parsley. It is important with any new drying method that either with or without a thermometer the herb should be constantly checked, and if only a few leaves get brown the temperature is too high or the method is somehow unsuitable. Evenly green herbs with as full an aroma as possible and the full flavour preserved should be the result of the drying.

Some of the flowers, such as collected lime flowers, can be dried in a cooling oven. There are reports of a flimsy nappy over a basket tray that has good results, but flowers such as verbascum or chamomile must be dried with utmost care. A specially-built drying cupboard should make it possible to retain the full yellow colour of the verbascum flower or the chamomile flower. This is important as the therapeutic qualities of these flowers are connected with the colouring substance in the herb.

2 STORING

The method of storing the green-dried herb is as important as the method of drying. Once the herbs have lost their moisture it is not intended that they should pick up moisture again from the air, and the air of this country is notably humid, particularly during the many cool and damp days. The herbs should be allowed to cool when they come from drying and then be stored in air-tight dark containers. Glass is still the best material for containers; no other material, such as plastic or cardboard, is as safe or as air-tight. Glass containers with screw tops or with the lids of Kilner jars or with well-fitting glass stoppers are all suitable; but though glass is safe it still allows the light to enter and nothing will bleach and destroy the qualities of a herb more quickly than exposure to light. It is therefore advisable to store any glass container, unless it is opaque or dark, in a cupboard away from the light. It should also be stored in a room which is dry and possibly heated to keep an even temperature throughout the changes of weather. The kitchen with its cooking steams, however, is only a good place for the herbs which are used immediately; even then they should be in a glass jar with screw top; any containers for herbs to be stored in larger quantities must be hard and more like tubs, bins or hard boxes, but not bags or sacks, so that the herbs do not become crushed or bruised.

Paper bags are highly unsuitable; they are not air-tight and give no protection against crushing or bruising. Therefore, bags of cotton or other materials are also quite unsuitable. Different herbs, even if kept separately in little bags, should never be kept in the same container because nothing will mingle more quickly than the various scents of the herbs and therefore their flavours will get mixed. None of these bagged herbs kept in the same container will have the individual scent of each herb any more.

Wooden tubs or boxes may be useful, but if any tins or containers, lined with foil, are used, the herbs should be separated from the metal by a linen or cotton bag. The well-closed lids are of importance. No different smell, no light and no sun should have access to dried herbs.

If the herbs are stored in this way, they can be kept for a long time and retain their aroma and flavour.

3 FREEZING

Freezing is probably the simplest of the preserving processes, but there is not, up till now, sufficient experience available to justify definite suggestions. All experiments with freezing herbs still carry the risk inseparable from a new technique and each herb gardener will have to make his own experiments; the main question being that the herbs must not only retain their colour, which most frozen products do, but must definitely retain their fragrance and their aroma, those elusive qualities by which the frozen herbs will have to be judged.

Freezing of herbs can be done as for vegetables, but, of course, on a smaller scale. There are suggestions that the herbs should be blanched either in steam for 60 seconds, then cooled, or by immersing them in boiling water.

It is, however, possible to snip the herbs in the morning just after the dew has evaporated, exactly the moment when one would cut them for drying, then they should be washed, shaken free of moisture and slipped into little plastic bags or wax containers; the plastic bags should be sealed with a warm iron or sealing appliance or have the tops twisted and fastened with a small rubber or wire band, and then they are put into the freezer.

Herb growers have to make up their minds whether to choose for their experiments the blanching process, which is required for all vegetables and is supposed to retain the flavour texture and colour. It may not always suit the herbs, as they are so often used uncooked and the experimenters have to find out whether blanched or unblanched will retain more flavour. Blanching can be carried out in two ways, and immersing in steam may be easier to carry out, but may not be as good for the herbs. The herbs may be put into a colander (not a metal one, but an enamelled if possible) and be immersed either in a container of strongly boiling water or, preferably, in steam. The water can be used over and over again but it must be, each time, brought rapidly to the boil. During this blanching the container must be shaken vigorously from time to time.

Herbs should always be packed in very small separate quantities; therefore very small cardboard containers or bags, which must be entirely moisture proof, are suitable for storing in the deep freeze. They must be placed in a clearly labelled carton before storing. To eliminate the tedious chore of labelling each packet, only one combination or one herb should be frozen at a time and the small amounts needed each time may all be stored in the same labelled box.

All herbs may be frozen in sprigs, except chives; chives are easier to handle if they are chopped before freezing. Though frozen herbs are probably close in flavour and fragrance to the fresh ones, they do not have the same crisp texture; they are good for cooking but not as a garnish; nor perhaps as a salad dressing, for which dried herbs are likely to be more suitable.

It is better not to freeze herbs singly but to have ready-made bouquets for instant use, such as for:

Meat, sauces and soups: Summer savory, lovage, marjoram and parsley in equal parts.

Tomato sauce: 2 parts basil, 1 part marjoram and thyme.

Chicken dishes: 1 part rosemary, 2 parts each of marjoram, chives and tarragon.

Fines herbes: 2 parts parsley and chives, 1 part chervil and tarragon.

Strongly flavoured stews: parsley, thyme, marjoram and rosemary of equal parts.

Delicate broths: 1 part chervil, 2 parts parsley and chives.

Salads and delicate dishes: 2 parts dill, 1 part parsley, chives, and chervil.

Tomato purée: Dill and chives in equal proportions.

Omelettes and egg dishes: 2 parts parsley and chives, 1 part each of tarragon, marjoram or rosemary.

PART II

Growing and Using Individual Herbs

Individual herbs, described with directions for growing and using, are given here in alphabetical order.

The original intention to divide the herbs into sections of useful, uncommon, culinary, medicinal, cultivated and wild, and into those groups calling for either more or less detail, does not appear to work out well. Though some of the herbs, flowers and fruit can be found wild, they may also be grown. The aforementioned sections become arbitrary, and made it difficult to find the herbs in the book, and so they were abandoned.

It does not seem advisable to impose values of judgment on usefulness by fitting the herbs into watertight departments. The importance of each herb, its value to the individual grower, the problems of soil, position and available time must be considered by each herb gardener. Thus all the herbs follow here together in the 'democratic' order of the alphabet. It may be unoriginal, but for ease of reference and avoidance of confusion it has much merit.

ANGELICA

(*Angelica archangelica*)

Virtues Angelica—one of the few plants with scented leaves which is a native of northern Europe—was introduced into England in 1568 and is now found in the countryside near river banks as an escape, or is cultivated for its use in flavouring and confectionery. Legend reports that it was revealed by an angel to cure the plague and though it has medicinal properties it is best known nowadays for its bright green candied or crystallized stems. The flavour resembles juniper berries, and angelica is used with them for gin. Angelica tea, which has medicinal qualities, resembles China tea in flavour.

Description Angelica is a tall umbelliferous plant, cultivated as a biennial but if left to sow itself it will become almost perennial. The plant can become more than 8 ft. (2 m.) high and with its deeply indented, very large leaves, strong stems and wonderfully big umbels, can provide a most attractive border to any herb garden. The colour of the stems, the somewhat decurrent leaf segments and the flowers are greenish white or light green.

Growing Angelica does best in a shady spot in rich but not too heavy soil and a medium damp position, but even on sandy soil it can reach 6–8 ft. (1¾–2 m.). As angelica seed loses its germination power quickly, it is best to buy plants and in two or three years these will sow themselves out abundantly. The best seedlings should be selected and the appropriate distance be allocated to them. As seeds germinate very shortly after the harvest it is advisable to use young plants and later propagate the plants by root division. If raising angelica from seed, it should be sown in drills 1-in. deep as soon as the seeds are ripe. The seeds can also be sown in boxes in September and planted out later. The seedlings should be thinned out to 6 in. (15 cm.) in the first year, in the following hear the distance should be 24 × 24 in. (60 × 60 cm.) and the final distance between plants to be

5 × 5 ft. (1½ × 1½ m.). Sometimes angelica does not flower until the fourth or fifth year, it usually goes on growing until it does flower and then it dies. If the plants are not allowed to bloom they will go on another year before they die.

Harvesting If the leaves are harvested they should be cut about May or June while they are still a good colour. The flowering stalks and leaf stalks should be picked in April or May as otherwise they become too hard to be used for candying and the colour goes if left too long. If some of the leaves have a very big stalk, it is best to strip the leaves off and dry them separately. If the leaves are carefully dried in the dark or on trays which are well ventilated they retain a most lovely light green colour, not only excellent for making a tisane but their lovely colour and scent can be used for potpourri. The leaves begin to turn yellow once flowering starts. If the flowers are continually cut there may be a succession of good green leaves during the summer. If roots are to be used they should be dug in the first year in autumn before they get too woody. They should be washed and then be plaited and dried as quickly as possible.

Uses Angelica has a particularly strong content of volatile oil in all parts of the plant, and in particular in the roots. Used as a digestive, as a bath addition for stimulating the skin, and the dried roots in winter or spring for a blood-cleansing, diuretic tea, which also has an anti-spasmodic and anti-flatulent 'effect. Further constituents in angelica are resins, tannins and bitter principles. The herb is used for herb pillows for a calming effect.

The most useful part, however, is the leaf stalks, which are candied and used for decorating cakes and pastry. The tips of angelica are also used for making and flavouring jams. The roots and stems of the plant are cooked with rhubarb to remove the tartness, as when rhubarb is cooked with sweet cicely.

BASIL

(Ocimum basilicum)

Virtues The name basil, which is derived from *Basileus*, the Greek word for king, gives it royal status amongst herbs. From the culinary point of view everyone today agrees that it is a strongly masculine herb with a power and pungency which dominate even garlic. In spite of all its strength of flavour it also gives a sweet delicacy to foods. Italy, where it is used in egg, cheese and fish dishes and where no tomato dish is ever served without it, seems to be responsible for the present almost striking popularity of basil.

As well as being extremely rich in volatile oils, basil contains some tannins. Oil of Basil is used for perfumes and the dried and powdered leaves are used in snuff because of their biting strength; this follows the theory that basil helps to clear the brain and disperses headaches, and this is repeated again and again by old herbalists. Medicinally it acts as an expectorant, a laxative and as a sedative for gastric spasms. A handful of leaves left for several hours in a bottle of wine produces a digestive tonic. It is also known that a pot of basil will discourage flies.

Originally from India, where it grows in abundance, and is used in curries, the plant needs warmth and shelter. It was brought to Europe by the monasteries, though it only seems to have arrived in England about 1548. Basil is a powerful herb and of great importance to the herb lover; it does, however, pose a few problems to the grower in this country.

Appearance of the Plant Common or sweet basil is a member of the Labiatae family, growing about 3 ft. high. The stem is quadrangular and has light green leaves, sometimes with a purple tinge on the underside. The leaves can attain a size of $3 \times 1\frac{1}{2}$ in. (8×4 cm.). The flowers are whitish and stand in whorls in the axils of the leaves, the calyx with the upper lobe rounded and spreading. The leaves, greyish green beneath, and dotted with dark oil cells, are opposite, stalked and smooth. They are soft and cool to the touch, and if slightly bruised they exhale a delightful scent.

Basil

There are several varieties, differing in size, shape, odour and colour of the leaves. Most of the basils are horticultural forms of either *Ocimum basilicum* or *Ocimum minimum*—a dwarf variety. Apart from the sweet or ordinary basil, which has the finest flavour, there is a lemon-flavoured basil, and some varieties smell like fennel or tarragon.

There are other varieties of sweet basil which, apart from their value for flavour, provide reddish and yellow flowers and attractive, sometimes colourful foliage for annual borders; and this makes the basils a herb with a double use. In this country one usually finds the common basil listed, but if any herb nursery should describe other forms of the species by leaf description such as purple or curly-leaved green, these are usually varieties of sweet basil.

Bush basils and dwarf forms reach a height of only 6 in. (15 cm.) with tiny leaves in both purple and green. Though their flavour may not be as strong as that of the sweet basil, they are particularly suitable for planting in pots.

Growing Though basil is a hardy perennial in hot countries it can only be considered a delicate annual in this country. The Asian origin of basil makes a warm sheltered position in full sun essential, and we have therefore to consider an annual propagation; we can only grow by seed. About one packet of seeds is needed for growing plants in a frame. Germination is supposed to take ten to fourteen days. If a cold wet summer is expected the sowing of basil seeds may not succeed out of doors and they should then be sown indoors possibly with artificial heat. As seedlings do not transplant well, best results are obtained if seeds are sown two or three to a small pot in a heated glasshouse and then planted out when hardened off without disturbing the roots. Otherwise, basil seedlings should be treated much the same as outdoor tomatoes—they should not be planted until the first week in June, when the soil is warm and no more frosts can be expected. It is essential that the soil be well drained; basil will not thrive in a moist clay or loamy soil unless lightened by sand, shingle or similar material and with adequate attention given to drainage. The seeds, which are black in colour, change to a characteristic shade of light blue and form a covering of a jelly-like substance after watering.

Basil

When transplanting, it is necessary to find a position where hedges or walls give the plants protection, unless cloches are used. The plants should be placed 8 in. apart in rows 1 ft. (30 cm.) apart as each plant needs a lot of space for maturing. Transplanting should not be done during a drought, but if it has to be done during a dry period a great deal of watering will be necessary. If the seeds should be sown on the site it is better to sow thinly, as plants do not transplant well.

While basil is growing no special attention is needed other than to keep free from weeds and to watch out for signs of massed centre growth. The tops should be pinched out as the tall flowering spikes rob the plant of good leaf development and flavour. The soil must be kept moist, and the plants should be watered regularly to keep the leaves succulent. In dry hot summers basil should be watered daily, but the soil should be allowed to dry out before the next watering as basil does not like to have its 'feet' constantly in water; therefore, a continuous moist soil should be avoided if possible. This experience was confirmed by finding in one of the old Herbals (Matthiolus, 1626) that basil prefers to be watered in the midday heat rather than in the evening. This advice is probably based on the fact that the midday sun will help to dry out the soil quickly. An occasional overhead watering keeps the foliage green and bright.

As the seeds do not ripen well in the British climate there is no point in collecting them, for they are not always reliable.

If sown and transplanted at the right time of the year it should be possible to cut basil twice in a good summer, but as drying presents as many difficulties as growing it may be advisable to use basil only for fresh herb foliage.

WINDOW-BOX AND INDOOR GROWING Basil dies completely at the onset of winter and it should therefore make the transition to the indoor garden. If the plants are potted early in September this will ensure a good supply of fresh basil leaves well into the winter. Before the frost can kill them, a few plants should be lifted and placed in pots in a frame or heated greenhouse until they can be taken indoors. It should be the first herb to make the transition to indoor growing, as the first breath of frost will kill it. For this the plants should be cut back to the first leaves above the base of its stem, and the soil in the pot should be richer than the garden soil and be kept just moist.

For growing in pots the variety with the finer leaves is more suit-able than the common or sweet basil, and it is the bush and dwarf varieties which should be planted. Basil can be grown successfully in pots, and half a dozen seedlings of bush basil are recommended for an 8 in. (20 cm.) pot. The tops of bush basil should be nipped off.

Even if basil grows well in the garden it is worth having one or two pots in the kitchen and dining-room because of its scent and its fly-repelling qualities. Also basil is really easier to grow in a pot or a window-box than in the open in this country.

How to Harvest and Dry Fresh green leaves can be cut for kitchen use as soon as they unfurl from the stem. If the plants are cut down for drying in the late summer or early autumn, they will shoot again, and in a good year give a further supply of green shoots. Basil leaves should be cut for drying just before the plant flowers on a dry day after the dew has dried off.

The extreme high content of volatile oils in the oil cells at the back of the leaves is responsible for aroma and flavour and should be re-tained at all cost. The herb when cut is very sensitive to touch, to exposure, to light and to high temperature; all of which will turn the leaves black. As it is a very succulent herb it needs a long time for drying, and if exposed too long to the light during drying will lose all value. The length of drying is not only dependent on the succu-lence of the leaves, on the humidity at the time of harvesting, but also on the weather in general of a given season.

If basil needs to be washed prior to drying it should be carefully immersed in tepid water. The leaves have a characteristic 'slimy' feel-ing when wet and care should be taken not to handle roughly at this stage. Basil should never be exposed to a temperature above blood-heat and it is better to dry basil in a dark airing cupboard with the door ajar or possibly in a darkened corner of a greenhouse with a small fan providing ventilation, or in a slow clean oven or plate-warmer of a solid fuel cooker. It should be spread thinly and evenly on frames covered with nylon net which will allow ventilation, and drying should be done as quickly as possible. When dried, the leaves should be stripped off and packed in tightly sealed air-tight containers.

Basil

What Basil Can Do for Our Food The addition of sweet basil is the secret which accounts for the many delicious Italian tomato and spaghetti dishes, salads and sauces; it lends a new and interesting flavour to practically all other foods. Sausages were and are flavoured with basil, among them the famous Fetter Lane sausages. Eels and other fish are improved if crushed sweet basil is used with them. Also small quantities of the dried herb can be used in the water in which peas or potatoes are boiled. Being one of the few herbs which increase in flavour when cooked, it is valuable in egg and cheese dishes, with poultry and game, in shell-fish, soups, stews, stuffings, and when added to the water or oil for cooking courgettes or aubergines (egg plants).

Basil in combination with parsley and summer savory gives a delicious peppery flavour. This combination is therefore useful for people who like their food spicy but cannot have pepper because of its effect on ulcers and the intestinal tract. Basil can be sprinkled on raw, boiled or fried tomatoes. It may be used to make herb butter by adding parsley, particularly if this is to be served fresh or melted with shell-fish.

CULINARY USES

Hors-d'œuvre: Tomato juice cocktail; tomato sandwiches and *canapés*; sea-food cocktail.

Salads: With other herbs in French dressing; a 'must' with tomatoes; good with cucumbers.

Eggs and cheese: Pinch in herb mixture for pancakes and omelettes, with creamed eggs; cheese *soufflés*; Welsh rarebit; *fondue*.

Soups, stews and sauces: In tomato soup; packeted soups; minestrone; pea soup; mock turtle soup.

Meat and fish: Beef; liver; veal; lamb; pork; sausages; marinades; stuffing; basil sauce; basil butter; sole; shell-fish; mackerel.

Poultry and game: On poultry before roasting. In stuffings; chicken and rabbit stews; with all game.

Vegetables: Indispensable in tomato cookery. Excellent with mushrooms and fungi. Flavours insipid vegetables; sauces with spaghetti; rice.

Sweet and beverages: Try *very little* with stewed fruit; tomato juice.

Bay Leaves

STUFFED TOMATOES WITH BASIL

Ingredients:
6 tomatoes (halved) sprinkled liberally with fresh or green-dried basil

Stuffing:
4 oz. fresh wholemeal breadcrumbs
4 oz. shredded cheese
3–4 tablespoons onion green or chives chopped or green-dried
Approx. ⅓ pint yoghourt and sour cream and top of the milk with a little more sour cream

Method of Stuffing:

1 Mix crumbs, cheese and onion green with sour cream; mixture should become a smooth and firm paste.
2 Place mixture on to halved tomatoes; a heaped mound of approximate height of halved tomatoes.
3 Dot each with a little sour cream.
4 Place in medium oven (350°) for approximately ¾ to an hour.

BAY LEAVES
(*Laurus nobilis*)

Virtues Sweet bay from which the bay leaves come, is the true laurel and the only one of the genus which is used in cookery. These were the leaves and berries wound into wreaths in ancient times for poets and heroes—the term poet laureate recalls this custom. With other evergreens, branches of bay were used to decorate houses and churches at Christmas and though years ago they were considered a cure for almost any illness, down the ages their best-known use has been for flavouring. Bay leaves have a strong, pungent, almost bitter flavour which becomes more apparent when the brittle leaves are crushed.

Description The sweet bay is an evergreen aromatic shrub-like tree which can reach a height of more than 30 ft. (10 m.); usually shaped like a pyramid. The spreading branches are covered with smooth, waxy leaves which are oval or ovate 1–4 in. (2–10 cm.) long, pointed, dark shiny green. The leaves are elliptical and taper to points at the base and tips, and the undersides are pale, yellowish green. The inconspicuous flowers are greenish yellow in small umbels. The fruit is globose and a dark purple when ripe.

Growing The sweet bay tree grows well in the shade of other trees; it needs slight protection. In the south of England the climate is quite suitable for treating the bay tree as hardy, but the winter of 1962/63 showed that practically no bay tree is quite safe in severe frost and long periods of cold and snow. In many parts of northern Europe the bay tree is mostly grown indoors, and if they are grown in tubs and are shaped, this allows placing them in a sunny greenhouse or indoors during winter. Otherwise, the cultivation of bay trees presents no problem; they will succeed in any soil of moderate quality, but love full sunshine. Bay trees can be propagated rapidly by cuttings of half-ripened shoots.

Harvesting The leaves can be picked all the year round and as they have to be dried they should be picked early in the morning and allowed to dry in thin layers on trays in a warm shady place; a low temperature should allow the leaves to remain exactly the natural colour. When they are dried, they have a tendency to curl up, and should be lightly pressed under a board and after two weeks packed tightly into well-sealed containers. Though thick and tough, bay leaves give the impression that they hold the volatile oil better than other herbs, but they are in fact exuding oil all the time. Therefore, glass containers are infinitely preferable to paper bags or cartons. They should never be dried in the sun as this will cause loss of volatile oil and changes in colour Crushed or chopped bay release more volatile oil available for flavouring and great care has to be taken not to use too much of it.

Uses Dried bay leaves stimulate the appetite and are added to many commercial products preserved in oil and vinegar. Bay leaf has al-

ways been a part of *bouquet garni*, which, in a classic combination—
for instance for roasting and boiling fowl—should consist of 2 sprigs
of parsley, 1 of thyme, 1 of marjoram and half a bay leaf, or the
equivalent in dried herbs. Bay leaves in stock in which fish should be
boiled (*court bouillon*) or in mixtures of herbs for fish dishes, for
poultry and game, sauces used with spaghetti dishes, are amongst the
well-known uses. They give a subtle flavour when boiled with carrots,
artichokes, beets, aubergines, potatoes, and above all smoked
tongue; also in rice dishes, sea-food, aspics and wine sauces. They
should be used in every marinade to flavour and tenderize meat, such
as venison, normally considered to be tough. They are essential in a
roasting-pan with meat, chicken or duck. Bay leaves have been considered the foundation of French cooking, but it is dangerous to
follow the casual advice 'just use a bay leaf or two' as in most cases
half would be sufficient—experience and discretion should be the
best guide.

BERGAMOT RED

(*Monarda didyma*)

Virtues Though red bergamot is an old-fashioned flowering plant it
was fairly recently discovered as a useful *tisane* in Europe for induc-
ing sleep and soothing. In America it has been popular for a long
time. It is called Oswego tea because it was used by the Oswego
Indians who used the plant extensively as tea. It was used by patriotic
American colonists during the time when they were boycotting
British tea at the Boston Tea Party. It is a delightful drink by itself but
can also be added to wine drinks and lemonades or to Indian tea.
On the Continent it is called Gold Melissa tea and its dried red
flowers as well as its leaves have a soothing and relaxing effect.

Description Bergamot is a beautiful old-fashioned perennial flowering plant which grows up to a height of 18–35 in. (45–90 cm.) with
ovate-lanceolated serrated leaves and red flowers which stand in
whorls at the top of a square stem. They flower from July to September. The colour of the flowers can be crimson, scarlet, purple,

lavender, white or pink, but it is mainly the scarlet flowers which are wanted for bergamot tea.

Growing Bergamot likes a rich moist soil, almost as moist as near a pond or stream; unlike the mints, to which it is closely related, it does not succeed well in dry soil and full sun. Bergamot can be propagated by division and should be planted out at a distance of 2 ft. (60 cm.) apart. It is advisable to split it up annually; the dead centre can be thrown away and younger bits should be planted out in fresh soil. Bergamot must be kept free from weeds for it otherwise deteriorates quickly. Two years is the longest bergamot plants should be left in any one position. The propagation can be done by rooted cuttings in the same way as balm, any time in late summer. They can also be planted in spring.

Harvesting Flowers and whole leaves should be carefully dried so that both retain their colour.

Uses The equivalent of 1 teaspoon of dried flowers or leaves per cup of boiling water and 1 teaspoon for the pot should be allowed to draw for about 5 minutes. When served hot, Bergamot tea induces sleep and relaxes. Whole fresh or green-dried leaves added to wine or cocktails or to Indian tea produce an interesting flavour.

BORAGE

(*Borago officinalis*)

Virtues Sometimes called beebread or starflower, the beautiful borage plant is believed to have had since the days of the Greeks an exhilarating effect, stimulating the mind and spirit and 'making men merry'. This perhaps accounts for the old English saying, 'I, borage, bring always courage'—which was originally a Greek proverb and came to England via the Romans.

There is a mucilaginous juice in borage which gives a coolness to beverages in which they are steeped. The herb also has a cucumber-like fragrance and when mixed with lemon and sugar in wine or water it makes a restorative drink. It used to be placed in tankards of cool wine or cider and has for many years been added to claret cups; even today it is used in Pimm's No. 1.

As all the parts of the plant are considered to have the same exhilarating effect, borage is one of the few herbs of which the leaves and flowers are used to the same degree. The lovely blue flowers make an edible garnish for salads and they were preserved and often candied in the time of our great-grandmothers, though as a decorative and wholesome sweet rather than as an exhilarating one!

Borage contains potassium and calcium combined with mineral acids, and in its fresh state it has more nitrate of potassium than after it is dried. The stems and leaves supply much saline mucilage, also contain resins, saponine tannins and traces of volatile oil. Attributed to the saline constituent is effectiveness in reducing temperatures and fevers and promoting perspiration and activity of the kidneys. It has always been considered mildly diuretic, demulcent and emollient.

Appearance of the Plant Borage is a sturdy annual herb growing to a height of $1\frac{1}{2}$–3 ft. (45–90 cm.). It has a rough foliage with a stinging hairy surface. The large ovate leaves of greyish green colour are pointed and are about 9 in. (24 cm.) long and 4 in. (10 cm.) broad before the plant produces its flowering stems. Later on smaller leaves grow on this stem. The lower leaves are stalked, with stiff one-celled hairs on the upper surface and below; their margin is entire but wavy. The round stems are hollow and succulent. The herb has a brownish root with many tendrils. Borage is a well-shaped boldly upright plant but its real beauty is in the heavenly blue flowers, sometimes called Madonna blue. The flowers are in a five-pointed star with pendants about 1 in. ($2\frac{1}{2}$ cm.) across, forming drooping clusters with central appendages. The anthers—the part of the stamens which contain the pollen—form a cone in the centre. There are also rare white and red flowering varieties. The fruit has four brownish black nutlets.

Growing Borage is an annual and can only be propagated by seed. The seed, which must be well covered with soil, should be broadcast or sown in shallow drills 1 ft. (30 cm.) apart in March but seeds can also be sown from April to July. If borage is wanted in a herb or rock garden it is advisable to make one-inch deep holes three feet apart and drop three seeds in and later thin to one plant per position. They germinate early and the plant self-sows freely needing only to be kept free from weeds. A loamy soil is good for borage but a light or, even better, sandy loose chalky soil if there is sufficient moisture. Like all herbs it should be grown in well-drained ground, and borage prefers a sunny position.

Once the plants are established after a spring sowing there will always be borage in the garden; and although it is an annual it often flowers right through a mild winter. The plants are ready in approximately eight weeks. From then onwards it is usually more difficult to keep the borage in its place than to raise it unless the soil is uncommonly poor. It is, however, important to keep borage under control. Plants will seed themselves, not only quickly but seedlings may appear year after year in unexpected places. While the seedlings are very young they can be transplanted but the weak ones should be thinned or pinched off at ground level. The mature plant can be 3 ft. (90–100 cm.) tall, perhaps even taller and will need at least two square feet of garden space. The plant remains in continuous bloom until heavy frost comes, when it will quickly become a mass of black leaves only suitable for the compost heap. To have a continuous supply a second sowing should be made. Borage is one of the few annual herbs which can be raised to flower twice in the summer season. If sown in March the plant flowers in July, but in mild areas they will flower in May, seed themselves out and flower again in August. Borage can also be sown in September when it will flower in the following May if the right conditions prevail: mild winters such as are found in the southern counties and a sheltered position on light soil.

Unfortunately, in most gardens the plants are left without any care during the summer. The growing cycle of the individual borage plant is short; it flowers, seeds and eventually dies. If borage plants were cut more often or the dead leaves removed and a few seeds sown again, one would have attractive borage plants all the year round. They would not look so much like weeds, and juicy leaves and lovely flowers could be harvested continuously.

If in autumn they sow themselves out again the new leaves can be used in late winter salads. This can also be intentionally achieved by sowing a few seeds at certain intervals and particularly in autumn if conditions are favourable. The older plants should be taken away after flowering. Usually these beautiful annuals are allowed to grow far too close to each other. They should be given enough space to allow them to branch out: they would then last much longer. A slope in the herb garden is the place for borage. As the pure blue flower clusters droop, the beauty of the plant can be enjoyed most from below, and it can therefore also be planted on high levels of a rock garden.

WINDOW-BOX AND INDOOR GROWING If climate, position and soil of the garden do not allow borage to grow outside during winter, seeds can be put into window-boxes or seedlings bought in spring. They may also survive the winter if sown or planted in autumn in a sheltered position or indoors.

How to Harvest and Dry The herb is ready to be harvested and cut when it flowers but only the young leaves should be used, even if it is cut for the purpose of drying. Borage is not easy to dry domestically as it is succulent and full of humidity and can easily turn black, either if dried at too high a temperature or—if the opposite situation arises—drying takes too long owing to too low a temperature. If the leaves are dried at all, this should be done quickly at a low temperature, and that needs good ventilation. Borage will lose its aroma unless the drying can be done carefully. It can only be kept for a short time unless stored in air-tight containers and in the dark. Flowers can only be used fresh or picked when at their best for the purpose of candying.

What Borage Can Do for Our Food Herb gardeners often do not quite know what to do with borage other than using the occasional leaf for a 'cup'! but the fresh leaves with their cucumber flavour are a delicious addition to salads and vegetables. Chopped up, the young leaves are also eaten on bread and butter and occasionally they have been used like spinach or as an addition to spinach, using half spinach and half borage. This herb improves all cabbage cooking, especially during winter. Certain soups such as green pea and bean, and stews, will benefit from the added borage flavour. As it has a slightly salty flavour, it is an important seasoning for *salt-reduced* diets.

All the qualities in borage extend throughout the plant and therefore a sprig of flowers and leafy tips should be placed in the claret cup or any alcoholic drinks just before serving. Borage is equally useful as an interesting flavouring in fruit drinks such as pure apple juice, and the leaves are also an excellent addition to iced tea as well as to a hot tisane. The flowers impart a blue colour to fluids in which they are steeped and use has been made of this for dyeing vinegars; it could probably have the same effect on white wine cups or clear apple juice drinks if desired.

Last but not least, the flowers make the most attractive decoration for any salad or herb dish, and even when candied and used as confectionery, retain some of the qualities of the plant.

CULINARY USES

Hors-d'œuvre: Tomato juice cocktail; raw vegetable juices; chopped on bread and butter.

Salads: All green salads.

Soups and stews: Green pea and bean soups; meat stews.

Vegetables: As a vegetable on its own; added to spinach; improves cabbage when cooked with it.

Sweets and beverages: Candied and crystallized; fruit cups; claret cup; wine cups; iced tea; hot tisane.

CLARET CUP WITH BORAGE

Ingredients:

A large teaspoon white sugar (best dissolved in a little boiling water)

Thin rind of lemon and strip of cucumber rind, each in one piece

1 bottle claret

Sprigs of young borage, possibly with flowers

1 glass sherry

½ glass maraschino

½ glass brandy

Soda water or Perrier or similar table water

Celery or Celeriac Leaves

Method:

1 Mix lemon and cucumber rind with sugar and ½ bottle claret.
2 Add sprigs of young borage.
3 Allow to stand for approximately 2 hours.
4 Add remaining claret, sherry, maraschino and brandy.
5 Remove borage, but decorate with fresh sprigs and flowers.
6 Add soda water very shortly before serving, according to taste.

CELERY OR CELERIAC LEAVES

(*Apium graveolens*)

Virtues The dried leaves of celery or celeriac will improve soups, sauces and stews if added shortly before serving. The dried leaves of celery are deemed in America an excellent addition to the herb and spice shelf. They are wanted in all recipes where celery-flavour is called for. Celery leaves are, in fact, a bi-product of the vegetables, one of which at least most herb gardeners will have in their garden. Celery was used as a medicinal plant by the ancients and during the Middle Ages, and has a particularly rich variety of vitamins, mineral salts and many active principles. It is even reported to have a hormone which has a similar effect to insulin. It is considered an excellent seasoning for diabetics, or for anyone on a salt-reduced diet.

Description Celery as a vegetable is well known. The base of the stem in the upper part of the root becomes swollen and forms the edible portion of the plant. While celery is grown for its blanched leaf-stalks, used in salads and as a vegetable, celeriac is a turnip-rooted form of the biennial celery. The leaves of both these plants retain their lovely light green colour.

Growing The seeds of both vegetables are sown at the same time: in late February or early March for the main crop, choosing an early variety, and in mid-March or mid-April for the main crop. They should be finely sown in boxes of light soil and the boxes are stored in a warm greenhouse; they are slow to germinate. The seedlings should be given plenty of air and hardened off before planting out. When the seedlings are about 2 in. high they should be pricked out about 3 in. apart in a cold frame. Protection should be given in frosty weather and very cold winds. Watering must be carefully carried out until the plants are large enough to go into a permanent position. Celeriac prefers a damp position with not too much sun. It is advisable to buy plants during the middle of May and plant them out at a distance of 16 in. (40 cm.) in a soil deeply dug and well manured with old manure or compost.

Harvesting The leaves may be cut at any time when the need for flavouring arises or otherwise cut and dried when the vegetables are about to be harvested. They have to be dried with the same care as all other herbs to retain the colour and flavour of celery.

Uses Celery leaves increase the strength of soup, sauces, stews, clear broth and stuffing if added at the last moment; they should not be cooked with a dish, no longer than two or three minutes. It is as well to keep not only the flavour in mind but at the same time the whole medicine cupboard of virtues which particularly take effect when celery is regularly used.

CHAMOMILE

(*Matricaria chamomilla*)

ROMAN CHAMOMILE

(*Anthemis nobilis*)

Virtues Chamomile flowers had at one time more significance as a medicinal herb in this country than at present, and even now more importance is attributed to chamomile in other countries. This may be due to the confusion of the two different kinds of chamomile, which have different qualities. The annual 'true chamomile' (*Matricaria chamomilla*) is the one used more for medicinal purposes, while the perennial 'Roman chamomile' (*Anthemis nobilis*) is the plant which in this country has been used for making lawns for centuries.

Chamomile

Each of these types is called in certain countries 'true chamomile' or Roman' or 'German', but *Matricaria chamomilla* is the one with the healing blue oil which is infinitely more valuable for medicinal purposes, and wherever it has been used the chamomile tradition is much more alive.

Flowers of the 'true chamomile' have a pleasant flavour and a cleansing and soothing action on the gastro-intestinal tract and, in fact, on all organs lined with mucous membrane. They contain volatile oil, resins, bitter substances, wax, fats and glycoside which has an anti-spasmodic effect. The oil of chamomile when freshly distilled from *Matricaria* has a blue colour which is part of a chemical substance called Azulen. This is responsible for the anti-inflammatory effect of the chamomile flower and the more of this contained in the flower or oil the greater the effect. The chamomile flower is curative, healing, warming, soothing and softening, but never a tonic.

Description 'True chamomile' (*Matricaria chamomilla*) resembles very similar-looking weeds, to which belong about twenty species, e.g. Stinking Mayweed. The best way to distinguish the 'true chamomile' is to look for the yellow receptacle which is markedly conical from the beginning and—above all—it is hollow. The ray-less *Matricaria*, which looks similar but has no ray-florets, has the same hollow receptacle and pleasant scent, but no blue oil; it can be added in small quantities to the other *Matricaria* flowers. Both have an erect glabrous stem 6–7 in. (15–16 cm.) high, but only 'true chamomile' can grow to 15 in. (40 cm.) and has the fifteen white rayflorets, approximately 6 × 9 × 2–3 mm., which reflex soon after flowering begins. This type is often found on the fringe of wheat-fields unless artificial treatment has either destroyed them or reduced their value. It can be collected wild, but preferably not from where it is known that chemicals are in use. It should, however, never be confused with *Anthemis nobilis* or with the allied *Chrysanthemum parthenium*, which is the herb 'fever-few'. However, they can easily be cultivated as an annual.

The 'Roman chamomile' (*Anthemis nobilis*) has double white flowers giving out a pleasant scent when crushed. It also has aromatic scales on the receptacles, which are broad and nearly as long as the centre florets.

Growing The 'true chamomile' (*Matricaria chamomilla*) is an annual which has to be sown each year and, as it seeds itself easily, it appears again and again in different places. It can be sown early in spring or in autumn in rows of 8–12 in. (20–30 cm.) or in three rows at a distance of 8 in. (20 cm.) apart with alternatively a gap of 20 in. (50 cm.) between each set of three rows. The very fine seeds should be sown on a humid day, mixed with sand or wood-ash; while they are germinating watering is advisable.

The 'Roman chamomile' (*Anthemis nobilis*) is propagated by division and cuttings in April; the plants should be placed about 4 in. (10 cm.) apart. It is suitable for making lawns in dry soils where it will remain green when grass has already started to become brown because of a drought. It has a pleasant fragrance when walked upon but cannot be relied upon for games lawns; the interest in these lawns is diminishing because of the labour involved in weeding them.

Chamomile is also medicinally helpful to other plants and nothing is as important to the health of a garden, and particularly to an organic herb garden, as a number of chamomile herbs growing in it. One of the organic schools, the bio-dynamic method of growing includes chamomile as an important factor in their herbal preparations which are used as activators and fertilizers. If a plant in the herb garden is drooping and apparently dying it has been observed that it will often recover if *Matricaria* plants are planted near it.

Harvesting *Matricaria* flowers from May to October. The flowers appear eight weeks after sowing and then are ready for picking. The flowers should be fully open and can be picked every few days, but only when it is dry and sunny. On wet and foggy days the chamomile flowers have only half the content of oil of chamomile. Only flowers without or with very small stalks should be picked, either by hand or with a comb. They should not be pressed down or heaped up, and should be placed in thin layers on a frame with nylon net. They should be quickly dried in a temperature not above 95° F. (35° C.). Good ventilation should help the flowers become dry even inside the receptacles, as quickly as possible. They should be touched as little as possible before and after drying, as they crumble easily. The dried chamomile can be kept in air-tight containers in a dry place as it easily absorbs humidity from the air and then starts to go mouldy.

Uses Chamomile tea is drunk in France as an aid to digestion after heavy meals; it deals with disturbances of the intestinal tract, has a cleansing, disinfectant and anti-spasmodic effect, and is helpful in the case of intestinal pain; an infusion is also used for enemas. For a general 'tummy upset', especially if connected with vomiting, a tea made partly of chamomile flowers, partly of peppermint leaves, is most settling. The anti-inflammatory and anti-bacteria qualities are helpful when an infusion is used as a gargle for inflamed gums or relaxed throats, alternatively with sage or combined with it. Chamomile is valuable in facial steam-baths, for improving the skin or against heavy colds; as an eye-bath in the case of inflamed eyelids or as a hair rinse, particularly for blonde hair. (The flowers of the 'Roman chamomile' can also be used as a hair wash or rinse.) Excellent for external use: for nose rinse, as a mouthwash after dental treatment, for a sore mouth, and for compresses.

The anti-pain effect comes into its own when dealing with toothache either by rinsing with a warm infusion or using small linen bags filled with chamomile flowers warmed on a kettle or hot-water bottle to hold against the cheek or other painful parts. Two teaspoons of flowers per cup of boiling water allowed to draw for 5–10 minutes make an infusion which should not be allowed to boil; no more than two cupfuls should be drunk per day. They will increase perspiration; also used for skin troubles or eczema, particularly those of old age.

CHERVIL

(*Anthriscus cerefolium*)

Virtues Chervil is a most useful herb and its delicate aroma can be enjoyed almost all the year round if sown at intervals. Famous in France and Central Europe for flavouring, it is used for making the delicious chervil soup and many famous sauces. The subtle, very special, flavour of chervil has to be experienced—it is difficult to describe it other than that it has a slightly sweetish, pleasantly aromatic scent and taste. Apart from its own aroma chervil has the quality of improving the flavour of any herb with which it is mixed, making it an important and constant part in *fines herbes*.

Chervil was brought to England by the Romans and as it was also used in Anglo-Saxon times it has been cultivated in this country probably uninterruptedly for a very long time.

The blood-cleansing and diuretic qualities of chervil have been known since early days. Whether they are the reason for qualifying chervil in particular for Lenten dishes, such as the Frankfurter Green Sauce, a German speciality originally used for Maundy Thursday, or whether this was due to the fact that chervil is one of the first herbs in spring available in larger quantities, is difficult to decide nowadays. But these two qualities made it one of the Lent herbs and the refreshing spicy flavour may account for people's wishes to use it in spring. The juice of chervil was originally used as a cleansing treatment, for fever, jaundice, gout and chronic skin troubles; it was also taken to increase perspiration and is said to have a special effect on the glandular system, and—above all—it has been considered a good digestive.

Appearance of the Plant The plant looks similar to parsley but is more delicate and feathery. The foliage is lacy and fernlike, in fact chervil has three-pinnate twice divided leaves, bright green in colour but of a lighter shade than parsley. The stems are hollow, striated (slightly ridged) and the plant has a thin whitish tapering root with a smell reminiscent of aniseed. The plant reaches a height of 12–20 in. (30–40 cm.). Minute (2 mm. in diameter) white flowers grow in umbels and flower from June to August. There are curly and smooth varieties and in some countries the curly varieties are preferred particularly as the wild chervil can be confused with fools' parsley and hemlock. The garden variety, however, is smaller and more delicate than either of these plants.

The fruits look like caraway but are longer and thinner when ripe. But if the herb is continually cut for using or drying it will not seed.

Chervil

Growing Chervil has the features of a hardy annual and also those of a biennial plant. It can be sown in the garden at any time of the year when the soil is workable and is one of the few herbs which can be cut during the winter and early spring if a careful sowing programme is planned. Chervil does not require any special soil but will not thrive in a heavy soil which is badly drained. Sometimes it can be found that in one row the plants vary from poor to well matured and this is usually due to the fact that in certain spots the soil is too wet. It is also necessary to find either a half-shady position or create a situation in which chervil will have full winter sun which it enjoys, and a half-shady position in summer.

As chervil cannot tolerate hot dry conditions it is more difficult to establish sowings during the months of May, June and July when the days are long and the plants more likely to be subjected to long periods of sunshine. Sowings made in February, March and April if well watered and kept shaded can be cut several times during the summer, depending on the type of weather. A typical English summer with plenty of cloud and rain creates good conditions for chervil.

The best time to sow chervil is in August when the days are already beginning to shorten and the morning dews, even in spells of sunny weather, help to moisten the soil and foliage of the young plants. Therefore, if a continuous supply of chervil is wanted throughout the year, August provides a good start for a sowing programme. These August sowings provide chervil for cutting at the end of September and will give a second cut in October if the weather is not too cold. If these plants are left in the ground during winter they will give a further one or two cuttings in early spring. If chervil is protected by cloches or frames it will give a crop two weeks earlier.

Chervil can be sown monthly from January onwards if the soil is workable (best results experienced when sowing two days before each full moon), and the plants will be ready from May onwards.

The seeds should be sown in drills 1 ft. (30 cm.) apart and the soil trodden in lightly or rolled if the conditions of the soil permits. Once the plants are established they will sow themselves out provided that not all plants are used for cutting and the new plants will come up amongst the old ones. Seeds must be sown where the plants are to grow as the delicate root system does not stand transplanting well. The seedlings should be thinned out when 2–3 in. (6–8 cm.) high by pinching off at the ground—around 9 in. (24 cm.) to be allowed for plants to mature.

After that it requires little care other than keeping the weeds at bay and keeping the soil moist by watering or irrigation. It is a definite danger with chervil that if it becomes too dry it will flower too quickly and is therefore no longer useful as a flavouring herb. Therefore bolting and fading in the direct sun has to be avoided if chervil is wanted all the year round. As the plants cannot be moved from place to place, for this would cause the young plants to flower immediately, the sowing may have to be done in different places at different months of the year.

During the summer rows of the herbs may be sown between rows of tall herb groups particularly during their first year. For instance as well as dill, chervil can be sown between other garden rows. The tall plants of herbs or vegetables or soft fruit can provide the semi-shade. If one arranges it so that annual herbs will be out of the way in winter, chervil can benefit from the winter sunshine which it needs and enjoys so much.

If sown in March, flowers appear sometimes early in May, often seeding in June. Later on, stalks and leaves turn mauve and then tawny red. Flowers should be plucked off as soon as they appear, as with all other herbs. In reading about chervil one will find that controversial opinions are offered on the subject of growing. There is hardly any other herb of which people state with such certainty that it is one of the easiest to grow, while others complain that they find it difficult. But, if its special requirements with regard to soil, position, sun or no sun in different seasons, and the short germinating power of the seeds are considered carefully, it should not be difficult to have plenty of chervil when it is wanted, even in winter or during summer, which is actually the more difficult growing period.

WINTER PREPARATION As mentioned before, if chervil is sown in autumn in the right kind of position which will provide it with shelter and with the winter and autumn sun, supplies will be available during winter, as chervil matures rapidly. As the plant is very hardy, the thinning of new plants can be done during winter and these can be used for flavouring even during this season.

WINDOW-BOX AND INDOOR GROWING Small quantities may also be sown in boxes in the greenhouse or indoors if the outdoor supplies run short and these sowings can be repeated at intervals. This herb is also particularly suitable for growing in a pot or trough.

A good spot is provided by the kitchen window-sill where it is in easy picking distance, for use with—for instance—scrambled eggs for breakfast. As it has to be used generously and is reduced to nothing in cooking, it should be sown in not too small quantities and a whole box should be given over to growing chervil. It will also be necessary to repeat sowing to have the same quantity again at a later time.

How to Harvest and Dry As soon as 6–8 weeks after sowing, chervil can be cut and used for flavouring in cooking. Leaves for immediate use should always be picked from the outside, as with parsley, as this will allow the plant to keep growing from the centre. Great care should be taken that chervil is not permitted to flower. If cut almost down to ground level it will grow a new leaf crop and will continue to do so even after the first frost until a really heavy frost comes. If the plants have been covered by cloches they can be kept until an early spring cutting, when it is most wanted. In March new leaves will shoot from the winter plants.

Chervil is not suitable for drying unless special precautions to retain its delicate flavour are taken. Drying must be done at a low temperature, and this low temperature must be maintained. As the thin, delicate leaves dry down to very little (1 to 10) domestic drying is not advisable particularly as it is almost easier to sow a cutting crop in autumn which will become available during winter and spring. It is more difficult to have a continuous supply of fresh chervil during summer unless growing in 'temporary or semi-shade' is made possible (see paragraph on Growing, page 74).

When chervil is dried—in a dark airing cupboard in thin layers on nylon-covered frames—it must be kept in air-tight containers in the dark.

Chervil

What Chervil Can Do for Our Food Chervil is one of the oldest seasoning plants of the north of Europe, and is used more today in France and parts of Central Europe than anywhere else. The mild flavour of chervil makes a generous use necessary—in fresh or dried form—particularly with all dishes in which it is the predominant or the only herb. There is hardly a dish which could not be improved by this fresh and yet spicy flavour. It is also such a lovely garnishing for any dish that might otherwise be decorated with parsley. It may wilt more quickly than parsley and therefore garnishes should be added at the last moment.

Chervil is, of course, at its best and most noticeable if added to food which need not be cooked, but if it is added to a soup or sauce it should be added last and the dish only be allowed to come to the boil once, unless the chervil is sautéd and cooked as in the famous Chervil Soup for which a recipe follows. This, however, as well as the similar Chervil Sauce can only be attempted if 2–3 good handfuls or 3 tablespoons of dried chervil are available for each recipe. This soup has been praised as one of the most delicious dishes of this world; it has in fact two values for the gourmet: its unique flavour and its wholesome effect on the one organ which has to serve the gourmet well.

Last but not least chervil can be used everywhere as it glorifies the flavour of the other herbs. Therefore it is found in all recipes combining other herbs, as well as in special ones. It will even help to improve sweet dishes such as custards and it plays an important part among the herbs which contribute and create the flavour of famous liqueurs. It is certainly a herb which can make in its modest and not overpowering way a great contribution to our enjoyment of food.

CULINARY USES—LIST OF DISHES

Hors-d'œuvre: Piquant with crab; all vegetable cocktails; canapés; as a garnish.

Salads: On lettuce, all raw vegetable salads; potato salad; any green salad. As a single herb in French dressing.

Eggs and cheese: Pancakes; omelettes; use generously in chervil omelette; any egg dish; in cream cheese.

Chives and Onion Green

Soups, stews and salads: Chervil soup; spinach and sorrel soup; green or spring soup; all sauces; Béarnaise sauce; green sauce.

Meat and fish: Generously (before serving) on roast beef, lamb, veal, steaks. Melted chervil butter over veal cutlets and fish. Herb butter; fish sauce.

Poultry and game: Broiled chicken; butter sauce; in melted butter for poultry. Chervil butter.

Vegetables: Sprinkle on peas, tomatoes, aubergines, spinach, before serving. On boiled, buttered vegetables.

CHERVIL SOUP

Ingredients:

3 tablespoons chervil	1 pint hot stock
2–3 tablespoons butter or oil	Salt
2 teaspoons flour	1 tablespoon cream (fresh or
½ cup cold water or stock	sour)

Method:

1 Sauté chervil in butter or oil.
2 Add flour, sauté again.
3 Smooth with cold water or stock.
4 Add hot vegetable stock and salt.
5 Cook for 20 minutes.
6 Add cream shortly before serving.

Note. Instead of using flour a raw potato can be grated into the soup as a means of thickening. It also improves it dietetically.

CHIVES

(*Allium schoenoprasum*)

ONION GREEN

(*Allium fistulosum*)

Virtues Chives have been called 'the little brothers of the onion'. The smallest of the onion tribe, they have the most subtle flavour of them all, while the similar-looking green leaves of the Welsh Onion are a little stronger in flavour and coarser in blade. Both have different parts to play in cooking. Chives is an unassuming plant with little glamour, its history goes back to the days of the ancient Chinese in 3000 B.C. and was used throughout Asia and the Mediterranean region centuries before the beginning of the Christian era.

Since the Romans introduced chives to this country they have been cultivated in the British Isles under the local name of 'Rush Leek', a translation of the Latin name, and they can be found as a native plant growing locally in rocky pastures usually near limestone.

Chives contain iron, pungent volatile oils, pectin and in small quantity, sulphur. In a mild way chives are an antibiotic and have the reputation of strengthening the stomach, reducing high blood-pressure and producing a beneficial effect on the kidneys.

The volatile oil and sulphur have also a stimulating effect on the appetite of invalids and it is therefore advisable to offer salads, ome-lettes and in fact all egg dishes with plenty of chives during con-valescence.

Chives is a most useful herb all round, but particularly for those who do not like a strong onion taste.

Small quantities of finely chopped leaves are reputed to be good for newly hatched turkeys and chicks, mixed with their mash.

Appearance of the Plant Chives are 'grass-like' hardy perennial members of the Allium family. The leaves are cylindrical, sub-glaucous (slight bloom), 4–10 in. (10–24 cm.) × 1·3 mm. Scape (stem) 6–16 in. (15–40 cm.), cylindric. Spathe (sheath) usually two valved; vales ovate (egg-shaped), shortly accumulate (tapering to a fine point) and scarious (dried and shrivelled).

The slender leaves appear early in spring and are long, cylindrical and hollow, tapering to a point and about the thickness of a crow's quill. The flowering stem is usually nipped off with cultivated plants as they are grown solely for the sake of the leaves or 'grass', but when allowed to rise it seldom reaches more than a few inches to, at most, a foot in height. It is hollow and has no leaf, or one leaf sheathing it below the middle. Chives differ in the thickness of their leaves.

Chives have relatively tiny white flat bulbs compared with other members of the onion family. The bulbs grow very close together in clusters and are of an elongated form with a white rather firm sheath; the outer sheath is sometimes grey.

The stem supports a close globular head or umbel of pale mauve to purple or pink flowers. The umbel is sub-globose, dense flowered without bubils; pedicels shorter than the flower, the stamens about half as long as the perianth. In other words, the numerous flowers are densely packed together and supported from slender little flower stalks shorter than the flowers themselves which lengthen slightly as the fruit ripens; and this causes the heads to assume a conical instead of a round shape. The anthers (the pollen-bearing part of the flower) are of a bluish purple colour.

The seed vessel or capsule is very small and completely concealed within the petals which are about its length. The small seeds which it contains are black when ripe and similar to onion seeds.

Chives make a neat attractive edging for a herb garden and the giant variety is best suited for this. It can grow as tall as 15–18 in. (38–45 cm.) with flowers the size of half-crowns which remain in flower for two months. This variety has not however the same flavour as the small culinary chives.

Growing The important point for the gardener is the fact that chives will be available for use early in the year before other onions are ready.

It is often said of chives that any kind of soil and position will suit them. Roughly speaking this may be so but chives have certain preferences which if observed will help to 'grow Chives rampant' and avoid failure. Chives prefer for instance an average light, medium rich, damp, sandy, loamy or chalky soil full of humus. They are really inhabitants of humid meadows and therefore need a great deal of humidity, in fact growing them near a water tank or tap is a good idea because they prefer not only to be kept damp but almost wet, particularly during dry summers. Careful watering can help enormously. It is not necessary for them to be in a warm position, though a sunny one is a help, but they could also be in half shade. The herb is not difficult to grow. It loves strong humus; some soot, though well-weathered, or coffee grounds can do wonders for its growth.

Propagation can be by sowing in spring and by root division in spring and autumn. When dividing into small clumps of 3–6 bulbs in spring and then resetting in rich soil, the distance between the rows should be 10 in. (25 cm.) for the fine-leafed variety and 15 in. (40 cm.) for the coarser variety. Chives may suddenly die and disappear. In this case the bulbs should be divided in the autumn to prevent overcrowding; a tiny clump will spread to a fine clump in the course of the year and may then be divided again. In fact, at any time of the year when the ground is not frozen, this can be done. The giant variety should be 12–15 in. (30–40 cm.) apart.

At the beginning of May, little seedlings look like grass and can be planted out on the site in clumps. If Chives are sown in the open ground which has a hard top layer the germinating power sometimes is not sufficient to break through it and the chives will therefore grow irregularly. The long-living chives take a great deal out of the soil and a good amount of compost should be used to replenish it.

Chives absorb nitrogen (0·64 per cent and potassium (0·33 per cent). The nitrogen content is the highest of any onion and leek plants. Also their requirements of chalk are higher than that for other onions and they should therefore never be grown before or after another member of the onion family on the same ground. If there is lack of food in the soil it leads to early yellowing of the tops.

Chives are about the most satisfactory of all the herbs to grow. Once plants are well set out, all there is to do to keep them vigorous and happy, is to cut them back for use; this is both good for the gardener and good for the plants. In any case, chive plants should be cut back periodically, particularly when they bloom. If this is not done the outer leaves will wilt and turn brown. It is, however, important to cut chives in the right way as the clumps may otherwise die. The 'grass' should be cut to within 2 in. (5 cm.) of the ground; but severe cutting requires enrichment of the soil afterwards. Unless the seed is wanted for propagation, all flower stubs should be shorn off as soon as they fade, otherwise they seed themselves so abundantly over a wide area that they become a nuisance.

If the plants seem crowded their thick clumps of bulb-roots should be dug up, divided and replanted wider apart. If they increase rapidly they will grow too quickly; they should be divided every third spring and dressed with some compost or well-rotted dung in autumn.

Chives and Onion Green

It is important that chives should be kept clean from weeds from the beginning—particularly if the plants are wanted for several years —as it is very difficult to get between clumps at a later stage.

In July chives sometimes weaken. It is recommended that compost be added during the hot months, or the chives be replanted elsewhere.

WINTER GROWING By careful cropping, 'grass' can be obtained quite late in the season until the early frosts come. Then it withers and disappears, pushing up again in the first warm days of February. The plants will produce new growth from their hearty bulb structure each spring, and no protection is required throughout the whole winter, but cloches can be placed over the chives to encourage earlier crops.

Sowing can be started early in a greenhouse. As early as January and definitely at the beginning of April chives can be sown in warm boxes. Chives need warmth, particularly when grown from seed. They can be raised from seeds sown as soon as ripe, in drills $\frac{1}{4}$ in. (5 mm.) deep. The seeds germinate slowly in the dark but unless they are of last year's harvest they should not be used, because after one year germination rate diminishes. The fine-leaved variety can be sown thicker than the medium or coarse variety.

Even the severest frost does not damage chive plants. In late autumn they can be dug up for division, the root bulb structure separated and the smallest bulbs with the surrounding soil taken indoors in order to supply chives for the whole winter. These should be put into pots or window-boxes after cutting back the stalks to a bare 2 in. (5 cm.) above soil level, but they must be watered regularly. The plants should be cut back repeatedly throughout the winter as the green shoots grow strong and bright. If left after reaching their full height they will wilt and suddenly die.

During the winter months chives can be sown in boxes in a greenhouse at a temperature of 80° F. (25° C.). Small clumps of the young plants can then be put into pots or deeper boxes. After a few weeks the chives are ready for cutting. It is important that the soil should be sufficiently rich in compost. Chive plants are very successful in window-boxes, even in London.

Often little pot plants which are purchased will not last because the container is almost always too small for the root structure. These should be repotted in layer containers.

How to Harvest and Dry Chive clumps are ready for cutting approximately five weeks after planting in spring. Otherwise, in whichever way chives are propagated, once the leaves have reached their normal height they should be cut. If chives are well looked after and repeatedly cut to within 2 in. (5 cm.) above the soil several cuttings are possible during the year. The leaves will soon grow again and be found more tender each time of cutting.

The harvest of chives varies very much in quantity according to seasonal conditions. A dry year will produce much less. Also coarser chives give larger quantities than the medium and fine.

Chives have been mainly used fresh until recently. Unless colour and with it the mild onion flavour can be fully retained, it is not advisable to dry chives and to use them in a dried state. Chives have therefore not been dried commercially until very recently. They can only be dried by very careful methods in low temperatures. If chives are dried the loss of humidity varies between 83 and 86 per cent. If it is possible to retain colour and the mild onion flavour, chives will reconstitute in any liquid and be surprisingly near fresh chives.

What Chives Can Do for Our Food Chives is without doubt one of the best culinary herbs, with extremely varied uses. It imparts a mild onion flavour to dishes and is therefore often liked even by those people who are not able to either appreciate or take any other onion.

Certain care has to be used with very delicate vegetables as it is always possible that the mild onion flavour will overpower subtle and delicate aromas; but wherever emphasis is wanted, chives are the right herbs.

In melted butter it gives a finishing touch to mashed or boiled potatoes. Chopped chives can also be added to mashed potatoes when accompanying grilled chops or steak, and a little can be put in dripping when frying. It is excellent mixed with meat and fish rissoles, scrambled eggs, sandwich fillings, very good with cucumber or tomato salad.

Chopped chives worked into fresh butter—Chives Butter—makes

an excellent accompaniment for grilled meat or fish, and can be spread on toast.

Chives is also the main part of the famous Frankfurter Green Sauce (see recipe p. 85) which is so good with the first new potatoes, boiled beef or cold joint. Chives make a fatty soup more digestible and this applies to all fatty dishes. It is really one of the most indispensable herbs for our daily food.

The bulbs of chives can be pickled like small onions, and they have also been used as a delicate addition to sausages.

Other ways in which chives can add piquancy to our food are as follows:

Hors-d'œuvre: With almost any hors-d'œuvre.

Soups: In cream of asparagus, bean or cauliflower, potato; important in Vichyssoise soup.

Salads: Potato, cucumber, mixed vegetables and green salads.

Salad dressings: Suitable in all French dressings (oil and lemon).

Eggs: In omelettes, scrambled and stuffed eggs.

Cheeses: In cream and cottage cheese.

Sauces: In white and tomato sauces; chives butter.

Fish: In fish casseroles.

Meat: In stews and rissoles.

Unless otherwise stated fresh or green-dried chives are equally suitable.

COLD SPRING SAUCE

There are two versions of the Cold Spring Sauce, one of which is the famous Frankfurter Green Sauce. In both cases seven spring herbs are used which can be slightly varied according to the availability in spring. They can be either chopped fresh or green-dried.

Ingredients:

1 hard-boiled egg per person
1 tablespoon oil (for 3 eggs)
$\frac{1}{2}$ lemon
Salt
2 tablespoons chopped or green-dried chives

1 tablespoon chopped or green-dried herbs; mixed of: tarragon, dill chervil, sorrel, salad burnet, borage
1 pinch of summer savory
1 cup (approx.) sour cream mixed with a little top of the milk and yoghourt

Chives and Onion Green

Method:

1 Separate yolks from white.
2 Mash yolks with fork and mix with 1 tablespoon oil into smooth paste.
3 Add juice of ½ lemon and salt.
4 Chop white of eggs.
5 Add herbs to yolks and mix well.
6 Mix in cream to a thick constituency.
7 Add white of eggs.

FRANKFURTER GREEN SAUCE

1 raw yolk of egg mixed carefully and slowly with oil as for mayonnaise.

Add while constantly stirring 1 teaspoon lemon, a little salt if liked.

When all is well mixed add finely chopped capers and gherkins, or fresh cucumber.

One hard-boiled egg finely chopped and the following finely chopped herbs add to the mayonnaise:

7 fresh or green-dried herbs such as: dill, borage, chervil, parsley, sorrel, salad burnet and above all two thirds of the bunch should be chives.

or 2 tablespoons green-dried chives and 1 tablespoon of all the other herbs mixed.

Note. Both are excellent with boiled beef or new potatoes.

ONION GREEN

(*Allium fistulosum*)

Virtues For those who like their onion flavouring a little stronger than that of chives, the green tops of the Welsh onion, often called onion green, are most suitable. They are not known wild, but probably originated in Eastern Asia. The taste is between the mild onion flavour of chives and the stronger one of the onions and shallots.

Appearance of the Plant Leaves are circular in section, the scape inflated near the middle. Inflorescence is many flowered and the flowers are yellowish white.

Growing Welsh onions are a hardy perennial and should be spaced 1 ft. (30 cm.) apart. They multiply rapidly through division of roots. Their chive-like stems can be available as a flavouring right through the winter without any protection.

How to Harvest and Dry As onion green is available also during winter, it is one of the mild onion flavourings for those who can grow herbs throughout the year, but for those who cannot, onion green is now green-dried commercially and can be obtained and used in the same way as chives, provided that the green tops have retained their full colour and flavour.

What Onion Green Can Do for Our Food Added to the sautéd onions in vegetables and meat cookery, soups, stews and casseroles they enhance the taste which, though hardly noticeable in the dish, nevertheless adds zest to the wide range of onion flavour. When vegetables are cooked in their own juice, onion green is indispensable because this method is usually begun by sautéing onions, parsley and onion green, the vegetables being added later. In this way not only are the juices, the flavour and the important nutrients of the vegetables retained but also the stronger flavour of parsley and onion green is added to them. This is the secret of many vegetable dishes, and in particular, casseroles and stews found all over Europe.

Onion green can be used sprinkled over a dish shortly before serving though if green-dried onion green is used it should be moistened in a salad dressing or lemon juice to reconstitute it. If onion green is used for cream cheese or sandwich spreads, it should be allowed to permeate the mixture outside the fridge for at least one hour before serving. Otherwise onion green can be used in exactly the same way and in the same dishes as chives.

BREAD STUFFING
(Basic Recipe)

The quantity of soaked bread depends on the purpose for which the stuffing is required.

Dandelion

Ingredients:

1 lb. stale bread
Oil for sautéing
2 onions
2 tablespoons parsley
2 tablespoons onion green, celery, 1 tablespoon lovage

Pinch each of marjoram, thyme and rosemary
Salt, grated nutmeg, ground ginger
1–2 eggs

Method:

1 Soak bread (preferably wholemeal) in cold water until the crust is soft.
2 Take it out and squeeze well so that it is mashed and fairly dry.
3 Sauté chopped onion in oil, in a large frying-pan, until it looks golden.
4 Add the parsley and sauté again.
5 Add an equal quantity of onion green and other herbs and sauté again.
6 Add to this the squeezed bread and mix well.
7 Sauté, turning over all the time, until the mixture is fairly dry.
8 Allow to cool, season with salt, grated nutmeg and ground ginger according to taste.
9 Add 1 to 2 whole eggs and mix all well.

Note. This stuffing can be used for cabbage rolls, spinach rolls, tomatoes, potatoes, and all stuffings. It can also be made into dumplings. Cook 1 dumpling and if it does not hold well together, add another egg.

Dumplings should be cooked in salted water or stock; some dumplings can be served in clear broth, larger dumplings can be served with butter and fried onions on a hot dish.

The bread mixture can also be made into a loaf and baked like a joint in the oven. To make a full meal 1 or 2 hard-boiled eggs can be put into the centre of the loaf.

DANDELION

(*Taraxacum officinale*)

Virtues Dandelion and nettle are a disgrace in the garden, but they are both of such highly nutritious value that they should be considered for growing—at least in a corner—unless they are already found in abundance in the grounds. Dandelion is also full of remedial qualities. Though dandelion leaves are mainly taken in spring as a fresh salad, as a freshly pressed juice, together with spinach, or made like spinach purée, the young leaves can really be used throughout the year. The substances which cause the various effects of dandelion have not been sufficiently examined, but continental writers claim that in dandelion can be found potassium and calcium salts, also manganese, sodium, sulphur, silicic acid, next to vitamin A, B, C and D and a substance called choline, which is also found in the gall-bladder; the root contains inulin.

According to new chemical investigations dandelion is supposed to contain more nutritious substances than the best spinach. Dandelion salad in spring has a very high efficiency as a blood cleanser owing to its slightly diuretic and digestive qualities. Taking green-dried dandelion during winter is used as a means to improve the functions of the gall-bladder and even is supposed to help to free the system of gall- and kidney-stones.

Dandelion stimulates the glands connected with the digestion, and encourages the gall-bladder and pancreas to increased action. The whole plant has medicinal properties useful in liver disorders and in jaundice. The juice of the fresh root or an infusion made of the dried root is used to stimulate the production of bile.

Description Dandelions are variable perennials, which may be anything from 2–12 in. (5–30 cm.) high, well known as a difficult lawn weed, but on the other hand producing an attractive golden blaze in May meadows. Dandelion has a milky juice and the basal rosettes of leaves are sometimes downy, occasionally purple spotted, deeply lobed or toothed, with the teeth usually pointing backwards and a large, rather blunt, terminal lobe: the name *dent de lion* originates from these teeth. The large flowers are composed of numerous bright yellow ray-florets and are always solitary on hollow fleshy, rubbery leafless stalks, narrower at the op. The fruits have a beak surmounted by a non-feathery spreading pappus, which together make the well-known dandelion clocks. They are abundant in grassy and waste spaces throughout the year but in great profusion in April to May.

Dandelion

Growing The seed may be sown in any odd corner of the garden, provided the plants can be kept in check there. Almost full shade is still useful for dandelion. Some humus should be added to the soil in the form of leaf mould or a small quantity of manure. The seeds should be sown in April and there are improved strains available which will make larger and more succulent leaves. The leaves can be blanched before use as otherwise they tend to be bitter. Four or five plants should be allowed to remain in each clump to be covered with a forcing pot over a deep box or large plant pot. They will probably have less chlorophyll, but for those people who do not mind the bitterness, blanching is not necessary.

The plants have a root which will penetrate the soil deeply and this is one of the reasons why they are so difficult to eradicate. They flower from April to autumn, but the flowers, or later the 'clocks' should be pinched out to prevent dandelions appearing in unwanted places.

Harvesting The leaves can be collected from April to September, the root in spring or autumn. The leaves can be picked from the root because the root will send up new shoots so that there can be several harvests during the 4–5 months. The collected leaves should be carefully dried to retain their green colour and when they are really dry they should be rubbed and kept in an air-tight container away from the light. The roots, which have to be dug out with forks, are freed from the parts which are above the soil, brushed and washed and dried in a similar way to valerian roots (see p. 211). The roots must be brittle so that they break, and then they can be ground and roasted for use as 'coffee'.

Uses Young dandelion leaves are used as a salad or on sandwiches, or as a freshly expressed juice, or added to spinach purée or made like one, and green-dried leaves are sprinkled over food and used like a culinary herb. A tea can be made of them for regular use for gall-bladder and rheumatic conditions (1 teaspoon per cup).

The dried leaves are used to make a 'stout' and this is often mixed with burdock. A wine made from the older leaves and flowers, which is excellent for the digestion, is made by country people.

The dried root, roasted, is used for making dandelion coffee as a substitute for coffee (without caffeine). The coffee should be made with boiling water, strained, milk and sugar added as required.

DILL

(*Anethum graveolens*)

Virtues Dill is a herb with a pungent sharply aromatic and yet slightly sweetish flavour, quite its own. Though primarily a culinary herb it was mentioned for medicinal purposes in old Egyptian texts. It came to us with the Romans whose poets sang praises of its delicacy and fragrance in their gardens. In the seventeenth and eighteenth centuries and probably later, dill seeds, also called 'Meeting House' seeds, were nibbled during church services to dull the agony of listening to long dry sermons and to prevent people from feeling hungry. As dill seeds have a mildly soporific effect, they were given to babies to quieten them and make them sleep. The name is derived from the Norse word *dilla*, 'to lull', for it was believed in early days to be a cure for sleeplessness, while another favourite use for it was to sharpen the appetite.

The difference between dill herb and dill seed lies in the degree of pungency. While the seed has a slightly bitter taste and is much stronger, the dill herb has a delightful bouquet. Its tendency is to improve rather than to dominate. The dill herb therefore is ideal for all delicate vegetables, salads and fish while dill seeds have been used in babies' gripe water, for carminative effect and excellent digestive purposes. Its richness in minerals—it contains potassium, sodium, sulphur and phosphorus—makes it a valuable supplement to our food.

Appearance of the Plant Dill is of medium height, approximately 3 ft. (90 cm.) and over. Its dark green erect stem is hollow, finely serrated and has alternate white and green stripes reaching to the umbels. The leaves are feathery and bluish green, bipinnate, threadlike and similar to fennel, but a little farther apart. The lower leaves are stalked. The single slender main stem carries at its top a flat cluster of tiny yellow flowers. The flower umbels are large, approximately 8 in. (20 cm.) and flat. They have no involucre or bracts, and flower from June to August. The root is weak.

The fruits are oval, compressed, about 5 mm. wide with three longitudinal ridges on the back and three dark lines of oil cells between them and two on the flat surfaces. The taste is strongly aromatic and though resembling caraway, it has a distinct flavour of its own.

Dill and fennel leaves look very similar in the garden but the difference in shade, the slightly upturned umbels of dill, and the hollow stalk, will help to distinguish one herb from another.

Growing Dill is an annual and can only be propagated by seeds. It can be grown in every kind of garden soil and has no special requirements. It will be found that certain conditions are more helpful than others and quite a number of gardens exist in which it has not been quite so easy to grow dill.

Dill is a tender, fragile plant which has difficulties in withstanding adverse conditions. With favourable soil and weather conditions dill grows rampantly like weeds. It has therefore to be avoided that dill should become dry in light soil during a drought or become mouldy in stagnant humidity. A well-drained soil in a sunny spot gives dill the best chances.

Dill requires fine tilth; seeds have to be sown as flat as possible and should then be slightly pressed in.

Germination takes place after fourteen days in the dark at 15° C. It can be unsatisfactory when seeds are used which are not fully matured. On the other hand dill seeds have a long germination power and it has been observed that even after five years' storage the seeds could still germinate. To try out whether seeds will still germinate they should be sown in boxes at a low temperature of 15–18° C.; after twenty-one days they should have germinated.

To have a constant supply of fresh leaves, dill should be sown from April to June consecutively. Even in July it is possible to sow dill. It should be sown on the site and rows should have a distance of 8–12 in. (20–30 cm.). If the plants are kept well watered they will grow quickly, produce a mass of foliage and then flower. During a drought dill may flower while still short and the leaves may hardly be worth gathering.

It is not advisable to grow dill near fennel. Cross-pollination can produce leaves and seeds which are neither dill nor fennel; also when harvesting, the mature plants are so similar in appearance and flavour that it is difficult to sort them out satisfactorily. However, when dill is cut before going into seed this crossing can be avoided.

As dill grows quickly it is usually not difficult to keep the ground clean until the plants close up together. Transplanting should be avoided because of the delicate root system, but dill needs protection from wind and it may become necessary in exposed places to stake dill when the plants become 18 in. (45 cm.) high. Dill must be weeded to produce thriving plants. Dill self-sows readily and the resulting plants are often stronger than those from the first sowing.

In some countries in which dill is cultivated in large quantities, such as Germany, there are two types of seeds, one which is particularly useful for growing leaves (Chrestensens Herkules which came originally from East Germany) and a 'leaf or fish dill' from West Germany. These varieties are suitable for damp positions. Any other variety of dill is suitable for growing seeds and those prefer a dry position. In the same way there are different times for sowing, depending on the purpose one hopes to achieve.

If grown for seed, dill should be sown during the month of April as a longer time is needed for the fruit to mature. If grown for leaves there is a longer margin of time available for sowing, for instance from April to the end of June. Whenever dill is grown, particularly for preserving cucumbers in brine, it must have reached a height of 10–12 in. (25–30 cm.) and developed seed heads, part of which are still in flower, by the time the cucumbers are ready; it thus necessitates sowing from the end of April to the beginning of May. If the leaves are used for the kitchen, dill can be sown in succession to have a constant supply.

It is advisable to sow and thin so that the plants do not touch when in full growth, because they may harbour greenfly. This can spread from plant to plant and can harm and even kill dill. Ladybirds and their grubs appear on the flowering dill.

If dill is not grown in a herb garden it can be grown in the vegetable garden between such vegetables as carrots, lettuce, spinach and onions, which finish early, and such herbs as chervil and parsley.

WINDOW-BOX AND INDOOR GROWING As dill needs so little from the soil it is a very useful plant to grow in a pot or window-box. It looks most attractive even between flowering plants, as its delicate foliage is as decorative as that of asparagus.

Dill can well be grown in a flower-pot but when grown in a flat container the roots are restricted and therefore the plants will shoot up quickly, but will not grow to the size reached in a garden, nor will it develop seed heads for picking; it will, however, provide an adequate amount of the pungent-flavoured dill leaves.

How to Harvest and Dry Dill grows quickly, and the aroma is at its best before flowering. Opinions have been expressed that the maximum content of volatile oil is reached at the beginning of the formation of the buds but there are other opinions that shortly after dill has finished flowering the herb has its highest content of volatile oil. This may have something to do with the difference in purpose, as the variety used for leaves and that used for seeds may have different peak periods of volatile oil content.

The leaves can be used all the time from six weeks to two months after planting, in fact from the time the plant is hand-high up to the time it dies off in November. Dill grown for drying leaves is better cut when 10–12 in. (25–30 cm.) high.

It is advisable to let some of the plant flower and seed. For pickling they should be cut at the moment when flowers and seeds are on the head at the same time. If seeds are wanted for sowing or flavouring, they should be left longer until they become brown, approximately when the whole plant turns a purple red; but as they easily fall to the ground they should be harvested before they are fully matured and allowed to ripen. They usually start to turn brown in August.

The seed heads should be dried and then either shaken or threshed. The residue can be used for cattle or any other animal fodder. It should be cut with a hook.

Dill

If dill leaves are dried they have to be handled carefully and they should never be dried in a temperature higher than blood-heat, under 100° F. (38° C.). They must under all circumstances retain the light green colour and full aroma, to be useful for flavouring. If this cannot be achieved it may be more useful to dry the seeds without using any artificial heat or with a very low temperature. Seeds should be spread flat in a thin layer. When dried they should be stored in a tightly sealed container.

If dill is wanted for the purpose of flavouring, fresh leaves can be used from June to November and at other times, dill seeds can be used or green-dried dill which can be obtained commercially.

What Dill Can Do for Our Food The lacy leaves of dill are delicately aromatic, and when finely chopped they give a very special sharp interesting new flavour. There are three main flavouring purposes for dill: accompanying fish, particularly as a sauce; flavouring bland vegetables; and the usage, much found in other countries, of putting leaves and flower-seed heads into cucumbers while pickling in brine, or when pickling white cabbage for sauerkraut.

Once dill has reached the stage of forming green seeds in the large still yellow umbels, it combines well with other herbs such as borage and tarragon for cucumber pickled in brine.

Dill is a good flavouring for diabetic patients and for everyone on a low-salt diet.

DILL SEED The seed is very pungent and stronger than the dill herb and therefore best used for certain strong vegetables such as cabbage. It will also make soups very tasty. It is a good addition to many vegetable salads such as potato, cabbage, cucumber; also used with grilled or boiled fish or lamb stew. The ground seed may also be used instead of whole seed. Some cooks prefer the ground seed when using it with fish, in a broth, or with herb butters and sauces.

A tisane made from dill seeds, unsweetened, is considered an effective help in the case of hiccups or vomiting. The chewing of dill seed is supposed to remove bad breath and a tea made of dill seed, aniseed, chamomile and hop shoots is considered to have a sedative effect.

Dill

CULINARY USES

	Fresh or Green-dried Dill Herb	*Whole Seeds*	*Ground Seeds*
Hors-d'œuvre	In all spreads; for canapés; avocado pear filling; in all preserves (whole with flower heads) crayfish	Fish cocktails	
Salads	Potato, lettuce, tomato; in salad dressings, in herb dressings; with sour cream on cucumber; with pickled cucumber; in brine	Salad dressings	
Eggs and cheese	Egg sandwiches; pancakes; omelettes, hard-boiled eggs, cream cheese	Cream and cottage cheese; herb butter	Cheddar cheese
Soups, stews and sauces	Bean, pea, tomato, chicken soups; (2 teaspoons dill). Fish soups, all fish sauces, cream white sauce with 1 tablespoon chopped dill; dill sauce with pike and green eel (serve with boiled or steamed fish)	Sparingly with bean, beet, and cream of tomato	Sparingly with all the soups mentioned
Meat and fish	Steaks, chops, corned-beef, grilled, garnish with freshly chopped leaves. Lamb stews, Beef Stroganoff with sour cream, halibut, mackerel, sea trout, sprinkle lightly before grilling or frying. All sauces with boiled fish (see sauces); snails	Lamb chops, lamb stews	Halibut, salmon; all fat fish when boiling
Poultry and game	Creamed chicken; rub dill into poultry before roasting; spread 1 whole stem over poultry, leave 1 stem in the bottom of roasting pan.	Creamed chicken fricassé	

CULINARY USES—*continued*

	Fresh or Green-dried Dill Herbs	*Whole Seeds*	*Ground Seeds*
Vegetables	String beans, cauliflower, cabbage, brussels, tomatoes, young peas, petit-pois, courgettes, aubergines, mashed potatoes, dill potatoes, mushrooms and fungi, dumplings with dill sauce, stews, avocado pears, asparagus, salsify	Beets, cabbage, cauliflower, sauerkraut, turnips	
Beverages		Dill tea from seeds	

DILL POTATOES

Ingredients:

1 lb. potatoes

1½ oz. oil or butter

1 onion

1 garlic

1 tablespoon sour cream

Stock (very little)

Salt

2 heaped tablespoons dill (freshly chopped or green-dried)

2 tablespoons sour cream

Method:

1 Boil potatoes, skin and cut in fairly thin slices.

2 Sauté finely chopped onion and garlic until golden.

3 Add flour, sauté, smooth with stock or cold water, salt.

4 Add dill and simmer for 5 minutes.

5 Add potatoes and allow to simmer.

6 Add cream shortly before serving.

ELDER, THE

(*Sambucus nigra*)

Virtues The elder is closely connected with legend and folk-lore and it is probably due to the fact that it was believed to be unlucky to uproot elder trees near houses that elder trees are found particularly near old houses. It was supposed to be a protection against witches and even now country people are sometimes afraid to cut elder owing to the old heathen witchcraft myth of northern Europe.

All parts of the elder tree were used; the hollow stems, the wood, the leaves, the flowers and the fruit. The elder flowers are chiefly used for medicinal or cosmetic purposes. The uses for medicinal household purposes are so varied that only a few can be mentioned. The dried flowers, containing volatile oil, mucilage, tannins, glycoside, choline and vitamins, are diaphoretic (increasing perspiration), diuretic and are supposed to purify the blood, also dealing with skin troubles. Elderflower tea is helpful in stimulating the glandular system. Elderflower water is chiefly used for eye and skin lotions because it is a mildly astringent stimulant.

Description The elder is a genus of about twenty herbs or small trees and belongs to the family *Caprifoliaceae*. The shrubs or trees will grow to a height of 9–30 ft. (2½–9 m.) high. It has large, opposite odd-pinnate dark green leaves with five broad, lanceolate, toothed, regular leaflets, long and almost smooth. The flowers are usually white and yellowish and announce themselves through their sweet and heavy scent in June and July. The flowers stand in flat cymes or umbel-like clusters, 5–8 in. (12–20 cm.) across. When the little fruits have ripened they usually become shiny black-violet.

Growing Elder trees need very little from the soil but prefer a fertile fresh to damp soil. They will put up with some shade but the real possibilities of development can only be seen when they are in a sunny position. Propagation can be done by cuttings of bare shoots in the open in autumn. Elder should be pruned in the late autumn or early spring before the growth begins. It is hardy and where there is no elder it can be propagated in the garden by root division. No special attention is needed. The elderberries, which are eaten by the birds by the hundreds, and these help to spread the seeds.

Harvesting Flowering time is June and July and the berries are ripe in September/October. The outer flowers open first, therefore it is always difficult to pick them; the flowers must be all out but by no means over. The flowers start blooming in June and therefore the flower heads can be dried before any other herbs are ready. If they are handled much or bruised, they go black. They must be spread out on trays immediately after being picked in order to keep cool; if they are left in a heap they become hot and it is not possible to keep the good colour. They should stand upside down on a tray with fine nylon net, but not touching each other and a circulation of air should pass around them. Only when they have retained their full colour are they useful. The leaves are used fresh or dried, collected in June or July. They are supposed to keep off the flies if bruised. They are reported to contain sambacine and resin.

Uses The dried flowers make a delightfully flavoured tisane strongly reminiscent of muscatel. It promotes perspiration in the case of colds and is a pleasant alternative to aspirin, particularly if mixed with equal parts of lime flowers and chamomile, and taken hot in bed.

For making elderflower tea 1 teaspoon elderflower per cup is used. The flowers should be placed in a warm but dried china or glass cup or teapot, boiling water is poured over them, and they should be allowed to steep for 3–5 minutes only, strained and sweetened with honey if desired. If a stronger infusion is required more flowers should be used from the beginning.

The flowers are excellent for making a refreshing summer drink popular with children. A jug should be filled with elderflower and boiling water added to it; sweetened, then allowed to stand and be strained when it is cold. The elderflower water can also be made in the cold way. In this case a cup or jug half-filled with elderflowers should be filled up with cold water and allowed to steep for at least one hour. Elderflowers add a pleasant sweet and distinctive flavour to milk dishes, jellies, jams, gooseberry or apple tart. They can be tied in a muslin bag, boiled or baked with milk or jam and removed before serving. India or china tea can be flavoured by adding one-third of elderflowers to the tea. The tisane is also sleep-inducing. One of the best summer desserts is elderflower fritters which can be made with elder-flowers picked from the hedgerow, or with dried elderflowers.

Elderflower water has been used chiefly for eye or skin lotions, and it is said to be good for washing and as a bath addition. For cosmetic purposes elderflowers are added to facial steam baths and there are many other external uses as they clear and soften the skin, and are good against freckles and faulty pigmentation, particularly in connection with whey and yoghourt. The face packs are stimulating and a tonic rather than soothing only.

The elderberries can be cooked in jam and also have medicinal properties, though of a different kind. They have the reputation of cleansing the blood-stream, and juice of elderberries is good for chills and for people who suffer from sciatica and neuralgia.

FENNEL

(*Foeniculum vulgare*)

Virtues Fennel is one of the oldest cultivated herbs, originating from Mediterranean countries. Medical papyri from the tombs of old Egypt bear witness to the fact that fennel, in all warmer zones and wherever vines are grown, already played a big part long before the Christian era.

It is a perennial relation of the annual dill and because of this it is of great importance that dill and fennel should never be grown in proximity in any garden, as they cross-pollinate and the resulting herb has neither a pure dill nor fennel flavour but one that has characteristics of both. However, fennel seeds clearly differ from those of dill for they have a strongly aromatic scent which is sweeter and less pungent than dill seed. It is said to be nearer to aniseed but has still a distinctive flavour all its own. The fennel seeds contain 4·5 per cent fatty oils, starch, sugar and protein, anethol, acid of anise and camphor. Altogether the effect of fennel can be considered as being antispasmodic, anti-inflammatory, appetite-stimulating, expectorant, carminative and anti-catarrh. It is one of the constituents of 'gripe water' used for babies with digestive upsets.

Throughout the centuries one of the qualities repeatedly reported on fennel is its effect on the eyes. Compresses steeped in fennel tea, placed on the eyes, or bathing the eyes with fennel infusion, is suggested for inflamed eyelids, watering eyes, strengthening the eyes and improving the sight.

As fennel helped to digest fish, fresh and salted, it was therefore much used during Lent, not only for its anti-flatulence effects, but also to satisfy the cravings of hunger on Fast Days. For the same reason seeds were nibbled in church during long sermons. There is also the fennel's reputation for reducing overweight, and all this could probably be applied to today's desire for slimming. The ancient Greek name for fennel is 'marathron'—a growing thin.

Fennel also has cosmetic properties, a facial pack made with fennel tea and honey is recommended against wrinkles.

Florence Fennel (*F. Dulce*) (called Finnochio in Italy) is sold in Italy and France and is imported as a vegetable into this country; but if planted here early under glass, or if it happens to find a long and warm summer, it will produce a bulbous base. It is not unlike celery; it is sweeter, and one of the most aromatic vegetables.

There is one other variety of fennel grown in southern Italy and called there *Carosella* (var. *piperitum*) which is the variety of which the young stems are eaten raw.

The garden fennel herb and the sweet fennel vegetable are two different plants, but the leaves of the vegetable variety can be used as a flavouring herb for fish sauces and fish cookery.

The strong connection of fennel leaves with fish shows in its habitat, because fennel not only grows along the coast, but also along estuaries where salmon run. These and any other oily fish, particularly mackerel, should be eaten with Fennel Sauce. Serve fennel with bass or red mullet in *Grillade au Fenouil*, where the aroma is not only used in the cooking but also in the serving, by placing the fish on a bed of burning fennel, imparting to it a delicious aroma; this is a traditional French delicacy. (Recipe, p. 106.)

Appearance of the Plant Fennel is a perennial but the cultivated fennel is often planted as a hardy biennial; it has a long, spindly, fleshy, whitish to whitish yellow root like a carrot or horseradish. In a loose soil the root can be as strong as a finger.

It is a stout, erect rather glaucous plant 20–50 in. (60–130 cm.) tall —height from 2 ft. (60 cm.) the annual variety (Florence fennel, Finnochio) to the 4 ft. (120 cm.) wild fennel, to the 4–5 ft. (120–150 cm.) height of the garden fennel. The stem is solid, developing a small hollow when old; striated and polished.

The leaves are first light green when young, then they are dark to blue-green, much divided; they have fresh green double feathers when young, threadlike and divided up into almost hair-like segments.

The flat terminal umbels are golden yellow, without calyx and with 1½–3 in. (4–8 cm.) diameter up to 6 in. (15 cm.)—with 13–20 rays; they flower from July to August. Flowers are 1·2 mm. of yellow colour. The umbels droop when seeds ripen.

The fruit consists of two carpels which adhere by their faces to a central stalk from which, as they ripen, they separate below and finally are attached to the upper extremity only, forming mericarps. The carpels have five bluntly keeled ridges and these are separated by channels in which are often found narrow cells, containing coloured oily matter, the volatile oil contained in the seed. It tastes sweet or aromatic and the colour varies from green to light brown.

In appearance the fennel plant resembles dill though the drooping flowers are distinguished from the slightly upturned umbels of dill. The leaves and seeds are similar in flavour, dill being more pungent, and fennel distinctively sweeter, reminiscent of aniseed. Fennel may be a little difficult to start, but once it gets going it becomes a tall graceful, bushy plant with light green, strong shiny stems. The cultivated fennel has its stems cut down to secure a constant crop of green leaves for flavouring and garnishing so that the plant is seldom seen as in the wild state. It varies very much as to habitat, shape, colour of leaf, number of rays in the flower head and shape of fruit. It has been cultivated so long that now there are several well-marked species.

Growing It is easy to grow fennel if one is not interested in harvesting seeds, as they ripen late, and therefore all early precautions such as starting the plants in a seed bed in March or April are only necessary if the length of the season is fully needed for maturing seeds. Other-wise seeds should be sown in spring on the site.

Fennel

There are three possibilities:

1 Garden fennel (*F. vulgare*) grown for the purpose of the green leaves for flavouring—that is, sowing on the site in spring.

2 The same plant (*F. vulgare*) grown for leaves *and* seeds. In this case they are cultivated as a biennial plant. The roots can be taken up in autumn and stored inside and planted out again the following spring. The flower heads, with some seeds, will only start from July and the seeds mature slowly.

3 Florence fennel (*F. dulce*) which is a different plant altogether, grown as a vegetable for the purpose of harvesting the swollen stem base to be eaten as a vegetable. The green leaves can only be used, when the stem base is harvested.

Any soil will suit fennel, although it delights in a really warm spot in the garden. The soil should be dug deeply enough and be rich and chalky; not too humid. Heavy chalky soil is unsuitable and there should not be any cakey layers, or the growing of the root will be disturbed.

Garden fennel is a hardy perennial and once established can take care of itself in most sunny fertile gardens. Plants can be raised from seed, sown in drills 18 in. (45 cm.) apart in April and May and the seedlings being subsequently thinned to stand 18 in. (45 cm.) apart. It is also possible to divide established root stocks early in spring.

Germination will be retarded if the temperatures are too low. The seeds germinate in the light and in the dark. Very often germination of fresh seeds finishes after fourteen days. Unripe seeds or those harvested when wet and not dried sufficiently become mouldy.

If propagated by division, the roots should be lifted in March, divided into portions and replanted one foot apart in rows 15 in. (38 cm.) asunder. The only attention needed otherwise is to keep down weeds and remove flower stems, directly they form. The plantations will last many years.

If required for culinary uses the plants should be spaced at 1 ft. (30 cm.) and the growth not allowed to exceed 1 ft. (30 cm.), for full growth at 5 ft. (150 cm.). This becomes an imposing plant growing to a height of 6 ft. (180 cm.). Tall varieties must be sheltered from the wind or individual plants staked when 18 in. (45 cm.) high.

Fennel

Both the wild and the garden fennel with their bright foliage and yellow umbels of flowers are also useful for the border. Except in cold climes both are hardy perennials and harvesting the seeds does not destroy the plants.

Florence fennel (Finnochio) is the bulbous-based vegetable fennel plant.

Florence fennel grows easily from seed after danger of frost is passed or it should be started earlier under glass. Seeds can normally be sown where plants are to be grown on light, limy, moderate fertile soil in a dry sunny spot; the vegetable needs a long warm season to finish growing the stem bases and should be given plenty of moisture. The plants remain much smaller than the perennial fennel, as all its nourishment goes down into the stalks.

The base of the stalk becomes thick and wide, overlaps and swells and then the soil should be cultivated and fed. As soon as the base is the size of an egg it should be earthed half-way as for celery in order to blanch the bulbous base; about two weeks later the vegetable can be harvested. Finnochio needs a soil richer in compost than any other form of fennel.

WINTER PREPARATION In autumn, fennel can be cut down to about 4 in. (10 cm.) above ground and in cold parts roots should be covered against frost or even taken out, also cutting the root to 4 in. (10 cm.). It should then be covered with sand and stored. In the second year the sets can be planted out again 20 in. (50 cm.) apart.

WINDOW-BOX AND INDOOR GROWING At the approach of winter some fennel plants are transplanted into pots which are kept in a glasshouse or indoors so that leaves can be gathered throughout the winter. The plant will also grow in a smoky atmosphere and in poor soil and is therefore suitable for town gardens and window-boxes.

How to Harvest and Dry The green foliage of fennel can be cut shortly before flowering until just before the frost. From mid-July onwards the centre umbels should be cut out and the remainder of the plant should be cut down in October before the frosts come. Sometimes the flower of fennel lingers on from July to September and sometimes even in October. The time for harvesting the whole of the fennel herb is when it has a grey-brown tinge, and that is usually during the middle of September.

The leafy part of the Florence fennel can be used for flavouring from the moment of flowering onwards and even before.

Seeds ripen from September until the end of October. The seeds are larger than those of caraway and dill and will therefore take a little longer to dry. If seeds are harvested they should not be fully ripe but light green in colour and never be dried in the sun as the quality suffers. The drying of seeds should be done at a very low temperature. When drying they should be laid in thin layers and moved often as they perspire. If left, there is a tendency for them to become black. They are also inclined to grow moulds and can become quickly musty. No part of the plant should be dried in the sun, as this will make a difference to the quality as with all herbs. If fennel is grown for seeds the seed heads can either be picked out or combed out with an iron comb.

The roots of fennel used for medicinal purposes can be collected from March to the end of April.

Fennel, like every feathery herb, is only suitable for drying if done with the greatest care and the lowest temperature. Until recently fennel was not considered suitable for drying, but if the usual precautions are taken, dried fennel can be as green and full of aroma as any other herb, but it is not suitable for domestic drying.

Any surplus fennel herb or seeds can be cut up and added in small quantities to cattle fodder to encourage appetite.

What Fennel Can Do for Our Food The chopped leaves of fennel are used in sauces, or a sprig of fennel may be placed inside a fish when grilling or baking. At one time, all fish was cooked with fennel, and today we like to add the acid-sweet flavour of fennel also to salad dressings for beetroot and carrot salads. The fine leaves cut during the summer can be used for marinades with fish and fish sauces.

The flowers and seeds of the umbels are always used in a semi-ripe state when pickling cucumbers and sauerkraut in the same way as the dill seeds are used.

Fennel herb is particularly suitable for giving aroma to freshly expressed juices and uncooked salads: it will add a very special and interesting aroma to vegetable cocktails and at the same time the herb may be able to add to the slimming effects of such juices.

The thickened base of sweet fennel (Florence fennel) which is grown for the herb as well as for the vegetables, is eaten as a savoury either raw or made into a salad with cheese. Fennel salad made from slices of this uncooked stem base with finely chopped fennel leaves is an excellent salad with a French dressing.

A salad can be made of the slices of the nutty raw fennel and some asparagus, all dressed with French dressing and a dessertspoon of finely chopped fennel leaves and chervil.

CULINARY USES

	Fresh or Green-dried Herb	*Whole Seeds*
Hors-d'œuvre	In all spreads for canapés; particularly with every kind of fish	Fish, shell-fish (crabs, shrimps, etc.)
Salads	Mixed green salads; with all dressings; with sour cream on cucumber, potato salad	Crabs, shrimps, etc.
Eggs and cheese	Egg sandwiches, pancakes, omelettes, cream cheese	Omelette, jelly Belpaese cheese
Soups, stews and	Fennel Sauce, fish sauce, fish soups	
Meat and fish	Fennel Sauce with lamb, broiled steaks, corned meats—add before serving. Eels, mackerel, bass, red mullet, salmon—grilled. In broth for all fish	Beef braised, or stewed lamb, mutton. Ground seeds for roast pork. Cod, halibut, lean fish boiled (add seed to water). Shell-fish (crabs, shrimps, etc.)
Poultry and game	Creamed chicken	

Fennel

CULINARY USES—*continued*

	Fresh or Green-dried Herb	Whole Seeds
Vegetables	Florence fennel, string beans, cabbage, cauliflower, tomatoes, young peas, courgettes, aubergines, mashed potatoes, mushrooms and fungi	Lentils, sauerkraut
Fruit		Apple pie
Bread, cakes and biscuits		Sprinkle tops with seeds and prepare fennel biscuits

GRILLADE AU FENOUIL
(Grilled Fish on Fennel, Flambé)

Red mullet (*rouget*) and bass (*loup de mer*) are the best fish for this world-famous, dramatic and elegant Provençale dish for festive occasions.

Note. This recipe is mainly for those who grow their own fennel because a large bunch is needed. The fennel sprigs have to be dried in a cooling oven approximately 100° F.—with the door ajar for ventilation—on a grid covered with muslin or nylon or perforated paper.

Ingredients:

2 fish (approx. 2 lb.)

Salt

Fennel } chopped or green-
Sage } dried

Oil

1 glass brandy (not too small)

Large bunch of fennel sprigs with stalks and leaves (green-dried)

Method:
1 Clean fish inside and out and dry.
2 Rub with salt inside and out.
3 Fill fish with small sprigs or chopped or green-dried fennel and sage.
4 Score across twice on each side.

5 Brush with oil on both sides.

6 Arrange a bed of dried whole fennel stalks and leaves on the bottom of the grilling-pan.

7 Put fish on the grid above the fennel bed and grill.

8 Turn fish carefully once or twice and brush again with oil if necessary.

9 Warm brandy in a ladle (on gas) or in a small, covered fireproof bowl (if using electric—starting earlier).

10 When fish are finished, remove the fennel bed on to a warmed, flat fireproof serving-dish.

11 Serve fish on top of fennel bed.

12 Garnish with lemon slices and parsley.

13 When serving, pour the warmed brandy over the dish, set alight and allow the fennel to burn out in order to impregnate the fish with the flavour and scent of fennel.

14 Can be served with new potatoes, tossed in butter and finely chopped fennel.

GARLIC

(*Allium sativum*)

Virtues Garlic is one of the oldest cultivated plants, having been used to keep the workers who built the pyramids healthy. It was used as a ritual as well as a therapeutic plant. Apart from its strong flavour-value it is a disinfectant, mentioned as a protection, and has the capacity to keep the intestines healthy and the blood-pressure down. The reason for its effect is found in the volatile oil which contains sulphur and traces of iodine and fruit sugar. It is best used as a daily seasoning but has to be used sparingly and its disagreeable odour can be overcome by using parsley and celery leaves at the same time. In spite of its reputation as a vulgar seasoning the sophisticated French cuisine cannot be without it, although in extremely small quantities. Often rubbing a salad bowl or a saucepan with a peeled clove of garlic is sufficient. Garlic is now far more commonly grown than before and there is no doubt that it has a strong influence not only on the human body but also on the plants which grow near it, as it has

Garlic

been found that garlic will cure leaf-curl if grown under a peach tree, and it also enhances the scent of roses when grown nearby.

Description Garlic is a perennial member of the onion family and grows 12–40 in. (30 cm.–1 m.) high. It can be planted as an edging at a distance of 9 × 12 in. (22 × 30 cm.). When the foliage dies down in summer the garlic bulbs contain a number of small divisions which are called 'cloves of garlic'.

Growing The soil could be light, but can be enriched by manure or compost but not fresh manure. Garlic prefers a sunny position and some dampness. It was customary in this country to plant bulbs in March but garlic is perfectly hardy and it may be better to follow the Italian method of planting in October or early November. The bulbs should be split into cloves, the smaller ones discarded. They should be planted 8 in. apart (20 cm.) in drills 2 in. (5 cm.) deep, in rows 12 in. (30 cm.) apart. If the cloves are planted in March the bulbs should be ready for harvest in autumn but in order to have garlic all the year round it is recommended to plant the cloves in spring (April) and autumn (October). Cloves could also be planted at the end of February on well-dug ground, raked to a fine tilth, using a dibble.

Harvesting When the leaves have died down the crop of bulbs can be lifted. They should be allowed to dry in the sun or before when the leaves are plaited they can be hung up to dry. If garlic is planted in October or November the bulbs can be harvested the following summer, as soon as the foliage has faded. Though garlic is hardy it is susceptible to humidity once the bulbs are harvested. The bulbs can be dried in the sun with their roots to the south but as the sun always helps volatile oil to escape the best method is probably to hang them up in bunches under cover but in a sunny shade or veranda. They are safest dried indoors as they are likely to decay during winter if left in a damp atmosphere but they have to be hung up in a dry frost-proof room. The dead leaves have to be removed.

Uses As garlic has such a penetrating flavour, do not be too lavish with it. But garlic not only stimulates the digestion, acts as an expectorant and has a diuretic blood-cleansing property, it also lowers the blood-pressure and helps to cleanse and purify the system; it will be helpful to the herb gardener not only for the extra flavour which, without doubt, it adds to most dishes. Even the famous Swiss Fondue cannot be made without rubbing the *caquelon* with garlic. The secret of Italian cuisine is garlic with a large quantity of parsley; and Spain and South America make the same use of it. In these countries garlic is often pounded with salt in a wooden mortar until the two have integrated, and this salt is used with caution to season rice, beans, soups, salads, vegetables and meat dishes. When sautéing or cooking the finely chopped garlic it loses some of its pungent odour. Still, caution is needed; remember that Homer reports that Ulysses owed his escape from Circe to garlic.

HORSERADISH

(*Cochlearia armoracia*)

Virtues The root of the horseradish has a delicious intense pungency and at the same time a cooling taste which is not only an excellent flavouring but is also considered a very healthy addition to the diet. The Sunday joint of beef, as well as boiled beef, is incomplete without it and it is an excellent addition to certain fish, e.g. smoked trout or avocado pears. At the same time, horseradish contains natural antibiotic qualities—substances which are hostile to bacteria—similar to those found in nasturtium, watercress and garlic. The many important constituents in horseradish, stimulating appetite and digestion, have a favourable influence on the liver, a strong diuretic effect and horseradish makes an excellent seasoning for diabetics.

Description Horseradish is a hardy perennial, naturalized in Britain. The plant has large dark green leaves which spread as much as 2 ft. (60 cm.) or more. All parts of the root are edible.

Growing Excellent horseradish can be grown here, but as it is difficult to eradicate roots once established it is best to confine it to a far-away corner of the garden where it may be allowed to grow rampant.

Horseradish

In order to accommodate the very large tap roots, the soil must be worked deeply for at least 2 ft. (60 cm.) and must be rich and moist. Planting should be done in early spring and trenches should be dug 2 ft. to 3 ft. (60–90 cm.) deep; 15 in. of the top soil can be thrown into the bottom, a layer of good manure or compost on top of this and dug in, then the trench can be filled with the remainder of the soil. The pieces for planting are put on top of the good soil and thinned to 12 in. (30 cm.) apart. Seed can also be sown in early spring and the plants be thinned to 12 in. (30 cm.) apart, while propagation can also be carried out by planting the roots in the autumn. It is only necessary to remove the side shoots and to keep hoeing the bed free from weeds.

Harvesting All parts of the root are edible and all those which are at least 8 in. (20 cm.) long and as large round as a pencil can be saved for planting. The larger roots are lifted and can be used for flavouring.

Uses Horseradish is used grated or cut in very thin strips. It is best used in connection with grated apple and cream as both have the effect of making the flavour a little milder and in this combination it can be added in careful doses to salad dressings. If other herbs are used at the same time horseradish will increase the flavour of the mixture. It is also an excellent addition to fish, such as river trout, carp or cod, minced or with cream. It is a delicious combination mixed with brown melted butter and so is horseradish with whipped cream and a pinch of salt. A similar combination, to which delicate herbs such as tarragon, parsley and chervil are added, makes an excellent filling for avocado pear. If used with boiled beef the pungency of horseradish should be preserved. Grated and mixed with grated sour apples or with sour cream, finely grated horseradish can be used with roast beef, sausages, ham and smoked meat. Grated horseradish can also be mixed with finely chopped, hard-boiled eggs seasoned with lemon juice, herbs and a pinch of salt. During the summer months the young tender leaves may be chopped or finely minced and mixed with green salads. It is also an excellent condiment in dips for fish and shell-fish. Many different recipes for sauces and other combinations with horseradish can be enjoyed as a regular addition to the diet.

HORSETAIL

(*Equisetum arvense*)

Virtues This herb is reminiscent of the type of tree of prehistoric times which had the same shape, but was gigantic in size. It has very many names in various parts of the Continent, probably due to its double use. It contains a large quantity of silicic acid and for this reason it was used for all medicinal purposes for which silicic acid is needed, but at the same time it was used for cleaning and scrubbing copper, brass, pewter and all fine metals. In German-speaking countries it was called 'Zinnkraut' (Pewter Plant). The plants are still sold in Austrian and German markets for scouring and cleaning. They clean metal to a fine shine without damage to the metal and are used by watchmakers and for precision tools to give them an extra smoothness after filing. Horsetail has been mainly used for diuretic purposes and was specially recommended by Kneipp, the South German priest who had such striking success with hydrotherapy in connection with herbs. All other medicinal used are connected with the use of silicic acid which has an astringent and strengthening effect on the tissue. Also bitter principles and the saponine equisitin are available in horsetail.

Description The rootstock of horsetail is generally a creeping rhizome, the stems are erect, hollow, grooved, jointed with a sheath at each joint, often with whorls of branches at the joints. The fertile branches appear before the barren branches in early spring and are brown and have no chlorophyll. The barren stems are green with black-tipped green teeth, as many as the furrows. Horsetail is widespread and common in cultivated places and on dunes.

Growing The plant can be collected in many country places, waste grounds, etc., but if it is to be grown it prefers loamy and sandy soil.

Harvesting The green barren shoots, which look almost like Christmas trees, are the ones to be collected during the summer months of June and July. They should be cut close to the base of the root. They have to be dried carefully so that they retain their green colour and are not broken up or bruised so that they do not lose their important constituents. Collection can be made from May onwards but is best done in late summer. The dried shoots should be kept unbroken in air-tight containers in the dark.

Uses When the dried tea is broken up, the equivalent of 2 teaspoons per cup of water are used for Equisetum tea. They should be allowed to boil for 20 minutes and be dried. In order to make the best use of the properties of the herb 1 teaspoon per cup can be soaked for several hours and then the herb should be boiled in the soaking water for 10–15 minutes and allowed to steep for another 10–15 minutes before being strained. It helps to stimulate the passing of water. For external use it is suggested for badly healing wounds and for bathing nails which are brittle. Useful for strengthening and toning the skin, astringent and antiseptic.

HYSSOP

(*Hyssopus officinalis*)

Virtues Hyssop is a fragrant member of the *Labiatae* family, a perennial fragrant sub-shrub which grows well in England and is sometimes planted as an edging. Mentioned in the Bible for cleansing purposes it was also used much in ancient times. The herb contains amongst other things volatile oil and tannins which are responsible for its refreshing aromatic scent. This attracts bees and butterflies who enjoy the blossom and are able to reach nectar and pollen and is much appreciated for use in perfumes. Hyssop is also part of the famous Chartreuse Liqueur. For healing properties hyssop tea is used as an expectorant in cases of catarrh of the bronchial tract.

Description The sub-shrub can be 2–4 ft. (60 × 120 cm.) but does not reach more than 2 ft. in cold parts. The herb flowers from June to August and with their one-sided spikes of bright blue flowers is a lovely plant and a decorative edging in the garden. The usual type has blue flowers but pink and white flower varieties are also known.

Growing Hyssop is quite hardy and is not particular as to soil; it prefers, however, a light soil and a sunny position. It can be raised either from seeds or cuttings. Seeds should be sown in drills of ¼ in. deep and the seedlings be planted out 2 ft. apart. The distance of rows should be 14 in. (35 cm.). The cuttings can be taken in spring or after the flowers have been finished in autumn and be struck in sandy soil and planted out the following season.

Harvesting The herb should be cut shortly before flowering or when the flowering has just started. Often a second cut is possible. The usual precautions for drying all other herbs should be applied to hyssop.

Uses The slightly bitter and minty taste is an excellent flavouring and it is particularly good in salads when young and finely chopped also as an addition to game, meats, soups and stews. Flowers and tops are used to flavour some continental sausages. Hyssop is helpful with the digestion of fat meat and it has been suggested that the addition of ½ teaspoon of chopped hyssop 'cuts grease'. It goes well with fat fish, such as eel; game (½ teaspoon rubbed into the bird or roast before roasting), and vegetable soup. It can be added also to kidney and lamb stews. In America fruit cocktails, especially those made with cranberries, are flavoured with one or two leaves in the bottom of the serving-dish. Pies made of fruit such as apricots and peaches should have ¼ teaspoon of chopped hyssop sprinkled over the fruit before covering it with the pie top crust.

JUNIPER BERRIES

(*Juniperus communis*)

Virtues In the distant past juniper was regarded as a magic shrub to be used against devils, evil spirits and wild animals. This reverence also lasted throughout the Middle Ages and in particular with all the nations living in the north.

Juniper is mentioned in the Bible as a symbol of protection, and there are legends that the Virgin and the infant Christ took refuge behind the juniper bush when fleeing from Herod into Egypt.

There is a strong aromatic scent, emanating from all parts of the shrub, and the taste of the berries is slightly bitter-sweet, fragrant and spicy. They need three years to ripen and during winter they hang first as tiny green, then bluish and eventually black balls in the coniferous branches. These small berries enliven game, all marinades to be used for game, and are excellent as a constant flavouring for sauerkraut. They were used for gin and all spirits which are supposed to be good for the stomach. They are used in certain blends of kitchen spices and for game, especially for beef and venison. The Laplanders make a herb tea of juniper berries and the tea was also used in continental countries and in Scandinavia; in Germany a conserve is prepared and served with cold meat (*Latwerge*).

Juniper has been considered to be one of the most useful medicinal plants. The berries contain volatile oil, bitter substances, tannins, resins and various organic acids, formic and acetic acids, an alkaloid called juniperin, resins, sugar and fat. They are considered to be stimulating for the appetite and the digestion, cleansing the blood and dissolving mucus; they also have a diuretic effect and increase perspiration. The berries are stimulating to the functions of the kidney and much used in various forms as a cure for dropsy.

The tea of juniper berries is advised for inadequate functioning of the bladder and its consequences, for gout and rheumatism, for chronic catarrh, liver and heart conditions. It is a natural medicine of universal use.

The aromatic scent of the tree made it popular as a strewing herb, because it exhales a pine-like odour which is extremely healthy, and must have disinfectant properties. Juniper has always been considered a protection against epidemics. In the nineteenth century the 'antibiotic' qualities were made use of, when burning juniper shoots on the fire to improve the air in an invalid's room. It was a custom to burn juniper in the morning in the classroom of Swiss schools to disinfect the air, particularly during winter when not much ventilation was allowed.

Description The juniper tree is a small, graceful evergreen shrub or bush 4–12 ft. (1½–3½ m.), quite common in chalky districts, spreading or tall erect according to its environment. On shallow soil and in exposed places it rarely exceeds a few feet in height, but in sheltered conditions it grows into a large bush with several main stems. It has needle-like leaves, reddish stems and will be found to bear green and bluish black berries at the same time. This is due to the fact that the berries take two or three years to ripen and are green at the beginning and black only when ripe. The leaves are awl-shaped, spreading, rigid, sharp pointed and persisting for three years; they are $\frac{2}{5}$–$\frac{3}{5}$ in. long. The flowers are small, yellow at the base of the leaves, male and female usually on separate plants; the shoots are a green berry-like cone turning a sloe-like blue-black colour in the second or third year. Juniper trees are found wild in many parts, sometimes on chalky and limestone formations, but others in ground that is fairly free from lime.

Growing Though juniper can be found wild in the right places, herb gardeners should if possible grow their own juniper trees for the berries for culinary and medicinal purposes, but it has to be remembered that male and female flowers are usually on different bushes and that only the female flowers produce the berries. It is also important to choose only *Juniperus communis* when buying juniper trees, as the many other varieties are not suitable for either culinary or medicinal use.

Harvesting The flowering period of juniper is April to May and the black berries, are harvested in autumn. The berries can only be dried when they *are* black and this should be done in a thin layer on a tray until they are slightly shrivelled. The leaves and shoots which can be collected any time of the year should be dried, stripped and sieved.

Uses Juniper berries for flavouring are unfortunately neglected in English cooking though they are one of the best spices. Three or four berries are roughly equivalent to one small bay leaf, which they can replace. They can be used fresh but are usually dried and stored. Juniper berries are an important flavouring for diabetics. They are used with game, grouse, meat, meat stews, poultry, sauces, sauerkraut, cucumber, beetroot and for pickling; for cooking game, venison, hare, pheasant and woodcock, in fact for all the animals who enjoy eating juniper berries during their life, if they can get hold of them. The berries added to the liquid in which grouse and wild duck are cooked take away the strong game taste to which some people object. Some cooks, before roasting game such as wild duck and grouse prefer to part-boil it in a good beef stock, to which lemon, bay leaf and juniper berries are added. The liquid is then strained and kept for use in preparing the gravy. The berries add a piquant flavour to meat and game stews and can be added to meat pickled in brine.

Wherever juniper berries are found in preserves, such as pickled sauerkraut they should always be eaten because they are not only a flavouring, but have important medicinal qualities.

Juniper berries are good for increasing perspiration and have a cleansing effect on the blood and digestive organs. They make a useful tea for all liver and kidney conditions and this is also reported to be helpful against stones. Kneipp suggested a régime which can be repeated four to five times and is most blood-cleansing and has also been used for migraine. It is advisable as a diuretic, if the elimination of urine is not satisfactory and is also helpful with gout or rheumatism, with chronic cystitis and with conditions of the liver, the heart or digestive troubles. It is really a universal medicine and is most useful for a spring-cleansing treatment.

Juniper berries have been suggested, together with certain herbs of a disinfectant nature, to people travelling abroad particularly in southern countries, as a protection against 'tummy' upsets which are so often encountered.

Uses of Juniper Berries

JUNIPER CONSERVE (LATWERGE) The berries should be cooked in water until soft, without breaking them, then the pulp should be pressed out and mixed with three times its weight of sugar; all this should be well beaten together. It is liked by children.

ROB OF JUNIPER The juice of juniper berries, well strained, should be boiled over a gentle heat to the consistency of honey. A 'rob' is the juice of the fruit made so thick by the heat that it is preserved from deterioration for some time.

JUNIPER BERRY TEA Juniper berries provide an excellent tea for liver and kidney conditions but this tea is not suggested for acute or chronic inflammation of the kidney. The tea is made by using twelve to eighteen crushed berries per cup, bringing it to the boil and boiling for 15 minutes. This produces a universal tea for a great number of conditions.

CHEWING BERRIES The régime suggests the eating of four berries per day at the start, and increasing the number to fifteen by taking one more every day, and then going back by one until arriving at four again. The berries have to be chewed carefully, and if it is a large number they should possibly be taken in two doses.

It is considered a protection against infection if eight to ten berries are chewed twice daily.

USES OF JUNIPER SHOOTS A tea can be made of the young sprouts of juniper for the same purpose, and one cup daily is suggested, or freshly pressed juniper juice can be taken as one teaspoon morning and evening. Young sprouts soaked for 24 hours before use in cold water and then boiled for $1\frac{1}{2}$–$2\frac{1}{2}$ hours can be used as a bath addition and are suggested for their effect on sciatica and rheumatism. Compresses made of juniper berries are suggested for skin conditions. The branches and berries, and the crushed berries, can be burned in an invalid's room to prevent infection and sweeten the air. The green shoots of juniper have a bitter scent, and they were also burnt as a kind of incense.

LADY'S MANTLE

(*Alchemilla vulgaris*)

Virtues Lady's mantle is a herb with a very old reputation and many healing qualities. The ancients knew its medicinal strength and gave it the name *Alchemilla*—'the magic herb'. There are a number of names of different origin which refer to its use as well as its shape: as 'Mantle of Our Lady'; the leaves were considered to have a shape like the mantle worn by ladies. It was originally a wound herb and

Lady's Mantle

was used against bleeding, but its universal reputation everywhere has been connected with female ailments and it has been called 'a woman's best friend'. Its active substances are not all fully understood but it contains tannins, saponine, and bitter principles, and the effect is binding and anti-inflammatory.

Description Lady's mantle is a perennial of the *Rosaceae* family. It is mostly found in mountains but can easily be cultivated. It is hairy and grows to 4–6 in. (10–15 cm.), with branched flower shoots. The almost circular leaves are 6–9 lobed and 2–6 in. (3–10 cm.) across, toothed, green beneath and long-stalked. The flowers are 3–5 mm., insignificant and yellowish green.

Growing Lady's mantle can easily be grown from seed and the plants spread rapidly. They can become a nuisance and have to be kept in check.

Harvesting The leaves of lady's mantle are cut when the plants are in flower, which may be from June to August, but they should be cut before August ends. The large leaves should be dried with good ventilation, at a temperature under 100° F., in the dark to retain their colour during the longer period of drying.

Uses Tea: 1–2 teaspoons of lady's mantle per cup of boiling water; it should be allowed to steep for 10 minutes, and one to two cups taken per day. This tea is of importance to all women and has been suggested to be helpful during pregnancy and in particular shortly before birth; also for drinking in good quantities for 8–14 days after the birth. It is supposed to have a regulating effect on the monthly cycle (to be drunk 10 days before it starts, until after); for easing 'the change' this tea should be taken from the fortieth year onwards for ten days each month. It has also been said that lady's mantle clears inflammations of the female organs; in fact it is claimed by a German writer that 'a third of gynaecological operations could be avoided if this herb was used in time over a long period'. Lady's mantle has been recommended by homoeopathy as helpful in the case of obesity, and generally against diarrhoea. Externally, the herb has been reputed to heal wounds and cuts if crushed and laid against the wound. The freshly crushed leaves or freshly pressed juice area help against inflammation of the skin and acne, as well as against freckles. An infusion is suggested for washing and baths, as well as compresses for wounds not healing satisfactorily.

LEMON BALM
(*Melissa officinalis*)

Virtues The lovely lemon balm, also called 'bee herb', has long been famous for its lemon-scented leaves and honeyed sweetness. It originated in the Middle East but very soon found its way throughout the Mediterranean countries. Of great importance to the Greeks, *Melissa*, the generic name, is Greek for honey bee. There is an ancient belief that bees will not leave the hive if melissa is growing in the garden, and it was Pliny, the ancient Roman naturalist, who discovered that 'when bees have strayed away they do find their way home by it'.

While lemon balm can be added to many foods, it imparts its delicious fragrant flavour best of all to teas and summer drinks; a few sprigs of lemon balm added to China tea make it most refreshing. Melissa tea is most beneficial because of its anti-spasmodic effect. It has also a calming effect on the nervous system, and stimulates the heart. Above all it helps relaxation and dispels over-tiredness and even an incipient headache or migraine. It is frequently used for this purpose on the Continent, and is now more regularly used as a morning or night-cap or an after-dinner drink in this country.

Appearance of the Plant Lemon balm is a perennial herb 2–3½ ft. (60–100 cm.) high and belongs to the *Labiatae* family. It forms a shrubby plant and the root-stock is short. The stem is square and branching, somewhat hairy, and has at each joint pairs of ovate or heart-shaped light green crenellated leaves. As the leaves are wrinkled and deeply veined, it makes them appear embossed and thicker than they are. Usually the leaves are 2½–3 in. (6–8 cm.) long and ½–2 in. (1·5–5 cm.) wide but they become much smaller towards the top and they are much smaller on the flowering shoots. The leaves give off a strong lemon scent when bruised, and have a distinct lemon taste.

The calyx has long spreading hairs with the upper teeth broadly triangular. The insignificant flowers, each one 12 mm. long, are creamy white and grow in small loose bunches of 6–8 in the axils of the upper leaves. The flowering period is June, July and August and there are, on the same stem, both male and female flowers which are pollinated mainly by bees.

The fruits are longish and ovate from 1·5–3 mm. long and 0·75–1·00 mm. wide and, when ripe, are shiny and a deep, almost black, brown in colour.

There is also a variegated balm but this is grown more for its appearance than for practical purposes although it is highly aromatic and smells strongly of lemons. Of creeping habit, it is most suitable for rockeries and edgings and looks attractive with its pale-gold foliage.

Growing There is hardly a herb easier to grow than lemon balm. It is not particular as to soil but grows best in a fairly rich, warm, moist soil in a sunny sheltered position. If the soil is too light or dry the leaves tend to become yellow. If the position is too damp and shady the aroma suffers.

Lemon balm can be propagated by seeds, cuttings or division of roots. The seed should be sown in March or April on well-prepared beds in a cold frame. It should germinate after 3 or 4 weeks, then the plants are ready in August or September to be planted out. Alternatively, the seed can be sown in June or July on the site and the planting out of the seedlings can be done in the second half of May in the following year. The distance between the rows should be 10 in. (25 cm.) and the distance between the plants 12 in. (30 cm.). The seed should keep its germinating power 2–3 years.

The young plants need plenty of space around them otherwise the development of the lower leaves is restricted. Lemon balm must be hoed and kept free of weeds, as the plants then develop luxuriantly and soon close up so that weeds cannot grow between them.

When lemon balm is propagated by cuttings or root divisions from 2–3-year-old plants, this should be done in the spring or autumn. If in autumn, it should not be later than October because of the danger of frosts and if in spring division should be made as early as possible in the year. In climates colder than the British Isles, for example Norway, lemon balm has to be grown as an annual.

The roots may be divided into small pieces with three or four buds to each and planted out 24 in. (60 cm.) apart.

A particular danger to lemon balm is a fungus (*Septoria melissæ*) which can attack the plants in damp weather and will discolour the leaves. This happens especially when the plants stand too near each other. Otherwise lemon balm plants can last in good condition for many years. If cut constantly though, the plants last only about 3 or 4 years.

WINTER PREPARATION If divided in the autumn the young plants should either spend the winter in a frame or be mulched with strawy manure to avoid being killed by frost.

For winter, mature plants should not be cut back too low as the plant shoots out from the stalks above the ground. It is advisable also to cover the roots with strawy stable manure, peat or leaf mould, especially if there is not much snow. For lemon balm is very susceptible to frost and it is advisable to protect plants in exposed positions in November either by earthing them up or placing a light frost cover over them.

Sometimes lemon balm shoots up very early in spring, if there is a warm spell, and then can suffer from frost while already in leaf. This is not dangerous to the plant but can delay the use of the leaves.

WINDOW-BOX AND INDOOR GROWING Lemon balm should be planted for indoor growing in October or in March for outdoor window-boxes. It needs good soil and plenty of moisture. After flowering it should be cut down to the ground.

How to Harvest and Dry During the first year there is very little to harvest of lemon balm. From the second year onwards however, two and three cuts are possible.

The best time for cutting is on a dull, cool day when the buds are coming into flower, because this is when the leaves contain the maximum amount of essential oils. Hot sunny dry days seem to affect the content of volatile oils, because the sun causes evaporation.

The first cut is usually at the end of June, beginning of July; the last cut being September or October. If the plants are cut frequently for drying many leaves form at the base so that few stalks get into the dried herb; the last cut is not often such good quality as the first. The cutting should be done with a hook about a hand high above the soil. The herb should be piled loosely and handled as little as possible as it bruises very easily and the bruised leaves become discoloured during drying.

The drying must be done quickly in the dark with plenty of ventilation otherwise the leaves turn brown. Drying by artificial heat needs care. The temperature should never exceed 100° F. The leaves when dried must remain green and the aroma preserved; they should be stored in tightly capped glass jars and kept in the dark.

The seed is harvested in August or September, which is when the little nuts are a yellow brown. The plant has to be cut carefully as the seeds fall out easily, then gently placed on trays or tarpaulins. When dried they should be shaken out and gently rubbed to clean them.

What Lemon Balm Can Do for Our Food Lemon balm is one of the more delicate flavouring herbs and can therefore be used generously in all those combinations for which it is suited. For culinary purposes it is the leaves, fresh or dried, which add a lemony-mint flavour to a dish.

When lemons were scarce dried balm leaves were added to marrow jam and apple-jelly, giving a distinctive flavour but without that hard sour spiciness of lemons. The chopped leaves can be used with great success as a lemon substitute or wherever a recipe calls for grated lemon peel.

Its flavour comes out particularly well if it is allowed to permeate fruit juices, wine cups or iced teas. It is extremely good in fresh orange juice. Sprigs of lemon balm in China or India tea are a refreshing addition, and the light green summer tea made of fresh lemon balm tops has an excellent flavour.

The fresh and dried leaves can be added to soups and stews and sauces; freshly chopped or rubbed dried they can also be used in salads, salad dressings, mayonnaise and egg dishes, and with any fruit dish where a faint lemony flavour is desired. Herb mixtures such as herb sauces or soups should never be without its distinctive flavour. All mushroom dishes, milk dishes, and milk shakes are improved by the flavour of lemon balm, if added to food or drink in the evening, has also the reputation of promoting sound sleep. It is also good with fish, with lamb, added to sage stuffing for pork; chicken is most delicious when wrapped in the fresh leaves and then cooked. Marinades are much improved by the slightly sour taste of lemon balm.

In spite of its emphatic reputation for health, the culinary possibilities are no small feature and can be much enlarged by experimenting more with its subtle flavour, above all with fruit, milk and sweet dishes.

CULINARY USES

Hors-d'œuvre: Melon, fruit salad, fruit juices, vegetable cocktails.

Salads: All salads and salad dressings, green salads, mayonnaise.

Soups, stews and sauces: All soups and stews if lemon flavour is desired. Asparagus soup; greens served with fish, herb sauces, fish sauce.

Meat: Roast lamb; add $\frac{1}{4}$ teaspoon to sage stuffing for pork.

Fish: Fish sauce; with fish; in marinades.

Poultry and game: Rub before roasting, wrap chicken in fresh leaves for baking.

Vegetables: Add to vegetable soup, all mushroom and fungi dishes.

Sweets and beverages: Fruit salads, jams, apple jellies, fruit cups, iced Melissa (balm) tea, sherbet, claret cup, wine cups, cooling drinks. Milk dishes and milk shakes.

MELISSA TEA

1 teaspoon lemon balm leaves per cup and 1 for the pot.

Place leaves, whole or freshly crushed, in warmed but dried cups or teapot.

Pour boiling water over herbs; allow to steep for 3–5 minutes only; strain.

LEMON BALM AND MARSHMALLOW CUSTARD

Ingredients:

½ pint milk

1 egg

1½ tablespoons sugar

6 marshmallows

1 tablespoon fresh lemon balm leaves

or

1 dessertspoon green-dried leaves

1 piece of vanilla pod (2–3 in.)

Method:

1 Butter a fireproof dish and put in the marshmallows.
2 Beat egg and sugar.
3 Add milk.
4 Cut vanilla pod open (⅓ of it), scrape and add to milk.
5 Beat well and pour over the marshmallows.
6 Sprinkle lemon balm leaves on top.
7 Place the dish in a shallow pan of cold water and bake slowly in a medium oven until set.
8 Serve with thin cream.

LIMES

COMMON LIME (*Tilia europaea*)
SMALL LEAVED LIME (*Tilia cordata*)
LARGE LEAVED LIME (*Tilia platyphyllos*)

Virtues The flowers of the lime, which can be collected mainly from three varieties of lime tree, make a delicious tisane which has 'the scent and savour of honey' (Grigson). Only the dried flowers are used but they are collected together with the large, oblong, leaf-like bracts. These flowers contain tannins, mucilage, sugar and the scent is provided by a volatile oil The flowers are mildly soporific and have demulcent and mucilaginous properties. A tisane of lime flowers not only induces restful sleep, soothes the nerves, allays spasms and aids digestion, but it is also useful in cases of chills and colds and is therefore a pleasant alternative to aspirin as it has febrifuge qualities and reduces temperature. Equal parts of lime flowers, chamomile and elderflower provide an excellent tea against colds and 'flu by increasing perspiration. Lime flowers are also anti-spasmodic and calming, useful against intestinal cramps. The tea not only tastes good but improves the functions of the digestive system and is therefore often used as a daily drink in France (*tilleul*). Externally, lime flowers are an excellent cosmetic against freckles, wrinkles and impurities of the skin. They also stimulate the growth of hair.

Description The most frequently found lime tree is the Common Lime (*Tilia europaea*) a fertile hybrid of the small-leaved *Tilia cordata* and the large-leaved *Tilia platyphyllos*. The limes are botanically a very difficult genus because of their readiness to hybridize. These hybrids become species with different botanical names and it is therefore, best when ordering trees for planting to stick to *T. cordata* or *T. platyphyllos* (the red-twigged) rather than the many other hybrids which are planted for decorative purposes.

Lime trees are large trees 80–100 ft. with spreading branches and a smooth bark; the small-leaved lime (*T. cordata*) has roundish, cordate leaves 1½–3 in. (4–8 cm.) long and wide, shortly pointed, dark green, glabrous above, with red brown axil tufts beneath. The large-leaved (*T. platyphyllos*) has roundish ovate leaves 2–5 in. (5–12 cm.) long and wide, sharply toothed, densely downy beneath. The large-leaved lime is one of the first to flower in June, while the small-leaved lime flowers late in July. The flowers are yellowish, heavenly-scented, hanging in umbel-like clusters, usually about six on stalks half-joined to a large oblong, leaf-like bract.

Growing Linden trees take quite a long time to bear flowers when planted and if the tisane is wanted it is best to collect from existing trees which are not only found wild, but also in old gardens, in parks and streets; they are lovely trees to plant in a garden, particularly in avenues.

Harvesting The flowers can be collected from the lime tree during June and July. When picking the flowers it is important to see that in addition to the actual small flowers the long bracts are collected as well. The flowers should not be heaped up or pressed when transported home for drying. The harvesting should be started early, not when the flowers are already overripe. They should be dried very carefully on trays in the dark and the temperature must be carefully watched so that it does not exceed 100° F. (35° C.). It is a most valuable flower and should therefore be very carefully handled, as the flowers break off easily.

Uses When making the tea a teaspoon of lime flowers should be used per cup, with one extra for the pot; it should be made in a glass tea-pot, if possible, to show the lovely flowers. The flowers and bracts should be left whole. Boiling water should be poured over the flowers and they should be allowed to steep for 3 to 5 minutes only. They should never be boiled, because the tea may become red from it, and during boiling all three important substances will be destroyed. The tea should be strained and served hot or iced and sweetened with honey if desired. If it is allowed to steep too long the subtle flavour of this delicate tea will be spoilt. If a stronger infusion is desired more flowers should be used from the beginning. One to two cups of hot lime tea are drunk after meals in France. If taken late in the evening when in bed, it will promote perspiration in the case of colds. An infusion of lime flowers is used externally against skin troubles.

LOVAGE
(*Ligusticum officinalis*)

Virtues Lovage—an immensely tall and spreading perennial—came with most of the other herbs to the north via the monastery gardens of the Benedictine monks. In this country it always has to be culti-vated—it does not grow wild.

The giant-sized herb with its strong unusual scent reminiscent of yeast and of the famous soup extract Maggi, is very different from any sweet-smelling herb in the herb garden. As a culinary herb the special yeast flavour of lovage will give strength to soups, broth and casseroles; an extraordinary herb which deserves experiments in many different ways. Lovage is used a great deal in all German-speaking countries, as well as in France and Italy, as a well-known ingredient for soups, casseroles and stews.

The seeds give the whole sum of the concentrated lovage flavour and are therefore as useful for flavouring as fennel and dill seeds. They are mainly used in Italy and America on bread, biscuits and meat. Even the Greeks and Romans chewed lovage seeds, believing they aided digestion. At one time in this country a drink called Lovage cordial was sold. It is either made from seeds or contains other herbs as well.

A bath addition of lovage improves circulation and in particular stimulates kidneys; it is also helpful in heart conditions. The leaves provide a fragrant tea, which served hot is a restful and relaxing drink. The tea tastes like a broth rather than a tisane made from one of the sweet-smelling herbs and can be taken with salt, if preferred to sugar; it has the same effect internally as a bath addition has externally and in both cases they act as deodorant.

Legends and folklore have been attached to lovage in all countries. The herb is reputed to be of help to those in love and the name, in many languages, seems to indicate a love potion or aphrodisiac, though it is really derived from *Ligusticum* and *Levisticum*.

There might well be other reasons for this herb's reputation as a deodorant—probably its effect on better functioning of the digestive system and its general cleansing effect may provide an explanation. Does the Czech girl who hangs a bag of lovage round her neck when going to meet her boy friend believe it to be a love-charm or a deodorant?

Appearance of the Plant This enormously tall culinary herb is umbelliferous, with strong fleshy roots. The stem is straight, round and hollow. The leaves are divided into narrow, ridge-like segments to form opposite branches towards the top. Their surface is shiny and their stems divided; their colour is dark green on the top, paler on the underside. As the stems grow higher the leaves diminish and eventually end in the flower umbels, which are approximately 5 in. (12 cm.) in diameter. They have countless greenish yellow flowers with plenty of nectar. Not sufficient is known about pollination but it appears that lovage is pollinated by other plants.

Lovage

The seeds of lovage grow in pairs in two carpels as with other *Umbelliferae* and resemble those of caraway. They are elliptical—slightly curved on one side with three ribs and flat on the other with two winged ribs which are serrated at the edge. They are brown when ripe and have an aromatic smell and flavour and contain volatile oil in the same way as the herb plant.

The main root is short and thick and has many different heads and long rootlets about a finger thick. In the fresh state they have pale yellow milky juices containing resin, as does the whole plant. The root stock or upper portion is usually about 1½ in. long and 2¾ in. thick, spongy and whitish, with glistening oil cells.

Growing Lovage is easy to grow; it does not ask much from the soil. It prefers a rich moist soil into which the roots can go deeply and a relatively damp position, but lovage does not really mind any kind of climate and does well in exposed positions in a chalky heavy soil which has been well worked. Heavy clay soils are not suitable.

Propagation is done by division and by sowing; the seedlings can be transplanted either in autumn or as early as possible in spring to their permanent site 20–24 in. (50–60 cm.) distance between the plants either way. From 4 years onwards the plants should have reached their full size and then they should be spaced 4 ft. (120 cm.) apart.

Seeds may be sown in spring but it is advisable to sow when the seeds are just ripe as the germinating power is only satisfactory for a short time. After 10 days it should be possible to see whether the seeds are germinating and after 28 days one should be certain of it. It may therefore be wiser to sow some of the seeds in autumn rather than in spring. Low temperature and darkness is good for germination. If they begin to sprout after 2–3 weeks the seedlings can be transferred out to a well-composted or manured deeply-dug bed. Well-rotted compost is by far the best food for lovage. The plant can then stay for several years in the same ground where it will become larger each year. It flowers in June, July and August.

The plants can also be propagated by division of roots. The roots should be cut in pieces, each with an eye, and planted out with the eye 2 in. below the level of the soil. They need the same kind of well-

Basil

Chervil

Dill and Fennel

Lovage

Peppermint

Sage

Sweet Cicely

Tarragon

composted, fresh soil in good cultivation as suggested for the seed-lings. For most families one of these larger plants is more than enough for culinary purposes throughout the year. If lovage is wanted the same year, sowing in March into frames or a seed-bed is advisable. The plants should be kept clean and the soil well hoed around. them.

WINTER PREPARATION Lovage can survive even very hard winters but in marshy soil there is always the danger of frost when the roots could break off and the development of the plant is hampered. The soil should be well drained, otherwise the big roots may become mouldy.

How to Harvest and Dry If the big and very aromatic leaves are wanted for flavouring, it is important that sufficient water be given to the plants. If they are kept sufficiently damp it is possible to cut the plant fully off at least three times a year: in May, beginning July and August/September. The herb can be cut to about hand-high above the ground but the 'heart' leaves should not be hurt.

If the leaves are wanted for flavouring the plant should not be allowed to flower and seed: but if the seeds are wanted they should be har-vested before they are fully ripe, then they are better for germinating. The seeds can also be harvested for flavouring, as they contain the same volatile oil as the other parts of the plant. The roots and stems can be cooked like celeriac or celery or used with salads.

The root is dug in spring for medicinal purposes and this is also the time to use it as a vegetable, but for medicinal purposes it can also be dug in October. If strong roots are desired, the flower heads should be broken off.

The green leaves dry well and retain, if properly dried, their light green colour. Yellow leaves should not be mixed when cutting or dry-ing and the drying should be mainly carried out with young soft leaves at a very low temperature. Only with great care can the leaves remain light green. The drying in relation to the fresh leaves is 10–1.

As lovage is quite a tough herb—like parsley—home drying can be successful in a cooling electric oven or second oven of a Rayburn or

Aga which provides a temperature descending from 200° F. (93–94° C.) with the door left approximately 2 in. ajar. Drying of small quantities may be done in 1 hour, though slower drying is recommended. The herbs should be brittle and light green; they should be allowed to cool then be rubbed off the stalks until they have a shredded appearance. They should be kept in air-tight containers in the dark. The tender stalks may be blanched and used like celery and the leaves like spinach. The seeds and stalks can be harvested for candying.

What Lovage Can Do for Our Food The clever housewife serves her soups, casseroles, stocks, stews and mixed vegetables, her salads and marinades with lovage. Because of its extraordinary yeast flavour lovage acts like a soup extract often made of yeast and herbs, and therefore gives to stocks and soups the extra strength which bones and meat normally supply to many dishes.

It is therefore an important flavouring for vegetarians as it provides to food what normally are the flavouring extracts from bones or meat, not usually associated with herbs or vegetables. It can, in fact, 'make' a weak soup or stew.

It also adds the flavour of celery which many people like in connection with soups.

It should be used economically to begin with, but many people will increase it when they appreciate what it does to soups, casseroles, stews, gravies, meat, particularly roasts, and to cooked ham; it is also good with fish, sauces, potato dishes, cabbage (sauerkraut), mayonnaise.

The leaves have also been used as a vegetable. In New England they are cooked like spinach or celery. Fresh leaves and stems can be cooked like celeriac or eaten uncooked in salads. When the herb is used for flavouring it need not be added at the last minute, in fact it improves if cooked with the food all the time.

Like all other herb plants which produce edible seeds containing a concentration of volatile oil, the seeds can be very useful; whether nibbling them like the American colonists or the church-goers of the past did fennel. The people in north-western Italy use them instead of fennel or anise on bread and cakes, because of their sweet pleasant taste. Spiced or cheese biscuits flavoured with lovage seeds are in a class quite different from all other biscuits. There are many ways in which lovage seeds can be used.

CULINARY USES

Lovage	*Fresh or Green-dried*	*Whole Seeds*
Hors-d'œuvre	Mayonnaise, fish chowders, instead of celery, herb butter	
Salads	Green salads (rub the salad bowl with crushed fresh lovage leaves). All raw salads. Vegetable salad (cabbage, roots, sauerkraut). With mayonnaise dressing	Mixed fruit salad
Soups and stews and sauces	All soups, stews and casseroles; clear stock or broth. Lovage cream sauce. Strong flavour for all sauces (fish sauce)	
Meats and fish	Meat stews, meat and poultry pies. Stews, gravies, fish	Beef, lamb, mutton stew. Removing seeds before serving. Pork meat and poultry pies
Poultry and game	Rub before roasting	Hare, rabbit, venison stew (remove seeds before serving)
Vegetables	Fresh leaves eaten as greens. Blanched stalks as celery. Improves all vegetables if used carefully	
Sweets and beverages	Stems candied like angelica, fragrant tisane, especially for nursing mothers	
Cakes and biscuits	Lovage cheese biscuits	Sprinkle over top. Lovage cheese biscuits

Marigold

Thick Lovage Soup

Ingredients:

1 lb. potatoes	Salt
1 onion	2 tablespoons green-dried lovage
½ oz. butter	or
½ oz. flour	2 tablespoons fresh lovage (chopped)
2 pints stock	1 tablespoon chopped parsley
½ pint milk	

Method:

1 Peel and slice onion and potatoes.
2 Sauté onions in the butter till the onion is soft but not brown.
3 Add the lovage and sauté.
4 Add potatoes.
5 Add flour and cook for a further few minutes.
6 Add stock, and salt. Stir until it comes to the boil.
7 Simmer for 20 minutes or until the potatoes are soft.
8 Add milk.
9 Put through a sieve or blender.
10 Heat up again and just before serving sprinkle with the chopped parsley.

Note. If the soup becomes too thick, add more stock or milk.

MARIGOLD

(*Calendula officinalis*)

Virtues Marigold is a member of the tribe *Calendulae* belonging to the family *Compositae*. It came originally from India and it is only the florets of marigold which are of medicinal value, already mentioned in the twelfth century, and used for culinary purposes today. The flower petals are used in salads, omelettes, marigold buns and as a substitute for the expensive and rare saffron. An old herbal reports that only to look at marigold will 'drive evil humour out off the

Marigold

head'. Marigold contains, apart from bitter principles, a colouring substance calendulin which is like carotin, and very small quantities of volatile oil.

Description Marigold is an annual reaching a height of 20 in. (50 cm.). They are simple and bold flowers in all colours from light yellow to orange-red. Particularly useful for drying are the strong orange-coloured or the saffron-yellow varieties. There is also a variety which has deep coloured simple ordinary flowers with or without dark centres.

Growing Marigold grows in any kind of soil but prefers loamy soil. A position in full sun is essential. Sowing can be done straight on to the site in March or April. If sown in rows it is advisable to thin out the plants to at least 18 in. (45 cm.) apart. If thinned to 2 ft. apart they make a bushy growth quite 2 ft. (60 cm.) across. If the dead flower heads are picked they will flower continuously till November.

Harvesting The petals can be used either fresh or dried and have to be pulled from the flower and dried in thin layers in low temperature in the dark with adequate ventilation, in order to retain the beautiful yellow or orange colour on which the flavour depends.

Uses Marigold petals are used in place of saffron and impart a subtle flavour as well as colour to many foods, e.g. rice and omelettes. Half a teaspoon of crushed petals added to fish and venison, stews, roast beef and chicken or any other broth makes a subtle difference. The fresh and dried petals as well as chopped leaves give a delightful tang to salads and the dried petals in buns and bread puddings make an interesting change. For buns and cakes marigold petals can also be soaked in a muslin bag in a small cup of hot milk; the milk can be used for baking after it has cooled.

The dried flower petals are an excellent food colouring and have also been used externally in oils and in ointments in the treatment of wounds and old scars.

MARJORAM

(1) SWEET MARJORAM (*Origanum majorana*)
(2) POT MARJORAM (*Origanum onites*)
(3) WILD MARJORAM (*Origanum vulgare*) (Oregano)

Virtues Marjoram is one of the oldest herbs in use, and one which has never lost its attraction during its varied history. It is, however, not generally known that this name covers three very different kinds of marjoram with different uses and histories. They all belong to the *Labiatae* family.

The *Sweet Marjoram* is an annual and the most popular for flavouring purposes, especially in sausages. It has a sweet subtle characteristic flavour. Originally from the eastern Mediterranean, it came to be used extensively by the Greeks who gave it its name, which means 'joy of the mountains'. It was the Romans, however, who brought it to this country, where it has been cultivated ever since.

Marjoram contains disinfectant and preserving qualities which, in the Middle Ages made it invaluable as a culinary herb.

The *Pot Marjoram* is a perennial, perhaps with less flavour but greater reliability for the gardener. It is reputed to have come from Sicily but it is uncertain whether it was originally developed from wild marjoram. It was most generally grown in gardens and was reported as being first introduced into this country in 1759.

The *Wild Marjoram* (*Oregano*) is a wild as well as a cultivated perennial with a strong flavour of its own which has a pungency varying according to where it grows. It is the kind of herb used in Italian, Spanish and Mexican dishes and known all over the world as oregano. Though wild marjoram is as old as the hills from whence it comes—it was used in the days of Ancient Rome—it grows nowadays all over the English hills, but its present popularity in American kitchens is probably not older than 25 years. It is supposed to have both stimulating and medicinal properties. It contains thymol which is a powerful antiseptic internally and externally.

Appearance of the Plant *Sweet* or *Knotted Marjoram* is a half-hardy cultivated annual though in southern countries it can be perennial.

Marjorams

Wherever ground freezes in winter sweet marjoram has to be considered as an annual and sowing should be started indoors to give them a season long enough to flower, though the seeds will not mature. In our climate sweet marjoram is sooner or later killed by frost.

The plant has a leafy, bush-like appearance, about 8 in. (20 cm.) high—only rarely growing to 10 in. (25 cm.)—with the knotty flower growth being produced at the top of the tough, but very fine woody quadrangular red stem. The leaves are small—smaller than those of pot marjoram—grey, opposite, oval, rounded at the top and have little glandular spots.

The knotty growth of the stems from which the flowers grow have caused it to be called knotted marjoram. About eight to ten flowers, or more, are contained in these small green pea-sized buds. These are really bracts and the flowers which come from them are white to pale mauve or pink, they blossom from June to September. The whole plant is covered very lightly with hair and has a strong aromatic scent. The plant does not spread. The fruit or seeds—little nuts—are very small, egg-shaped, rarely round. Their colour is yellow to dark brown.

Pot Marjoram is a hardy perennial, inclined to sprawl and layer itself. Though all marjorams have certain features in common, the main difference between sweet and pot marjoram is that the sweet marjoram produces the characteristic bush-like shape and retains it during the flowering season, while the pot marjoram produces 'mounds' of leaves from which grow long flowering stems, holding the flowers well away from the main growth of the plant. These beautiful mounds are about 6 in. (15 cm.) high and about 12 in. (30 cm.) across and from them shoots creep along the ground, rooting as they go. During the growing season flowering stems are thrown up from the plant to a height of 2 ft. (60 cm.). Flower clusters and bracts are purplish, also the stems and leaves show a warm reddish tinge. The distinction between pot marjoram and sweet marjoram is shown by the difference in shape, by the warm reddish tinge on the stems, smaller leaves, and by the fact that the whorls of mauve flowers appear much later than those of sweet marjoram: at the end of July and August.

Wild Marjoram is found as a perennial chiefly on chalky soils and has reddish brown stems with looser flower spikes than pot marjoram.

It grows wild but is also cultivated and has a rather different flavour from the other two cultivated varieties. Wild marjoram grows as a leafy bush with creeping roots about 12 in. (30 cm.). The woody stems are branched above, erect and often purplish. They have very short axillary sterile branches below. The leaves are opposite, about 1 in. (2 cm.) long, hairy beneath and are smaller than those of pot marjoram. Bracts are similar to the leaves but smaller and usually pink. The calyx is hairy within, tubular and five-toothed, the teeth are short, the corolla 6–8 mm., rose purple, the tube longer than the calyx. The flowers stand like pyramids and the considerable light red flowering crowns attract many visitors and are pollinated by different groups of insects and butterflies; therefore the wild marjoram is highly valued by beekeepers. The fruit or seeds—little nuts—are very similar to the fruit of sweet marjoram. They are about 1 mm. long, their shape is ovoid from broad egg-shaped to long egg-shaped. The flowers last from July to September, even November if there is no frost. There is a variety with white flowers and green stalks and another with variegated leaves.

The whole plant of wild marjoram is covered with hairy oil glands and the pleasant aromatic scent is reminiscent of thyme. The scent of wild marjoram is so lasting that even the dead leaves and stems do not entirely lose it during winter.

Growing Sweet Knotted Marjoram is easily affected by frost and should only be planted in the warmest and most sheltered spot the garden can offer. A medium rich soil with plenty of well-rotted compost in a medium warm and moist location results in good yields with high aroma quality. The soil should possibly have a pH between 5·6 and 6·4 but a neutral reaction is probably best for marjoram. A heavy or cold soil and one of stagnating humidity is not advisable. Also a crusty or cakey soil which makes it difficult for germinating seedlings to break through should be avoided.

Marjoram usually goes through a critical period between the end of April and beginning of May, when the seedlings are often lost. In order to protect them a combination of warmth and humidity is necessary. If these are missing at the right time a delayed poor growth is the result.

Marjorams

Marjoram should be sown in a frame at the beginning of March and transferred on to the site in the middle of May or the seeds should be sown on the site after the middle or at the end of May when it is certain that no more frosts will occur. When sowing, 10–12 in. (25–30 cm.) should be the distance between rows. When planting out 6–10 in. (15–25 cm.) should be allowed for two to three seedlings each time.

When sowing the fine seeds can be mixed with the dust of wood-ash or better with sifted sand and drilled as shallow as possible. Germination takes place between 8–32 days. At the beginning seedlings grow very slowly and owing to their slow development it is important to keep the seedlings carefully free from weeds. Seeds of sweet and knotted marjoram can already be sown indoors during February or under glass in March and planted out 6–10 in. (15–25 cm.) apart each way at the end of May. Seeds can also be broadcast on the surface, trodden in, and raked carefully and watered if there is the danger of the usual spring drought.

It appears advisable that the sweet marjoram seedlings should have some shade until they are well established. As all varieties are slow-growing they require frequent weeding and cultivation. They should not be choked with weeds which—as these are of much quicker growth—are likely to harm the marjoram if they are not removed. This should be done by hand until the plants are large enough for a small hoe to be used with safety. When the seedlings are about 1 in. high they can be thinned. During the slow development the seeds should be kept well watered.

WINDOW-BOX GROWING OF SWEET MARJORAM Sweet Marjoram needs good soil and a sunny sill. Seeds can be sown indoors in February or March and the seedlings be transplanted into window-boxes when sufficiently developed, or otherwise if well-developed plants can be bought in March they can go into the window-box but have to be protected from frost or otherwise be planted into window-boxes in May only.

Pot Marjoram, a perennial—about 2 ft. (60 cm.) high—prefers a warm situation and a dry light soil. It is generally increased by cuttings taken early in summer. These can be put under cloches and later planted out; the space should be 2 ft. (60 cm.) between rows and as much space from plant to plant, as it likes plenty of room. It can be on the same spot for many years if it is well looked after. It may also be increased by division of roots in April or autumn, or by offsets, that is by breaking off pieces of the plants with roots attached. They can be planted out but have to be well watered. From May onwards they grow quickly.

Pot marjoram can be grown from seed in March or April and should be sown thinly or moderately thinly in shallow drills $\frac{1}{2}$ in. deep and 8–9 in. (20–24 cm.) apart, well and evenly covered with soil. The seeds are very slow in germinating and it is some time before the seedlings are big enough to transplant to about 1 ft. (30 cm.) apart each way and therefore propagation by either rooted slips or cuttings is preferable.

Before propagating can be done successfully in spring the plants are exposed to the danger of long spring droughts in the same way as sweet marjoram. Owing to their shallow root growth the leaves may turn yellow and develop black spots. If this cannot be avoided even with sufficient watering, propagation can be done more easily in autumn. Whenever this is done the plants should be planted in full sun.

Within a year or so, pot marjoram will completely cover the space allocated to it. Then is the time for training this plant, but as perennial pot marjoram dies down to ground level in winter the trimming should be done before this happens. Any growth of pot marjoram which grows upright or in odd shoots and sprigs should be trimmed. This will discipline the plant to the low almost ground-cover shape. These cuttings may be used for flavouring or drying.

WINTER PREPARATION Normally, in England, pot marjoram needs no winter protection. In exceptionally cold winters or exposed positions or in places with hot summers and cold winters pot marjoram will benefit from protection from the weather during the hibernation period. The plants should be mulched with dead beech or oak leaves. The leaves should be placed around and on the plants gradually as the cold weather approaches. At the first frost, pile leaves over the plants and cover them possibly with a light open basket. The baskets should be weighed down so that the wind and winter gales will not blow them away. The main problem for this winter protection is to take care in uncovering it gradually in spring, perhaps re-covering it during frostly nights.

WINDOW-BOX AND INDOOR GROWING If pot marjoram is wanted for window-box or indoor growing, it should be trimmed back to about one-third of its original size before it dies down in winter. When the plants have recovered from their trimming they should be potted in soil with plenty of rotted compost and sand and be gradually adapted to indoor conditions. Again the cuttings can be used as fresh or dried, but a cutting may also be used to grow an indoor plant of marjoram from it. The light green leaves and tiny purplish flowers make a lovely and decorative house plant, as well as providing fresh aromatic flavouring during winter.

Wild Marjoram or *Oregano*. The wild marjoram, a hardy perennial, can be found on chalky soils as well as on gravel always providing that it has a dry and warm position. It loves to grow on hills and mountains. If cultivated, wild marjoram grows best in warm sunny gardens or similar fields. It can be propagated like the pot marjoram by seeds, divisions or cuttings, and all directions given for pot marjoram can be applied. The fruits—little 'nuts'—are very similar to the seeds of sweet marjoram. The germination trial takes about 28 days and can be carried out with alternating temperatures either in the light or in the dark. Sowing can be done early at the end of April. The distance between the plants should be up to 20 in. (50 cm.). If sown in drills the plants should be thinned to 8–12 in. (20–30 cm.). It is necessary to hoe well. Wild marjoram will be slow to grow but will develop with the first hot spell. If just the bud of its top leaf growth is patiently snipped at first, the plant will begin to thrive practically overnight.

WINTER PREPARATION It is advisable to give the fully developed wild marjoram a light covering around its roots in very cold winters. For indoor growing see pot marjoram (above).

Marjorams

How to Harvest and Dry

(a) *Sweet Knotted Marjoram*. The leaves and flowers are collected during the flowering season, July to September. The best moment is when the knots are about to break and start revealing the flowers. If possible cutting should be carried out in the morning starting about ten, because at that time the content of volatile oil is supposed to be at its highest peak. If cut for drying, sweet marjoram should not be cut too low: 2 in. (6 cm.) above the ground and some leaves must be left.

When marjoram has been grown from seed sown on to the site two cuts are possible even if the second one is carried out when the plants are not in full flower; but when planting seedlings which have been bought, well developed or cultivated much earlier indoors, two cuts are certainly possible: the first cutting should be carried out when flowering starts and the second cut can follow at the end of September or beginning of October in both cases.

As sweet marjoram is more strongly aromatic than pot marjoram and its aroma becomes even stronger when dried, it is one of the herbs which should be dried if possible. It is, however, important to see that it is dried well. The dried herb of good quality should be green and the typical marjoram scent should be noticeable. Mistakes in harvesting and drying may result in musty, earthy and other odours which spoil it. The drying of sweet marjoram should be done in even, thin layers in the dark at a temperature not above 100°. It is also important that it is cut at the right moment.

(b) *Pot Marjoram* and *Wild Marjoram*. All suggestions made for the harvesting of sweet marjoram also apply to pot and wild marjoram. The flowering herb has to be cut at the same height above the ground. It is important to watch that none of the runners shaped like rhizomes should be pulled out. Cultivated wild marjoram plants can be used for about 3–5 years, while pot marjoram can last for much longer periods.

The ripening of seeds of pot and wild marjoram—the seeds of sweet marjoram rarely ripen in this country—starts in good weather usually in the middle of September or October.

What Marjoram Can Do for Our Food Sweet marjoram has a sweeter and milder flavour than oregano, but yet is spicy. As it is a meat herb, pork, sausages, rissoles, also poultry and game such as chicken, duck, goose, rabbit, hare and venison, benefit from its addition and are improved by being rubbed with marjoram before roasting. Above all, sausages are given a characteristic flavour by marjoram, but as stated before only sweet marjoram produces this special flavour.

Marjoram has to be used judiciously at first as it easily overpowers other flavourings, but sweet marjoram being more subtle in flavour can and should be used in larger quantities than wild marjoram or oregano. All the marjorams are excellent in 'dry' cooking such as stuffing for poultry or forcemeat of any kind, where its permeating aroma is preserved. They are less successful in 'wet' cooking such as soups and stews, as the aroma is more elusive, and therefore more marjoram will have to be used.

The hotter flavours of the more delicate Mediterranean strain of wild marjoram and the more pungent Mexican strain are best enjoyed in tomato dishes, spaghetti, hamburgers, meat loves, meat sauces, stews and stuffings; also tomato or bean soup can be much improved with a small quantity of oregano added. Boiling or roasting pork or ham benefits from its pungency. Most grilled meats, pork, roasts and chops can be much improved if either of the marjorams is used intelligently. A touch of wild marjoram makes grilled tomatoes and tomato juice cocktail delicious and a few crumbled leaves give Pizza the authentic aroma, but either marjoram can be used.

CULINARY USES

Hors-d'œuvre: Tomato juice cocktail, stuffed mushrooms, cottage cheese, sea food, spreads.

Salads: Very small quantities, in chicken salads, green salads.

Egg and cheese: Omelettes, pancakes, scrambled egg, devilled eggs, cream cheese and other cheeses, cheese sauce.

Soups, stews and sauces: Onion, spinach, tomato, potato, lentil, pea, bean, clam, turkey, chicken soups. Small sprig in soups and stews, in bouquets for soups and sparingly in brown sauce, fish sauce, herb sauce.

Meat: Before roasting beef, pork, lamb and veal, sausages; liver dumplings, rissoles, stuffings, meat stews and loaves, in English pork and beef sausages, in German and Italian sausages.

Mints

Fish: Baked, grilled—sprinkle lightly before cooking; for creamed fish and shell-fish.

Poultry and game: Chicken, duck, goose, turkey, rub inside and outside but do not use marjoram stuffing as well. Rabbit. Stuffings for poultry and veal. Forcemeat.

Vegetables: Sparingly with carrots, peas, spinach, courgettes, aubergines, mushrooms, tomato dishes, lentils, beans and all pulses; with fried potatoes or any potato dish; in all stuffed vegetables. Put herbs into water in which vegetables are cooked.

Milk dishes: Milk puddings, milk shakes.

BEEF IN MARJORAM SAUCE

Ingredients:

1–2 lb. stewing beef (cut into 1-in. cubes)	1 tablespoon flour
Oil or butter	1 teaspoon marjoram (chopped or green-dried)
1 onion (finely chopped)	¼ pint sour cream
Stock	

Method:

1 Sauté onions in hot fat until slightly brown in a heavy saucepan.
2 Add beefcubes and brown.
3 Add a little stock.
4 Cover and stew until tender; adding more stock if necessary, stirring often.
5 Sprinkle with the flour and smooth with stock.
6 Add the marjoram and cook again.
7 Add sour cream before serving and heat up again.

Note. Serve with rice.

MINTS, THE

Virtues The mints play such an important part in the preparation and enjoyment of our food and also give such a delightful fragrance to the soil and air of the garden that every herb gardener should have a collection of them.

Mints

The mints, of the genus *Mentha*, belong to the *Labiatae* family and comprise several eminently useful species:

SPEARMINT (*Mentha viridis L.* or *Mentha spicata*)

Spearmint is the mint usually found in the English garden, also called green mint, pea mint and lamb mint. This is common or garden mint and the chewing-gum called 'spearmint' takes its name from this mint, the oil of which is used for its flavour.

BOWLES MINT (*Mentha rotundifolia*, Bowles variety)

Bowles mint is infinitely better in flavour and particularly so for Mint Sauce: it is woolly, more robust, much taller and not so subject to rust, the disease which can affect all mints. It is more difficult to dry because of its thick fleshy leaves.

APPLE MINT (*Mentha rotundifolia*)

Apple mint combines the flavour of apples and mint in one plant. It is smaller than Bowles mint and while some of it is better than spearmint it is probably not as good as Bowles mint.

CURLY MINT (*Mentha spicata* var. *crispata* and *Mentha crispa*)

Curly mint is a curly and stronger variety of spearmint. It is very hardy, and though it can be found in English Herb Farm catalogues it is more popular in German-speaking countries. Mint fritters and Mint Omelettes are made from it.

EAU-DE-COLOGNE MINT (*Mentha citrata* var. 'Eau-de-Cologne')

Eau-de-Cologne mint, the fragrant lemon mint, has lately come into favour because of its delicious scent and its use for drinks and potpourri.

PINEAPPLE MINT (*Mentha rotundifolia variegata*)

Pineapple mint—much appreciated in America—appears to be a variety of apple mint and fulfils more or less the same purpose as eau-de-Cologne mint in Britain. Once it starts wandering then it has to be curbed, possibly by a barrier of metal or slate.

Mints

These are the most interesting culinary mints but there are two delicious and useful medicinal mints:

BLACK and WHITE PEPPERMINT (*Mentha piperita* and *Mentha piperita officinalis*)

Black and white peppermint—though used for flavouring purposes —are mainly used as a beverage—Peppermint tea—a refreshing and wholesome drink; of the two types of peppermint, black peppermint is the strain to be preferred for making peppermint tea. Commercially they are used for distilling peppermint oil.

WATER MINT (*Mentha aquatica*)

Water mint is a rival to peppermint but can be cultivated and is found in some herb catalogues. It can be used with black peppermint and will have a stronger medicinal effect if used on its own. The famous nineteenth-century German expert on hydrotherapy, Sebastian Kneipp, preferred the therapeutic results of water mint.

PENNYROYAL (*Mentha pulegium*)

Pennyroyal belongs to the mints, but is not often used nowadays in the kitchen except for medicinal purposes. It is said to alleviate and ease a depressed state of mind. During the early periods of exploration and colonization, sailors used pennyroyal mint to 'purify' stale drinking water in the casks after long periods at sea.

Through the centuries man has held the mints in high esteem. They were found to be important herbs in the cultures of the early Egyptians, Romans and Greeks, as well as to the nomadic tribes of North Africa. Many curative powers were attributed to this herb by early man and its modern-day uses are still parallel with those of the ancient cultivations. Mint is native to the Mediterranean region and its frequent use as a drink in North African countries is still very much alive; mint tea is an important feature in the abundant hospitality of their people. Its use as Mint Sauce is reported as early as the third century, and by the sixth century it had already become important in preparations for cleaning teeth.

The mints have a high content of volatile oil, some bitter principles and tannins. This explains why mint and peppermint have many wholesome properties as digestives, strengthening the nervous system, stimulating perspiration and acting as anti-spasmodica. There is a high content of menthol, particularly in peppermint. Menthol is responsible for the specific sensation of coolness. Mint is considered to have a less strong effect in some cases than peppermint, for instance in easing pain, for headaches or stomach pains. Its volatile oil appears together with menthol, which has been extracted separately but it is also a part of peppermint oil.

Appearance of the Plants All mints have certain characteristics such as square stems, opposite single leaves, white to purple flowers in clusters or in terminal spike. They all spread rapidly underground and can virtually take over considerable areas in the garden. They are all perennial.

SPEARMINT (*Mentha viridis L.* or *Mentha spicata*). Spearmint or Garden Mint

The height is 12–18 in. (30–45 cm.). The plant has an erect stem, glabrous, usually branched with stiff upright shoots with long narrow leaves, finely pointed and with definite regularly toothed edges. Flowers are terminal, their cylindrical spikes are pinkish or lilac in colour, 1¼–2½ in. (3–6 cm.), with whorls becoming separated and clustered at the top of the main axis. The roots are stoloniferous; they produce freely underground stems or rhizomes called 'runners' by which the plant spreads rapidly. The little labiate flowers are followed by roundish minute brown seeds. Spearmint resembles peppermint in general but has no leaf stalks and has a light all-over green colour.

BOWLES MINT (*Mentha rotundifolia* Bowles variety)

Bowles mint is 2–4 ft. (60–120 cm.) high, shows vigorous growth with large round woolly leaves, entirely green. This is the variety that is often called woolly mint because of its large round fleshy, velvety leaves—though this name is sometimes also used for apple mint. In a favourable position it may reach a height of 4 ft. (120 cm.) on a strong quadrangular erect stem and can sometimes be used up to

Christmas. The leaves are generally all green, but some plants produce leaves with a white variegation.

APPLE MINT (*Mentha rotundifolia*)

Apple mint, also called 'Woolly Mint' because of the variegated soft woolly round leaves about 1 in. (2½ cm.) broad on round erect stems 12–18 in. (30–45 cm.) high, usually branched above the middle. The leaves are densely closed with white hairs and are 2–4 × 1·5–3 cm. oblong, ovate, round, crenate or dentate, grey or white tomentose beneath. The flowers appear in dense, interrupted spikes, bracts are longer than flowers, the corolla is pinkish, lilac, hairy outside.

CURLY MINT (*Mentha crispa* and *Mentha spicata* var. *crispa*)

It has deeply cut, crinkly, heavily veined, curled broad rugose leaves and pale purple flowers in terminal spikes. The stems are hairy, long and weak so that the hardy plant in late summer has a tendency to sprawl. 2–2½ ft. (60–80 cm.) tall, it looks similar to peppermint but is distinguished from peppermint by the curly leaves and the smell of caraway. There is also a curly variety of *Mentha spicata*; it represents a type of spearmint but the shape of the leaf is different. This is important because water mint also has curly leaves occasionally.

EAU-DE-COLOGNE (*Mentha citrata*)

Eau-de-Cologne mint resembles water mint and has branched stems with egg-shaped, smooth dull green leaves, edged with purple, which are oily and have a delicious scent of eau-de-Cologne.

PINEAPPLE MINT (*Mentha rotundifolia variegata*)

Pineapple mint is a low growing plant with smooth green woolly leaves, variegated with yellow; has pale purple flowers and has a refreshing aroma and fruity flavour. The more it is picked, the more luxurious it grows.

There are two peppermints:

BLACK PEPPERMINT (*Mentha piperita*)

Black peppermint is more purple and has a stronger flavour.

Mints

WHITE PEPPERMINT (*Mentha piperita officinalis*)

White peppermint is lighter green and more slender.

The stem of peppermint is erect, usually branched 2–3 ft. (60–90 cm.) high, reddish or purple, very thinly hairy and the tall square stems are lanceolate, sharply serrate, sub-glabrous to thinly hairy. The leaves of peppermint are shortly but distinctly stalked 2 in. or more in length and $\frac{3}{4}$–$1\frac{1}{2}$ in. broad. The underside of the leaf sometimes shows fine hair and a large number of oil glands. The coarsely serrated leaves can be pure green to reddish green. The whorled clusters of little reddish flowers are in the axils of the upper leaves forming loose spikes and rarely bear seeds. The corolla is lilac and the bracts lanceolate, about as long as the flowers.

Peppermint is not a pure variety, but a crossing of various kinds of mint; the plant is sterile and only propagated by its abundant runners, leading from a woody centre root. They run partly above and partly below the ground. The colour of the plant is light to dark green, sometimes bluish green and sometimes they have a purple tinge.

The difference between black peppermint and white peppermint is mainly in the colour of the leaves and the stronger pungency of the black peppermint. Black peppermint also has thicker stems than the white peppermint and grows higher; it is more prolific in oil and stronger. White peppermint is altogether greener and smoother on leaves and slender stems. The entire plant has this very characteristic odour, due to the volatile oil in all its parts, but all peppermints have a stronger odour and pungency than spearmint.

WATER MINT (*Mentha aquatica*)

Water mint is very pungent. It has erect hairy stems, sometimes reddish 6–36 in. (15–90 cm.). The leaves are oval shaped, hairy on both sides, 1–$3\frac{1}{2}$ × $\frac{1}{2}$–$1\frac{1}{2}$ in. (2–9 × 1·5–4 cm.). The flowers are pale purple and flower in terminal spikes. Water mint is a native and is found wild in marshes, fens and wet woods, along banks of streams and lakes up to 1,500 ft. (One parent of peppermint.)

Growing Mints are best if planted in a separate patch of ground preferably away from all other herbs. In order to keep them in check slate or metal strips should be imbedded in the ground to keep the roots from spreading. It may therefore be better to try out which of the mint flavours should be grown during one year and then give each of the mints decided upon a separate bed. A large separate bed of peppermint is useful if peppermint tea is wanted.

The plants are on the whole easily raised. A few runner with good roots are set in moist, rich soil after the danger of frosts is passed in the spring. A heavy soil with a tendency to 'crust' is most unsuitable and a warm sheltered position, facing south and half shade is best; if the sun is too strong the volatile oil seems to evaporate too quickly. To grow mint well, the soil should be well dug and be given a moderate dressing of well-rotted compost or manure. It is of little use trying to grow mints on dry soil. The ground is usually divided up in beds of convenient widths particularly if different varieties are grown.

The mints are propagated by division of plants in spring or autumn. Roots should be laid horizontally in drills 2 in. (5 cm.) deep in April and May. Stolons should be 3–4 in. (8–10 cm.) long with at least three well-developed shoots and the small shoots will develop roots. In dry weather drills should be watered before putting the roots in. Plants and stolons are sensitive to drought and should be put into water for several hours before planting. Drills should be at least 1 ft. (30 cm.) apart. If space is limited, and a large quantity of mint is required in a short period, these can be spread 6 in. (15 cm.) apart.

Also in September and the beginning of October, newly-rooted stolons can be used for propagation if they are not exposed to too cold a winter.

It is a great advantage if the soil between the plants can be hoed frequently for the first few weeks of growth, thus avoiding damage to the spreading roots at a time when seeds are germinating. Such beds provide large quantities of mint for two years, but it is advisable to renew the beds every two years. Mint takes a great deal of goodness from the soil and it is advisable to place manure along the shallow flat trenches, cover with soil in which the runners are placed and then fill in so that the pieces are well spaced and buried about 2 in. deep. New beds of mint can be made in autumn or spring from jointed pieces of the underground runners.

The mints should not grow entirely in the shade because in their

Mints

efforts to get leaves up to the light, on which they live, they are liable to form long inter-nodes and thus space out their leaves. Grown in the open the plant is stockier.

Renewing clumps of mint in spring after 2–3 years not only controls the extensive spreading of the plant, but also improves the vigour and quality of the foliage. Therefore, in March plants should be dug up and young shoots taken off about 6 in. long with a few shoots attached and planted out in new positions 6–9 in. (15–25 cm.) apart.

The spearmint runners which are almost half their length above ground should not really meet with hard-packed soil. The soil should be soft and not allowed to develop any cakey layers. The plants send out vigorous purple horizontal stems which lengthen until each top touches soft earth and then the stem comes down head first in the soil. This buried horizontal stem sends up a new stem from its tip.

Peppermint cannot be found wild and cannot be sown as this gives only rarely a true peppermint. Propagation is therefore exclusively through the planting of runners approximately 6–12 in. (15–30 cm.) apart. A wider distance per row but a smaller distance between plants is advisable.

The one hazard of mint is mint rust, a fungus disease which happens frequently in places where temperature changes quickly, while in parts with even temperatures rust does not seem to be so frequent.

This fungus grows inside the plant. It is detected by rust spores appearing on the underneath surface of the leaves, beginning at the bottom pair and soon spreading upwards, and by the swollen and twisted bases of shoots which are soon covered with orange pustules. The disease is not supposed to be covered by the underground parts of the plant. It is, therefore, advisable to plant in autumn, using only pieces of underground runners, cutting off any leaves and parts that have been above ground and washing them well to get rid of any soil. If rust appears it is well to hasten the cutting of the crop for leaves showing spores should not be dried and if a cutting is made in late June, if the summer is not too dry or the plants are well watered, a second cut in September may be possible. In order to obtain cuttings, leafy stools are cut from well-developed plants which must be put into a frame under glass, planted in to sandy compost and well weeded; these cuttings grow quickly. More rust can be found in plants in the south than in the north of England.

A constant renewal of mint plants may help to overcome rust. Some gardeners make a practice of burning straw over the plants during the winter months to destroy the spores of this disease which are found in the top soil.

WINDOW-BOX AND INDOOR GROWING Mints are useful to have during winter for flavouring purposes; if they have to be grown in window-boxes or pots it is important to control roots by division with slate or wood. Mint is particularly suitable for growing in a 4-in. (10 cm.) pot on a window-sill. Individual pots are better than a window-box as they can be turned regularly so that the sun reaches the plant from all sides and they will also keep the roots restricted. If using pots a piece of painted wood can be fastened round the edge of the window-ledge. This will conceal the pots and prevent them from slipping off the ledge. A saucer can be put under each pot to prevent dripping and make it easier to keep the soil moist.

Another suggestion for keeping the roots of mint under control, if planted in a larger deeper box indoors is to plant them in a small pail to keep the runners from spreading to other herbs in the box.

The height of mint plants should be kept to about 6 in. (15 cm.). The tops could be used for flavouring at any time. It is advisable to choose a well-flavoured variety. Usually spearmint is the basis of all the ordinary Mint Sauce and flavouring; people may prefer apple mint or Bowles mint for this purpose but this variety grows to 4 ft. (120 cm.) and is too rampant for window-boxes.

Mint wants a good soil which must be kept moist and possibly on a sunny window-sill for which partial shade can be provided. The plants should be put in in the spring, preferably from cuttings and should be watered frequently throughout the summer. The stems have to be cut down in September and the soil be dressed with rich compost. Propagation can take place by divisions in autumn or spring or by cuttings in early summer.

How to Harvest and Dry Mints should be harvested at the time when their volatile oil—on which the aroma and flavour depend—are at their highest peak. The content of volatile oil increases from spring onwards and reaches its height at the beginning of the flowering season. When the plant starts to flower it stops its growth and the content of volatile oil decreases. But before this point is reached young sprigs or leaves for culinary use can be cut at any time. In fact, frequent cuttings help the growth of the plant. The best moment of the day to harvest is the morning after the dew has dried, as this is the time when the content of volatile oil is at its highest. While the morning hours are good, the late afternoon is also recommended, before the evening dew settles on the leaves. While plants are damp, or wet, due to mist or rain, or during sunny hours, cutting is not recommended. Leaves easily become black if dried when damp.

The first general cut of mint or peppermint or the best time for using mint is while the flowers are in bud, or at the very beginning of flowering. That would probably be in most cases in the first or second half of August. During a dry season a second cut must be made during September, but it is necessary then to water the plants. A third cut is only possible in favourable positions or seasons.

Mint can remain on the land for two seasons or even longer, but although the plants continue to be productive, weeding becomes increasingly difficult and rust may reduce the crop. It may be a better practice to dig or plough and replant and this has the added advantage of nitrate put back into the soil with the old mint plants. In case of rust, mints have to be harvested immediately. If the rust is too strong, the whole plant may have to be destroyed to prevent it spreading, but no fungicide should be used; the new plantation will be rust free.

Peppermint plants can be cut down to the root; the plants should not be allowed to flower as this will reduce their strength and the leaves may become yellow and rusty after the first cool rain. The second cut has usually less leaves and more stems but peppermint should never, or all mints for that matter, be allowed to go to seed. If peppermint is cultivated as a perennial usually for 2 or 3 years in warm parts, one cut in the first year or two up to the third year are possible. This allows for stronger cuttings.

Drying Mints and especially peppermint should be handled very carefully so that they do not get bruised. The flower tops of all mints should be cut off while still in bud. Some people like to strip the leaves from the stems because that shortens the drying time but this has to be done very carefully as any handling or bruising of the plants loses aroma and makes them less valuable.

Mint leaves should be placed on frames—covered with nylon net—in loose flat layers and be dried in the dark with a low temperature 90–100° with good ventilation. It should be possible for fresh air to circulate freely. Too slow drying must be avoided and therefore circulation must be satisfactory. When the leaves are dried it is easier to strip them of the stalks.

If spearmint is dried, the leaves can be rubbed. If the drying is carried out successfully the whole leaves of peppermint should retain the exact colour which they had when growing. For instance, the green part should remain green and the purple, purple. After leaves have been stripped off, or spearmint rubbed, they should be placed in air-tight glass containers and stored in the dark. The rubbed spearmint and Bowles mint should be light green and show no discoloration.

When drying peppermint for use as tea, the leaves should remain whole, as the flavour of Peppermint Tea made from whole leaves is more subtle and very different from that of tea made from rubbed peppermint leaves.

What Mints Can Do for Our Food Spearmint is the mint most commonly used for adding a distinctive flavour to many foods, but for all the flavouring purposes for which spearmint is suggested, Bowles mint would be better, particularly for Mint Sauce or Mint Jelly. Both these mints, especially if mixed, are excellent for all purposes mentioned above, and are also good with spinach and will give some added interest to fruit salad and fruit dishes.

The young leaves of spearmint and peppermint can be used fresh: whole or chopped, or green-dried: whole or rubbed. The quantities used should be according to taste, always keeping in mind that peppermint or Bowles mint or mixed mints vary in strength.

The most common use for spearmint and Bowles mint is Mint Sauce, the inevitable accompaniment to lamb. It has, however, been made so often with such strong additions of malt vinegar that the original mint flavour has disappeared. Some people do not want to offer Mint Sauce when wine is drunk, as the vinegar makes it impossible for the palate to enjoy the wine. The greater appreciation of herbs and Mint Sauce made with lemon or cider or wine vinegar may lessen the general tendency to drown mint in strong vinegar. Mint Jelly made with apple or crabapple jelly or gelatine may also be preferred to be eaten with lamb.

Many herb honeys are made with mint; also a simple tea-time pasty can be made from equal quantities in volume of fresh chopped mint, brown sugar and currants together packed between a pastry crust. In the north of England this mint pasty is very popular.

In the flavour of three famous liqueurs mint or peppermint play an important part: *crème de menthe*, chartreuse, which contains 130 herbs, and Benedictine, all originating from the time when liqueurs were meant to be digestive or were used for minor discomforts, while nowadays they are mostly taken for their pleasant flavour.

Mint Julep is the famous cooling drink of the southern states of North America. It is made by pouring brandy or some liquor on sugar and broken ice to which were added sprigs of fresh mint, bruised or crushed, in sufficient quantity to flavour the whole. Not only a cooling drink, but a 'pick-me-up'.

Peppermint tastes a little more pungent and is more volatile and delicate than spearmint. It is excellent with roast beef and all those dishes for which spearmint is traditionally used, if a stronger and more spicy flavour is desired.

Peppermint leaves are dried whole for tea, which is either drunk as an enjoyable summer and winter drink or used in the case of certain ailments. A handful of freshly gathered or whole green-dried leaves, or the equivalent of a teaspoon per cup, placed in boiling water makes a tisane to which sugar or honey may be added if desired. The leaves should not be allowed to draw for more than 10 minutes, as the flavour changes. A few sprigs of peppermint placed in a jar of honey will give this a delicious flavour.

Peppermint is also excellent as a general 'night-cap' made in the following way:

½ pint boiling milk poured over 1 tablespoon of shredded peppermint leaves should be allowed to draw for 5 minutes and then

Mints

strained and served hot. In this case preferably chopped, rubbed or shredded peppermint should be used after it has dried.

Peppermint Tea is a good 'pick-me-up' when tired, and added to ordinary tea makes a stimulating drink. It is helpful in the case of an upset stomach and for indigestion but it is then advisable to add a few chamomile flowers. Peppermint Tea is a good substitute for coffee for people suffering from gall-bladder trouble. It can be taken up to three to four cups per day, if not more than the equivalent 1–1½ teaspoons are used for one cup; but Peppermint Tea should be discontinued for a break from time to time.

Eau-de-Cologne Mint. The flavour has distinctive culinary possibilities but should never be used in large quantities as it has a stronger taste and may easily become too much. Its fragrance however, is quite outstanding and most refreshing. It is more used for drinks; leaves infused in boiling water, sweetened with honey, provide an excellent summer drink hot or cold. Leaves can also be soaked in apple juice or in fruit drinks or squeezed into a jug of fruit drink and removed. Borage leaves can be added to such a drink. Little pots of cream flavoured with a vanilla pod and a little eau-de-Cologne mint are extremely pleasant and have an almost indefinable flavour. The same combination of scents could be used for soufflés.

CULINARY CHART FOR MINT AND PEPPERMINT

	All Culinary Mints	*Peppermint*
Hors-d'œuvre	Fruit juices, cream cheese	Fruit and vegetable cocktails, fruit juices, cream cheese spreads
Salads	Fruit and vegetable salads	Fruit salads; potato salad
Eggs and cheese	Cream cheese and in processed cheeses	
Soups, stews and sauces	Pea soup, mint sauce for lamb and veal, herb sauces	Lentil soup

Mints

	All Culinary Mints	Peppermint
Meat and fish	Marinades; with roast beef; lamb; baked, boiled and grilled fish	Roast beef, lamb, eels
Poultry and game	Rubbed on chicken before roasting	
Vegetables	Carrots, peas, French and runner beans, spinach potatoes, cabbage, courgettes	Carrots, potatoes, peas, courgettes, cabbage, spinach
Fruit and sweets	Pears, apple sauce, melons; mix into syrup for stewed fruit. Ice-cream, jellies, custards and icings. Mint syrup. Add 1½ teaspoons crushed mint to plain Madeira cake mixture, jellies and jams	Mint Ice; add to jellies and jams
Beverage, drinks	Whole leaves in fruit and wine punch, hot mint tea, chocolate, iced drinks. Mint Julep. Whole leaves, fresh or green-dried for making tea. Fresh sprigs as garnish in drinks	Peppermint Tea; whole leaves, fresh or green-dried for hot and iced tea; fruit cups; chopped or rubbed for hot chocolate

MINTED YOUNG CARROTS

Ingredients:

1–2 bunches young carrots
1½ cups water
½ teaspoonful salt
2 tablespoons butter, melted

2 tablespoons minced fresh or
1½ tablespoons green-dried
mint
Salt to taste extra

Method:

Select small, young, sweet carrots: scrape and wash; leave whole.

1 Pour water into saucepan over medium heat; add salt and bring to rapid boil.

2 Add carrots.

3 Cook uncovered 10 to 15 minutes (depending upon size), or until tender, but not soft.

4 Remove from heat and drain.

5 Season lightly, more salt if desired.

6 Return to heat.

7 Pour melted butter over carrots.

8 Add minced or dried mint.

9 Stir gently to coat carrots.

10 Serve piping hot.

Note: The same recipe can be used for fresh green peas, potatoes, spinach and runner or French beans.

MUGWORT

(*Artemisia vulgaris*)

Virtues Mugwort is a perennial member of the *Artemisia* family belonging to the *Compositae*. It is a native plant frequently growing wild, but also sometimes cultivated; it quickly grows so large that it becomes too much for any garden. The flower shoots, which contain a special volatile oil as well as bitter substances and tannins, are traditionally an indispensable seasoning for poultry, such as goose and duck or fat meat and fish. It has been used for such food because it not only contributes to the seasoning, but also neutralizes fat and thus improves the digestibility of such food. It has been well known in many countries for this use but it is sometimes difficult to disentangle from the history of herb usage in many countries whether a herb has been used because it is an aid to the digestion or because its flavour goes particularly well with certain dishes. This applies particularly to mugwort.

It has however been used for flavouring beer, before hops were used, hence the name 'mugwort'. It is also part of digestive liqueurs such as vermouth and absinthe, and is specially recommended as a seasoning for diabetics. A tea made of mugwort was used against rheumatism.

Description Artemisia are hardy perennial shrubs, the leaves are dark-green, hairy on both sides but in mugwort only the underparts of the leaves are hairy. The stems are purplish red, more powerful than those of other artemisia 2–4 ft. (60–120 cm.) in size, and the root stock is woody. The leaves are variable in size and shape, 1½–3½ in. (4–10 cm.) long, pinnately divided, each lobe with a few coarse teeth, dark and glabrous above, hoary with white down beneath. The flower heads are purple or dull yellow, ovoid, 1/16th in. long, forming terminal compound slender panicles, 6–12 in. (15–30 cm.) long. The flower heads are oblong and reddish and taller and more slender than wormwood. The plants grow in hedges and waste places. If cultivated, care has to be taken to keep them to their place and not allow them to encroach on other herbs. They flower from July to September.

Growing Cultivation is possible on any kind of soil. On a dry, chalky soil the plant will become particularly useful for seasoning. In the garden propagation is best done through division. The plants need a distance of 2 ft. both ways (60 × 60 cm.).

Harvesting The essential qualties of mugwort lie in the high flower shoots and it is these flower shots, when in bud, that are harvested. During July to September the top 5 or 6 in. (12 or 15 cm.) of each flower stem has to be cut when the buds are fully developed but before they open; the leaves can then be picked off and discarded, as only the buds are used for seasoning. When the buds are dry it is impossible to rub or shred them, as is the case with other herbs; they tend to roll together into a woolly ball. They must either be used dry or picked apart separately with the fingers or even cut off with stainless-steel scissors or knife. These downy flower buds remain fairly large but are excellent either as an addition to mixtures or used as they are.

Uses Mugwort is an aromatic culinary herb to be used in vegetable salads and in particular with raw salads to help a raw vegetable diet. It is reputed to have a good effect on the eliminating system; is also good against chronic diarrhoea and specially recommended as a seasoning for diabetics. Generally as a flavouring it is an excellent seasoning with meat and fish and, therefore, has been used with mixtures of herbs for poultry or fish or with goose, duck, pork and eel.

Nasturtiums

The German herbalist Adam Lonicerous explained the German name Beyfuss (by foot) from the fact that, when walking in the country with mugwort in the shoes the feet will not become tired. It is therefore still used as a bath addition and for foot baths for easing tired feet.

NASTURTIUM

(*Tropaeolum majus* or *Tropaeolum minus*)

Virtues Nasturtium leaves have been used for centuries. The leaves, petals and seeds are used in salads and the peppery pungency of the leaves makes nasturtium an excellent substitute for pepper for those who like their food spicy but should not take much pepper or salt. Nasturtium was formally thought to 'purge the brain and quicken the spirit'; today it is considered a valuable antibiotic, a kind of herbal penicillin, and is used as that in German-speaking countries. It also contains a great deal of vitamin C and it is possible that its antibiotic qualities are connected with the unusually high content of vitamin C. The highest vitamin C content is found in the leaves of the plant before they flower in July. The plant, which originally came from Peru, likes a hot and poor soil and will grow everywhere. The custom of eating the petals and using them for teas and salads came from the Orient. As the flowers do not dry well, but the leaves do, it is possible to have the leaves all the year round used as garnishes for foods and chopped up for canapés, while the flowers should only be used when fresh. They are not only a pleasant but also an extremely healthy food.

Description Nasturtiums are usually a strong growing, glabrous annual climber with orange flowers, but the more recently developed dwarf variety is a non-climber and similar in flower. The leaves are kidney shaped and the flowers grow in many colours from yellow, cream, orange to brownish and red.

Growing Nasturtiums like a light, sandy, moderately rich soil in a sunny spot. The best varieties to grow are those of compact habit

Nasturtiums

while trailers can be left to cover walls and boundaries. The Tom Thumb nasturtium should be used for bedding. All seeds can be sown where the plants are to bloom. Plants grown for leaves should be sown in ground rich in compost, but if more flowers than leaves are required, they should be sown in poor soil in a hot dry position. Nasturtium is a help in the organic garden for the natural prevention of pests. There are confirmed experiments in German-speaking countries that they are a protection against aphides for all kinds of beans, roses, soft fruit, etc. though they themselves are sometimes subject to them. Nasturtium should be planted near the plants to be protected. If they are grown in a herb garden among other herbs, it has been observed that they are not visited by pests.

Harvesting Leaves are best cut before the plants flower in July. They should be chopped or dried light green and rubbed or shredded.

Uses Nasturtium leaves should be used cautiously in food because of their peppery flavour. They are used in sandwiches with spreads requiring spicy flavour. In cream cheese, for instance 2 teaspoons to a ¼ lb. of cheese are excellent, but they must not be allowed to stand mixed with the cream cheese for a long time as the nasturtium leaves will make the cheese bitter. If mixed shortly before serving they are excellent; so they are for tossed, dressed or undressed salads and between bread and butter. Young leaves and flowers are delicious in salads and the seeds pickled when young and green are a good substitute for capers.

The strong peppery flavour when finely chopped-up leaves are used is an excellent substitute for pepper and in the case of a need for vitamin C to prevent infections or as a vegetable antibiotic to combat any existing infections, ways and means will have to be invented for chopped-up nasturtium leaves to be used. However, not more than ⅓–⅔ oz. should be eaten at one time, or 1 oz. per day, distributed over several meals.

NETTLE

(*Urtica dioica* and *Urtica urens*)

Virtues Nettle is a tenacious weed avoided by most people for its coarse stinging hairs, but the young leaves of stinging nettle have special curative values; they are haematinic (i.e. they increase the haemoglobin of the blood) and have a high content of silicic acid. Though science has not discovered all the riches contained in this plant, German writers claim that it contains: iron, magnesium, silicic acid, sodium, potassium, calcium, vitamin A and plant hormones with an influence on the blood sugar, further tannins and starch, and that the so-called nettle poisoning is not formic acid but a substance similar to histamin and also similar to the hormone secreted by the pancreas.

Nettle, with its outstanding number of important substances, should be used, if possible, almost daily, like a flavouring which can be added in small quantities to most dishes and in particular to salads. Small quantities of dried nettles are hardly noticeable in food. People on a salt-reduced diet and diabetics find in nettle an organic salt which is not a burden to the kidneys. Nettle, in fact, is both a flavouring and a medicinal herb.

Nettle is diuretic but also increases the haemoglobin and it has been found that in children the haemoglobin has been considerably raised by using spinach and nettles. This was confirmed when these foods were left out and the haemoglobin of these children dropped.

Description The stinging nettle (*Urtica dioica*), is an unbranched perennial, 2–4 ft. (60–120 cm.) high, often forming extensive patches, with toothed, heart-shaped leaves all longer than their stalks, with thin branched catkins of tiny greenish, sometimes purple, flowers; the male and female flowers are on different plants.

Urtica urens, the small nettle, is smaller, greener and less hairy than the stinging nettle, also annual, and often branched with the rounder leaves, the lower being shorter than their stalks. Male and female flowers have much shorter catkins, both on the same plant.

160

Nettles

Growing It does not seem necessary to explain how to grow nettle because in this country there is usually plenty available, even in well-kept gardens. Wherever nettles appear the ground is fertile.

Harvesting It is necessary to approach nettle with gloves, a pair of scissors and a large basket; armed with these they are quite easy to pick. Boiling water takes the sting out of them at once if they are cooked, and they also lose their sting when dried. They should be dried carefully, like all green leaves, and must retain their green colour fully, and with it their active substances and minerals. They should be rubbed when brittle and kept in air-tight containers in the dark. Only young shoots should be picked in spring, but it is possible to find young shoots on nettle plants at any time of the year. Dead nettle (*Lamium album*) should not be collected.

Uses The young shoots of stinging nettle in spring have a delicate flavour when treated like spinach or when green-dried and added to other vegetables as a flavouring herb. They are strongly recommended while young. They may be mixed with a little sorrel but not with other strongly flavoured herbs. They are very good prepared like spinach purée, mixed with lettuce or sorrel or as a similarly mixed soup or added to spinach, as an excellent spring vegetable or a spring food in general because of the cleansing qualities.

PARSLEY

(Carum petroselinum)

CURLY PARSLEY (*Petroselinum crispum*)
CURLY PARSLEY (*Petroselinum crispum*) var. *foliosum*
CURLY PARSLEY (*Petroselinum crispum*) var. *tuberosum*
HAMBURG PARSLEY (*Petroselinum sativum*)
(Also French, Italian Parsley)

Virtues Parsley is the most universal herb and should really never be left out of any garden. (The herb is actually a biennial but is often grown as an annual because this is easier, and the leaves are crisper during the first year. There are several varieties, from a dwarf variety suitable for an edging to the large fern-leaved Hamburg parsley which grows up to 2 ft. (60 cm.) and is mainly grown for its roots; other varieties—distinguished by their leaves—are smoothed-leaved, curly, moss-curly or ferny-leafed.)

Parsley can be used to give its characteristic flavour to almost everything we eat without one ever becoming tired of it. This makes it easier to use parsley in larger quantities than other herbs, and as the leaves contain vitamins A, B and C as well as a considerable quantity of various minerals—also the roots contain vitamin C—it is the kind of herb from which we can derive the utmost health benefit if taken every day in quantities larger than other herbs, which is usually done. Parsley is especially rich in vitamin C and as vitamin C is not stored in the body, parsley belongs to one of the minor sources which—if taken daily—will certainly add to the vitamin C supply, particularly in winter. The E.F.A. (formerly called vitamin F) factor is also reported to be present in parsley and is connected with the fatty acids necessary to utilize the fat-soluble vitamins. Parsley is rich in minerals of which iron is the main and most important one, but also calcium, magnesium, sodium and other minerals add to parsley's value as a daily food. The most interesting constituent of parsley is apiol, an oily non-volatile liquid which has a distinct odour and taste. It also contains a gelatinous substance—apiine—possibly a form of pectin.

However good the small quantities of apiol contained in parsley are for a daily intake as food, concentrated apiol can be damaging to health. The fruit or seeds of parsley contain a quantity of concentrated volatile oil and therefore should not be eaten or taken without advice as other seeds of herbs may, as a too concentrated dose of it may act as a narcotic.

The flavour of the roots has been described as celeriac and parsley combined; leaves and roots are able to give the same kind of character to dishes which is strong yet neutral at the same time. The flavour is difficult to define. A German poet said 'if the flavour and scent of all that is green and all the soil were put together and made into one flavour, this would be parsley'.

Parsley stimulates the digestive glands and that improves the working of the whole digestive system. It also has a mild influence on the working of the kidneys and this makes it a diuretic herb. Parsley has a very old medicinal reputation which may be connected with the small quantities of apiol. The old reputation of Parsley Tea as a remedy for rheumatism is most likely connected with its diuretic qualities, and parsley root and the seeds were used medicinally and were a part of the official pharmacopoeia. Parsley has been considered to belong to the anti-flatulence, anti-spasmodic and anti-fermentative herbs, but it must not be used by people who have an inflammatory process in the kidneys.

Parsley plays a big part in the natural rearing of dogs, in canine medicine and particularly as a daily addition to the food of dogs, in fact, as a canine tonic. Details about using parsley for many different conditions from which dogs suffer can be found in *The Complete Herbal Book for the Dog* by Juliette de Baïracli Levy (Faber & Faber).

Externally used, parsley water has the reputation of removing freckles or moles.

Appearance of the Plant Parsley is a hardy aromatic biennial herb which may be grouped in:

Curled varieties: the leaves are deeply divided and the segments curled or twisted over.

Fern-leaf parsley: the leaves are deeply cut but the segments are not twisted.

Plain or Hamburg parsley (also called French or Italian): plain fern-like leaves and edible roots for which it is specially cultivated.

Curly parsley The moss-curled variety is the prettiest for the garden and for decoration as it grows not taller than 6–8 in. (15–20 cm.). It is a member of the umbelliferae family with a hollow stem 12–24 in. (30–60 cm.) high which is mostly formed in the second year. The leaves are distinguishable by the different shades of green, lighter or darker green. The flowers are borne in compound umbels on stalks about 24 in. (60 cm.). The rosettes of bright green, finely cut leathery leaves develop during the first year's growth and the delicate greenish white and yellow-green flower clusters appear during the second year.

Hamburg parsley The vertical tap-root of Hamburg parsley is stout and fusiform. It is practically smooth. This root sends up in the second year an erect round striate stem which can grow to 24 in. (60 cm.). The leaves are three-pinnate, dark green and shiny on top. The umbels are 2–5 cm., flat-topped, the bracts are erect, entire or lobed. The flowers are yellowish. The fruit is broad, egg-shaped, and splits into two parts when ripe.

Hamburg parsley has one root which, according to the variety, can be either short, thick or long and is often compared to parsnips. Though the leaf parsley is mostly cultivated as an annual, the roots of Hamburg parsley *have* to be cultivated as a biennial.

P. crispum has two varieties; *foliosum*, grown for its leaves; and *tuberosum*, grown for the roots.

Growing It is surprising how many people consider parsley a 'tricky' herb to grow. Parsley is not really difficult but the nature of it has to be fully understood to achieve a reliable supply. There are two main factors: first, the enormously long time which parsley takes to germinate; in most cases it is not realized that the seeds sown have to be nursed along during the 5 to 8 weeks of their germination, if there is drought and hot sunshine, by watering and partial shade; secondly, that this plant is biennial and that sowing has to be done annually or biennially. It is important to realize that when growing parsley one is dealing with a slow-germinating, biennial plant which needs just this extra care and understanding. The safest way is to sow curly parsley every spring and to forget its biennial calendar, unless it is left to become a self-sown perennial.

As parsley is slow in germinating, it is advisable to wait for sowing until the spring-like weather has warmed the soil. The soil for parsley needs to be rich and well worked so that the roots can go deep down. The plants prefer a moderate humidity.

A light sandy soil is bound to produce weak plants with stunted growth and the roots may be impeded when these soils become hot in summer. Parsley has been known to grow well on a clay bank under the shade of trees, and any soil of loamy or clayey texture, which is fairly moist in summer, will give good results. Those who have too light or sandy soil will find it worth while to mix the soil for a special bed for parsley cultivation by forking in clay or heavy loam and plenty of manure. For winter growing it is an advantage if the soil is slightly drier and lighter to ensure that the plants will survive damp and cold winters.

As parsley runs to seed in the second year it has to be sown fresh every year to secure a succession. The seed can be sown any time from March to August in succession.

Sowing should be done at a distance of 8–12 in. (20–30 cm.) per row. Parsley is sown in drills $\frac{1}{2}$ in. deep and thinly covered with soil. As the seeds take anything from 5–8 weeks to germinate, the drills should be kept damp in dry weather until germination takes place.

Before sowing, the surface soil should be raked to a fine tilth and the soil should be made firm over the seed rows. It is good practice to mix a few lettuce or radish seeds as a 'marker crop' so that the rows are easily seen and seeds can be controlled. As soon as the parsley seedlings have come up, the indicator crop should be removed or, as in the case of lettuces or radishes, they may be allowed to develop to half-size and then be cut or pulled so that the parsley is not affected.

When seedlings are 1 in. ($2\frac{1}{2}$ cm.) tall they should be thinned to 3 in. ($7\frac{1}{2}$ cm.) apart and finally to 8 in. (20 cm.) apart as a well-matured plant will occupy nearly a square foot of ground. If the plants are too near to each other they quickly run to seed and are then useless. Eleanor Sinclair Rohde suggested that the secret of growing hardy plants is never to allow the leaves of any plant to touch those of its neighbour even in the seedling stage. Parsley that has been left huddled in rows even for a short time will never recover from this. The thinned plants form large spreading tufts and if they are prevented from flowering they will last over the winter so that cutting can continue until the following summer.

Parsley should be watered well in dry weather and kept free from weeds. Soot water made with soot which is about one month old is one of the best manures for parsley. The soot treatment will deepen the colour of the leaves. If not sufficient attention is given to the plants with regard to humidity, they will start flowering quickly during a drought. If the plants are not well picked in the summer their growth may become coarse. When the older plants begin to grow in spring the flower stem which then develops should be taken off at once so that the plant cannot go to seed.

The soil round the plants must be kept well stirred with a fork.

Parsleys

This is very often not done in winter, but it is more important during this time than during summer.

Curly Parsley Three sowings can often be made annually, the first on a southern border in February, the second in the open ground in May, and the third in sheltered and partially shaded spots in July. If the thinning can be done in showery weather those seedlings removed may be planted elsewhere to form another bed. Any flower stems should be removed at once. Towards autumn the whole of the old leaves should be cut off to stimulate the plants into making fresh growth. Since parsley is a biennial, only the tuft of leaves form the first year, but in the following summer the flower stalks shoot up and after flowering the plant dies down. The best leaves are picked the first summer and autumn although some may be had the following spring, particularly if the plant is not allowed to flower.

Plain or Hamburg Parsley The seed for this parsley—the roots of which are used as a vegetable—should be sown in shallow drills 12–18 in. (30–45 cm.) apart in March, barely covering the seeds with soil. The soil has to be prepared as for any other root crop; it should be dug deeply. When the seedlings are coming up the plants should be thinned out 9–15 in. (24–38 cm.) apart in the row. An even humidity is essential and it is therefore advisable to sow in half shade. Seedlings should not be allowed to stand too closely together in order to give the roots, used in cooking, a chance to develop well. Recently manured ground is unsuitable as it is with most root crops. It is apt to make the roots grow forked; ground on which celery was grown in the previous season is ideal for Hamburg parsley. The only other attention needed is to keep the ground free of weeds and to keep the hoe going between the rows.

WINTER PREPARATION Parsley has a long season. It can be planted at the same time as peas in spring and neither the occasional frosts in spring or autumn nor when the temperature stays at nearly freezing-point will affect the leaves, they remain green but in very cold weather they lose their flavour.

For spending the winter in the open the ordinary plain-leafed parsley is better as it is hardier and does not collect snow and rain in the leaves as much as the curled parsley does. Curled parsley for winter use should be covered with a cloche or be transferred to a cold frame where they should be covered, given plenty of air while the weather permits and the ground be kept open between the plants. (Another suggestion is to surround the bed or a portion of it with boards, place some poles or sticks across and cover with mats in severe weather, or protect plants with straw or bracken which is nearly as efficient as cloches.)

WINDOW-BOX AND INDOOR GROWING Parsley is a useful, low-growing edge for window-boxes inside as well as outside. The best varieties for this purpose are 'Triple Curled' 8–12 in. (18–30 cm.) and 'Green Gem' 5 in. (13 cm.). Parsley needs in a box a richer soil than outside and it should be well drained. The plants can be put in in the spring. Parsley likes partial shade but objects to stagnant dampness. When the leaves coarsen they should be cut back to stimulate young growth. It is best propagated by seed for succession from February to late summer and the seedlings are, of course, as slow in appearing as in the garden. They should be drastically thinned out when 1 in. high. The beginner seldom allows the seedlings enough room to develop.

During winter parsley can be grown in pots or boxes inside the kitchen window and with a few roots of parsley in flower-pots it is possible to have it as a flavouring and as an additional source of vitamin C throughout the winter. Some parsley seeds can be sown in June in boxes, which have then to be kept in a warm place (approximately 8° C. 45° F.).

Parsley plants to be brought in from the garden should be selected with care. The smallest plants with the smallest root structures are the best for transplanting. Since parsley has a good-size root structure it should be provided with an adequate pot. The foliage of the plant should be cut and just 2 in. (5 cm.) of stem length above the soil level be left, and the plant should be adjusted to indoor growing gradually.

How to Harvest and Dry *Curly Parsley*. When leaves are to be picked from plants of curly parsley, only a few at a time should be picked as the removal of a larger number of leaves at one time seriously checks the plant's growth. If parsley is wanted in bunches the stems should be up to 8 in. (20 cm.), but when the individual leaves are not wanted detached, or bunched, the plant can be picked close to the soil. For this purpose, dwarf compact plants grown close together are suitable.

If parsley is to be dried, the leaves can be gathered throughout the summer months and should be dried in the dark, laid out in single layers on trays covered with nylon net. Rapid drying is very important if the essential oils which give the herb its character, scent and flavour and particularly the green colour are to be retained in the dried herbs. Spring-dried parsley does not retain its colour as well as the young summer and autumn parsley.

Parsley is the only herb which requires a high temperature to finish it. It is not a good suggestion to follow the recommendation of some people and pour boiling water over parsley before drying. Some people suggest drying in the oven and if an oven can be regulated at a low temperature under 200° F. (95° C.) it might be possible to dry quickly and retain the colour. The door of the oven should be left ajar or some ventilation with the help of a fan should be arranged. The dried parsley should be rubbed immediately if it is crisp enough, but if parsley is not brittle when rubbed or shredded, and is not stored in air-tight glass jars and kept in the dark, it may re-absorb moisture from the air and become like rubber. Parsley, in fact, requires better conditions to retain flavour, colour and aroma than some of the other herbs. It should also be well washed before drying and should be shaken in a fine sieve before rubbing to be quite sure that no soil remains, which is inclined to splash up on low-growing leaves in heavy rain. The result of a good finished and dried parsley should show a strong attractive green colour and have an equally strong aroma.

Hamburg Parsley is mainly grown for the roots and as the roots grow best in autumn, the roots should be left in the ground for as long as possible. Before digging the roots, the dying leaves have to be cut off and the roots have to be taken out and covered with damp sand. If the roots are lifted in October they can be stored like carrots and beetroots. They can also be left in the soil during winter and weak roots which were taken up can be put back into the ground in spring. However, roots must be harvested in the second year before the plant flowers and takes all the strength out of the root. The best time to dig the roots is at the end of October or beginning of November. They can be dried at 170° F. (80° C.). If a lower temperature is used during drying it takes too long and the roots only dry outside, remaining damp inside where they start to become mouldy. The dried roots are excellent for flavouring purposes. If the roots are used for medicinal purposes they should be dug in spring after having wintered in the ground.

The roots can be dug in April or October to November, the leaves are ready when the plants are beginning to flower, and the seeds harvested shortly before they are fully ripe. The seeds are harvested by cutting off the flower umbels and putting them in tied bundles in bags which collect the falling seed.

Plain parsley has some similarity to fool's parsley (*Aethusa cynapium*) and the preference in this country for curly parsley may be due to the wish to exclude any confusion with the poisonous parsley. The most noticeable difference between plain and fool's parsley is the strong aromatic scent which is typical for true parsley, while fool's parsley has an offensive smell, reminiscent of garlic.

What Parsley Can Do for Our Food It is difficult to explain what makes parsley such a universal flavouring, but with all its strength and spiciness it has a neutral quality which neither adds such a strong accent of flavouring that it 'puts anyone off', nor causes anyone to get tired of it; somehow parsley seems to underline the taste of food but not add anything new to it.

Therefore, parsley is found with nearly every savoury dish. It flavours potatoes, peas, soups, stocks, sauces, salads, egg dishes; there are the special parsley dishes such as Parsley Sauce, Parsley Potatoes, Parsley Stuffing and Parsley Butter. It should not only be used at the beginning of cooking, when it often brings out the basic flavour, but it should also be added again shortly before serving. All those dishes which are served with a covering of parsley give pleasure from seeing this green and familiar colouring of chopped herbs. Green-dried parsley can be used in the same places where fresh parsley is used but it has to be stored in air-tight glass containers where it will retain its special properties of colour and flavouring all during winter.

The green-dried parsley should be reconstituted in a salad dressing or sautéd in heated fat before any further ingredients are added when cooking, and if sprinkled over salads and cooked dishes the initial humidity will reconstitute it anyway.

A special delicacy is fried parsley. Parsley must be fresh and very dry and can be fried in deep oil for about half a minute, drained on an absorbent paper and served very hot; a delicious garnish for baked or fried fish.

Hamburg Parsley, grown for its parsnip-like roots, also provides green leaves of parsley which can be used in the same way as curly parsley. The plain parsley is, in fact, considered on the Continent to have as strong if not a stronger flavour and the leaves are used much more for flavouring than the curled parsley which is used more for garnishing and decorating purposes. The leaves of the plain or Hamburg parsley have an excellent flavour and keep their qualities longer when dried; a combination of curly and plain parsley gives a particularly good flavour.

As a winter vegetable the roots of Hamburg parsley are very tasty either alone or in combination with other vegetables. Parsley in all its parts has not only a strong aroma and flavour which stimulates the appetite, but at the same time it affects the digestion, and stimulates elimination through the skin; parsley is therefore a very useful herb or vegetable for a 'spring-cleaning' of the body during Lent.

The roots also contain vitamin C and are therefore suitable for grating raw for salads, with chopped parsley leaves added. The roots are also used as a flavouring. They give strength and savour to all meat soups and stocks, and are part of a little bunch of vegetables and herbs called 'soup greens' (Suppengrün) which are bought as such from the greengrocers in German-speaking countries. They are cut up and added from the beginning to the water in which poultry or meat is boiled and from which a soup or sauce will then be made—in fact in *pot-au-feu* or boiled beef.

As in this country Hamburg parsley roots are usually boiled like parsnips, they have not found so much favour in English gardens, but grated raw in salads and added to soups and stews, or sautéd as a separate vegetable dish, they are of excellent culinary and health value (see recipe p. 171).

Parsley can be used with every savoury dish, therefore no list of special uses appears necessary.

HAMBURG PARSLEY ROOTS

Ingredients:

1½ lb. Hamburg parsley roots
(leave 1 raw root)

1 onion, chopped finely

⅓ oz. butter or oil

Stock

Parsley chopped

Chervil ⎫
Lemon balm ⎬ if available
Salad burnet ⎭

⅔ oz. butter or oil

2 tablespoons cream

Method:

1 Brush, wash and scrape roots.
2 Leave whole if small, or cut into strips.
3 Sauté onion in hot fat.
4 Add parsley and sauté.
5 Add roots and sauté.
6 Add stock, cover and simmer gently until tender.
7 Add herbs, butter and cream.
8 Grate 1 raw root into it before serving.

ROSE GERANIUM

(*Pelargonium graveolens, etc.*)

Virtues There are probably two hundred varieties of the sweet-scented pelargonium of herb gardens, but this is the most popular one. The lovely plant tastes and smells of roses, with a slight addition of spice. It is often thought of as a house plant because of its beautiful foliage but will grow from 3–4 ft. (90–120 cm.) high if given plenty of space in the herb garden. The dried or fresh leaves are used to give a delicate flavour to many interesting sweets, jams and jellies, also a fruit cup will be much enhanced by them. The dried leaves are used in herb teas, jellies, etc. and are a wonderfully scented addition to potpourri.

Description Rose geranium is a shrubby plant with deeply cut and divided leaves and clusters of pink and lavender flowers. The large soft hairy leaves are divided into three main divisions which are deeply cut around the edges; the larger the leaves the more fragrant their sweet and spicy scent will be. The flowers bloom in a rather loose umbel. The leaves vary in size in different varieties; the tiny leaves of the lemon-scented geranium have edges which feel almost crisp.

Growing Rose geranium needs a warm sheltered position; it can easily be injured by frost; it can be propagated by cuttings. The rose geranium has exactly the same growth habits as any of the unscented geraniums.

WINTER It may be taken in in the autumn and new plants started from cuttings in the spring. Rose geranium for winter use should be started from cuttings; after these are established the parent plant should be removed from its garden bed and hung in a dark dry, cool place to rest during winter. This should be done before any sign of frost appears. The rose geranium plants may be set out in the garden again after snow and frost have passed and the earth is well warmed. This applies to both the stored roots and the new plants which were started from cuttings in the autumn and wintered indoors. The acclimatizing of the winter season house plants to the outdoor garden is done in the spring when the plants are set out of doors in their pots during warm days and brought indoors during cool days; gradually they become readjusted to the outdoor temperature and can be planted in the herb garden.

Harvesting The scented geranium leaves can be used fresh from the garden and the large fresh leaves are the best for use in jams or jellies and other desserts. The leaves have to be most carefully dried as they may not always easily retain their colour, but if care is taken will certainly retain their lovely scent.

Uses The dry or fresh leaves may be used to give a delicate rose flavour to custard, baked fruits, puddings and ice-creams, to jams and jellies. The tiny fresh or dried leaf of the apple or lemon-scented variety will give attractiveness to a fruit cup. One of the small leaves in the bottom of a finger bowl will be a fragrant alternative to the usual lemon slice. The dried leaves are used in some parts with herbs or other teas and a tiny leaf in the bottom of a pudding dish will make all the difference. The leaves are also used in herb jellies and herb vinegar, brewed tea, fruit drink, lemonades, wine cups: if cold, garnish with a leaf after the drink is ready; for hot drinks one crushed leaf in the bottom of a cup is suggested before pouring the drink. One leaf under each piece of baked apple, pear or peach permeates the whole dessert and so does one leaf in the bottom tray of ice-creams before freezing, and also one leaf in the bottom of a pudding dish before baking. Rose geranium apple jelly is made by placing one small leaf in the bottom of a glass jar and the hot apple juice poured over it, a second rose geranium leaf at the top, then covered and sealed. A tea made of dry or fresh leaves can also be blended with mint and served hot or iced.

ROSE HIPS

Dog Rose, Wild Rose (*Rosa canina*) and *Rosa rugosa* (Shrubrose)
Sweetbriar (*Rosa rubiginosa*)

Virtues Rose hips are the fruit of the wild and the shrub roses. They are small red/orange berries which are left after the flowers wilt and are the fruits of the rose bush. These colourful berries are not just ornamental but are a nutritious fruit rich in vitamin C as well as A, B, E, and P. An analysis arranged by the author during the Second World War when no citrus fruits were imported found rose hips to be twenty times richer in this vitamin than orange juice and sixty times richer than lemons; and eventually the women's organization, Boy Scouts and school children collected large numbers of rose hips from the common hedgerows for making Rose Hip Syrup.

Rose hips contain, apart from the large content of vitamin C, vitamin A which encourages growth in children; also vitamin A deficiency causes night blindness. The bright red, sour/sweet fruits contain sugar, citric and malic acid, pectin, and above all vitamin C. They are diuretic if used together with their pips. It is important, according to Kneipp, that this stimulation takes place without doing any damage to the kidneys.

Rose Hips

Rose hip tea, which is now available in this country and which has been used on the Continent a great deal, contains pods as well as pips. The pods contain most of the vitamins and the pips have an age-old reputation of helping the work of the gall-bladder and the kidneys. Their diuretic quality makes them useful as a daily tea, particularly for people who like to eat uncooked fruit and salads.

Description The *English dogrose* is the most common and most variable wild rose in the south. The large flowers are pale pink or white, and fragrant, with numerous yellow stamens. The rose bush is tall, stout, and deciduous 4–10 ft. (1–3 m.) high with arching stems and hooked or curved prickles. The pinnate leaves with toothed leaflets are sometimes downy beneath; the fruits—the hips—are red, egg-shaped and nearly always hairless, losing the more or less pinnate sepals before they redden. The *Sweetbriar* (*Rosa rubiginosa*) is smaller in all its parts and is usually easily found by its sweet-smelling leaves; it is usually sticky and hairy below; altogether a smaller shrub with curved, oval prickles; the hips are also egg-shaped, with few or no bristles.

Growing Most of the hips used are collected wild. The dogrose is widespread on commons, in hedgerows and fields, while the sweetbriar is frequent on chalk and limestone in the south; there are certain parts of the country where hips abound. If the hips are to be collected in the garden it is a good plan for all those people who want a really impenetrable hedge to plant bushes of either *Rosa canina*, *Rosa rugosa*, or *Rosa rubiginosa*. The flowers are a lovely addition in summer and the rose hips a most valuable one for autumn and winter. A single free-standing bush is also most attractive and has the advantage that hips can be picked from all sides. The sweetbriar rose makes a dwarf hedge with fragrant foliage. All rose bushes should be planted at a distance of 3 ft. (approximately 1 m.).

It seems that the more northerly a country the higher is the vitamin content of rose hips; thus the hips of the dogrose in Scotland contains four times as much vitamin C as the same species in south England. When transplanted to the south of England it seems to retain its original vitamin C content. This opens a future field for select-ing special plants to increase the vitamin content of hips. It has also been found that the hips on a bush facing north are richer in vitamin C than those facing south.

Harvest Hips to be used for cooking purposes should be left longer on the bushes until the frost has touched them and they become slightly soft. If, however, they are intended to be dried they can be picked before they become soft, but they must be really ripe. It is therefore hardly useful to pick hips before October and they should, for all purposes, have had some frost. When going out for picking, a crooked walking-stick can be of help in bending down the tall branches for getting the hips from the top. Some people require gloves because of the thorns. Immediately after picking, particularly when they are soft, they should be made into purée, or used for syrups, sauces, creams, puddings or soups. When they are used for drying they should be bright red and firm and be spread on trays and al-lowed to dry until they are hard and brittle without losing their colour and becoming darker. When dry they should be crushed by means of a roller or some other means, or ground in a coarse mill; but as all contact with metal, other than stainless steel, must be avoided, the rose hips must be protected by a layer of paper when crushing. Any contact with metal not only loses vitamin C through oxidizing but also makes the rose hips black.

When dried and crushed they have to be shaken through a large sieve, preferably covered by a plate, preferably outside in order to get rid of all the hair. For this purpose they must be bone dry and the wind should not stand in the direction of the shaker. It is also advis-able either to wear gloves or to tie the sleeves of one's garment, as otherwise the hairs penetrate through the sleeves or the opening at the neck on to the body. They only cause irritation to people with over-sensitive skins, but they itch and make people uncomfortable. When the hips are freed from their hair they are ready to be stored in air-tight containers in a dark dry place.

Uses The tea is made as follows: 2 tablespoons of rose hips (pods and pips in a balanced proportion) should be soaked in 3 pints of water in an enamel or other non-metal pot for 12 hours or they can be soaked, covered with water, in a small container and the 3 pints added when boiling. They should be simmered gently for 20–30 minutes, but must never be allowed to boil quickly. They should be strained and then kept in a covered china or earthenware jar until needed. A few more hips can be added each time when heating up. The tea can be sweetened with brown sugar or honey. Two or three hibiscus flowers, called Karkadé in their African homeland, can be added to improve colour and flavour. Added shortly before serving or when warming up, they provide a beautiful burgundy colour and a new tart flavour. Rose hip and hibiscus teas are most attractive in a glass teapot because of the lovely colour.

The domestic rose hip purée, if properly prepared, contains the strong natural orange/red colour of the rose hips, and thus will most likely contain vitamin P, an essential part of vitamin C, connected with the orange colouring matter. It also retains the characteristic hip flavour which is a favourite, especially with children and is being used in all other countries. Also a sauce made of the rose hip purée is excellent to go with sweets as an alternative to custard or chocolate sauce, also providing the so necessary vitamin C.

ROSEMARY

(*Rosmarinus officinalis*)

Virtues Rosemary is a lovely evergreen shrub which is highly aromatic and has always been greatly valued for its use both in medicine and cooking, though originally it was a ritual herb. Indigenous to the Mediterranean, Rosemary or *rosmarinus* its Latin name, means 'Dew of the Sea' and was so-called because it grew all round the Mediterranean coast in the salt sea spray. To the ancient Greeks rosemary had a reputation for strengthening the brain and memory; thus it became the emblem of remembrance, love and friendship at christenings, weddings and funerals. The Greek students used to twine garlands of rosemary in their hair when taking examinations, to stimulate their minds!

Rosemary has a pungent, resinous taste with a delightful perfume,

Rosemary

and imparts its subtle but lasting flavour to many foods. It contains calcium, tannins, bitter principles and has a strong volatile oil similar to eucalyptus oil. Rosemary acts on a weak digestion, flatulence, neuralgic pains, and has qualities which help to stimulate the circulation and other functions; this because it increases the supply of blood and widens the tissues where it is applied. The results are obtained by drinking an infusion such as rosemary tea, wine or liqueur, or, externally, by rubbing affected parts with oil in which rosemary has been steeped.

Water in which rosemary has been boiled improves the skin when used for washing or as a bath addition; it also stimulates growth of hair when used as a hairwash or rinse. Rosemary twigs burned on the fire sweeten and freshen the air of an invalid's room and the leaves can be included in a moth repellent together with other herbs. It is also used extensively in the treatment and breeding of dogs.

Appearance of the Plant Rosemary is a perennial and a member of the *Labiatae* family. It grows to about 5 ft. in this country though in warmer climes it grows over 6 ft. tall. It has a woody trunk with many branches and the succulent leaves, which are about 1 in. long, curve slightly like pine needles. They are linear and revolute, green on top and woolly greyish green beneath where the oil glands are situated. The delicate pale blue flowers grow in clusters on a short shoot in the flower axils. Their calyces contain much of the active volatile principles. The whole plant, flowers, leaves and stems, give off a fragrant spicy aroma.

There are a number of varieties of rosemary: *Rosmarinus alba*— 'Miss Jessup's Upright' which has white flowers and yields long straight shoots; *Rosmarinus angustissimus* which comes from Corsica; this is highly aromatic, grows to about 3 ft. but is not a hardy plant. Another is the dwarf rosemary which is most suitable for a small garden as it grows only 18 in. high. The smallest variety of all is the prostrate rosemary, *Rosmarinus prostrata*. This is a rockery plant which grows 6–8 in. (15–20 cm.) high; it has shiny green leaves but is not a hardy plant and would need protection in winter.

Growing Rosemary grows best in a light, sandy, rather dry soil, preferably overlying chalk; this last because it needs lime, and to supply this a few egg-shells or wood-ash for use on one or two shrubs, or garden lime or ground chalk can be added to the soil around the plants. It requires a sheltered position with a southern aspect where it will get the maximum of sunlight, the best place being against a wall. The oil content of the flowers and leaves depends much on the amount of shelter and sunshine the plant can have. Other than its position it needs little attention; normal watering and snipping off of strong growth is all that is necessary. It does not require heavy pruning either, and once it is an established bush and is being cut and used frequently, there is no need to do more.

Rosemary can be propagated by seeds, cuttings, division of roots and layering. Seeds should be sown in shallow drills 6 in. (15 cm.) apart, outdoors in April. When the seedlings are a few inches high they should be transplanted into a nursery bed 6 in. (15 cm.) apart each way, finally being planted out 3 ft. (90 cm.) apart. It is said that the finest plants are obtained from seed but it is difficult to get it to germinate. It is quicker and easier to propagate from cuttings taken in February or March or at the end of May or June, after the plant has flowered. The cuttings taken should be about 6 in. (15 cm.) long, put into sandy soil in a shady spot having two-thirds of their length in the ground. If they are put under a cloche they will root and be ready for transplanting into a permanent position the following autumn,

Propagation by division of roots can be done from established bushes every two or three years. This prevents them from becoming leggy and ensures leaves of good colour. Layering is another easy way to propagate. It can be done any time in summer by simply pegging down some of the lower branches under a little sandy soil.

Rosemary is susceptible to cold biting winds and to frost if in an unsheltered position, and particularly so if grown on unsuitable soils. Though it will be found that rosemary plants are smaller in England than anywhere else, it grows not only better but is very much more fragrant, like lavender and peppermint. It is probably the moist climate and the longer daylight hours in the summer which accounts for this.

WINTER PREPARATION Rosemary should be protected in winter if it is to be kept successfully out of doors. It should be cut before winter, but not too low or too late, not later than August to give the shoots which start to develop a chance to harden off for the winter; then the soil which covers the root should be well covered with leaf mould. If there is a real danger of air frost, the whole plant should be covered with leaves and on top of this light open-weave baskets in which fruit are sold should be fastened to the soil, or some light hessian, sacking or other porous material be hung over stakes and weighted down or tied down so that the winter gales cannot remove the covers.

It can be gradually uncovered in the spring but at first it should only remain uncovered on fine sunny days. It has been found that after an extremely severe and long winter well-established rosemary bushes in a well-protected position—facing south between a house and a west wall—died rather than those in more exposed positions. This may be due either to the fact that the soil in this position is not sufficiently well drained or that it has not allowed the plants to become hardy enough to withstand such a winter, though their roots were protected by being well covered with snow.

INDOOR GROWING In many northern parts of this country it is too bleak for rosemary to grow outside and it can only be used as a pot plant. A small plant can be obtained from a nursery or raised from a cutting of the common rosemary. An outdoor rosemary plant to be converted into an indoor plant should be trimmed back to about one-third of its original size. The plant should be allowed to recover from trimming and to harden off the new shoots which form; then it should be potted in a soil with humus and sand and gradually adapted to indoors. There is a prostrate variety which is particularly suitable because its heavy stem weighs it down and the branches cascade down the sides of the pot. These plants, which can be put outdoors in summer, grow very well if set in sandy loamy soil with compost or well-rotted manure with a few pieces of broken limestone rock in the bottom of the pot. After the plants are potted they should be carefully watered every day from the top with lukewarm water. They will flower better if the plant is kept clipped.

How to Harvest and Dry Rosemary leaves can be picked for culinary use in small quantities, from the second year onwards at any time of the year. When harvesting rosemary for drying it is advisable to wait until the end of August to give the plant enough time to harden off the new shoots which will be encouraged by the harvesting.

Rosemary

The shoots should be severed just above the hard wood and be taken straight for drying so that the rosemary loses none of its volatile oil. When the leaves are required for flavouring purposes only, the green shoots, and what leaves can be stripped from the woody shoots, should be placed on trays in the dark in a well-ventilated cupboard so that they do not take too long to dry. When dried the leaves look rather like pine needles, but if dried successfully they retain their green colour and are equally good for flavouring as when fresh. When the flowers are needed for flavouring they should be picked just before coming out into full flower and this should be done on a warm sunny day. They have to be dried at a very low temperature to retain their beautiful colour.

If cutting is done in August, autumn flowering will hardly be experienced, but there are some circumstances under which plants will produce flowers in September.

Uses

For medicinal purposes:

Rosemary Tea: 1 teaspoon leaves per cup of water, two cups per day. Rosemary boiled with lovage and juniper—a most diuretic tea.

Rosemary Wine: Dried leaves or small chopped-up twigs added to white wine, allowed to draw for eight days, then filtered into bottles. Not more than two glasses of wine per day and not for longer than two months in succession.

Rosemary Liqueur: Good brandy can make liqueur in the same way. Not more than two small liqueur glasses a day.

Oil of Rosemary: Tops and leaves are allowed to soak in a good vegetable oil for a week in the sun and then be filtered.

What Rosemary Can Do for Our Food The unusually delicious, piny, pungent and lingering aroma—unlike any other herb—has made rosemary a very special flavouring, much in demand at present. This may be due to a new increasing interest in Mediterranean cookery. From turtle soup to marinades, from very strong-flavoured fish to quail, partridge and venison—rosemary is the herb to flavour the more unusual foods—as well as the everyday dishes of meat, eggs and vegetables. Rosemary freshly chopped gives a lovely flavour to jams, jellies and sweet sauces. Chopped or powdered rosemary added to a recipe for small shortbread biscuits makes a delicious and unusual tea-time food. It is also used for herb butters, herb jellies, vinegars and herb honey.

Rosemary as an addition to cider and claret cups will provide not only a rather special aroma to them but also help to act as a 'digestif' after a banquet, and will refresh at the same time.

For culinary purposes:

Rosemary is a herb which at all times should be used with care but this does not detract in any way from its attractiveness and once the cook has discovered how best its strength can be employed she will never want to be without it.

Hors-d'œuvre: With tiny biscuits—ham filling; fruit and vegetable cocktails.

Eggs and cheese: Omelettes; scrambled eggs; cream cheese; Cheddar cheese sauce.

Soups, stews and sauces: Chicken, pea, spinach, turtle soups; Minestrone; meat soups.

Meat and fish: Beef, lamb, pork, veal broiled and roasted; in marinades for meat and strong-flavoured fish like salmon, eel, halibut.

Poultry and game: Sprinkle inside and outside lightly before roasting chicken, duck, pheasant, quail. Stuffings; rabbit; partridge; venison.

Vegetables: Beans, green peas, cauliflower; mushrooms and fungi; vegetable broth; dumplings; risotto; baked potatoes.

Sweets and beverages: Apple jelly, jams, jellies; in biscuits; summer fruit drinks—cups; fruit salad; wine and cider cups. Rosemary sugar.

ITALIAN LAMB

Ingredients:

2 lb. of the meat of a young lamb
3 tablespoons oil
Clove of garlic (minced)
2 teaspoons crushed rosemary

Salt
(3½ oz. 1⅓ cup) dry white wine
½ oz. lemon juice
2 oz. stock

181

Sage

Method:

1 Cut lamb into 1½-in. cubes.
2 Heat oil in a heavy skillet or heavy saucepan.
3 Then sauté garlic.
4 Brown meat on all sides, adding rosemary and salt.
5 Add wine and lemon.
6 Add later stock if more liquid desirable.
7 Cover and simmer over a low heat for 25–60 minutes, according to the tenderness of the meat.

Note. If a little gravy is desired add before serving:

1 teaspoon flour smoothed with 1½ oz. stock and allow to cook for a few minutes.

SAGE

(*Salvia officinalis*)

Virtues Garden sage is a highly aromatic herb with a strong penetrating smell and rather an astringent taste. Now essentially a culinary herb, sage was highly valued in the past for its great curative and healing powers. Its very name is derived from the Latin *salvere*—to save—and it came to be regarded as a universal remedy for all ills. Sage is, in fact, one of the most effective medicinal herbs produced by nature, for it contains oils which increase the circulation of the whole digestive system, act as a disinfectant, and an expectorant on the lungs and is helpful to health in general. Sage tea was a popular drink in England for years before China tea was introduced, not only because it was good medicinally but because it was very pleasant to take. Originally from the mountain slopes of southern Europe it came to this country by way of the monastery gardens of France and Switzerland and for centuries was used to flavour rich meats such as pork and mutton, fat fish and poultry stuffings. In fact, as a German herbalist said in 1551 . . . 'it serves the doctor, the cook, the kitchen and the cellar, the poor and the rich'.

Appearance of the Plant Sage, one of the *Labiatae*, is a perennial, subshrub which grows about 2 ft. (60 cm.) high with strong woody stems.

Sage

It throws out new branches every year from the woody base of its stalks. The hardy leaves are stalked 1½–2 in. (4–5 cm.) long and ¾–1 in. (2–2½ cm.) broad, greyish green in colour, oblong with serrated margins. They have clearly visible veins which make the leaves appear crinkly. The violet-blue flowers come out from June to July and fade to a pale lilac.

There are many varieties of sage, most of them ornamental, but the following are those used for culinary and medicinal purposes: *Broad-Leaved English Sage* has a good flavour and is the best for drying. *Narrow-Leaved* or *Bush Sage* has an excellent flavour for cooking; the flowers are purple and they make good bee plants. *Red Sage*, a beautiful plant with reddish stems and leaves, can be used in cooking, but is mostly used medicinally for a disinfectant gargle. An attractive type is the perennial *Dwarf Garden Sage* which lengthens the season of green leaves in the herb garden as salad burnet does. One plant is often enough for a family. This sage has a compact branch structure and will always stay where it is planted and will not extend its root system into areas where it is not wanted.

Growing Sage makes an attractive border plant and needs little attention for it is unplagued by insects and has a strong resistance to weather. It does not require any special soil preparation. It grows best on a light dry chalky soil in a sunny, rather dry position. On a heavy soil it may die out in a hard winter; though, an exception to the rule, it has grown successfully near Evesham in Worcestershire on heavy clays.

(a) *Broad-Leaved Sage*. This never flowers in this country but is the best to grow for harvesting. It is grown as a perennial propagated by division of plants or by layering or by cuttings. It cannot be grown from seed. As a perennial, established plants provide a cut in June and a further crop in August, giving the plants sufficient time to develop again before the winter. Cuttings should be taken from well-established plants in April or May. The cuttings taken with a 'heel' root best if set in a cold frame, but they can be put straight into open ground. When rooted they can be planted out in their permanent position again 15–20 in. (40–45 cm.) apart with the rows 2 ft. apart. It is important to keep the soil well hoed and free from weeds. Propagating sage by layering the stems is very easy to do and the layered stems will produce numerous rootlets which can be taken from the plant in May.

Another way of dividing sage is by earthing up the fully grown plants in October or March leaving just the tops exposed. The shrub then produces roots from the buried stems. The plants can be lifted about May or June and divided into pieces each piece having fringed roots on it, and placed into a new permanent position. If established plants become leggy the growing tips should be nipped out.

When sage plants are 4–5 years old they are usually exhausted and should then be dug in and the plantation renewed. If, however, cuttings are taken each year, thus ensuring a good crop, then old plants can be dug in every two years. Red sage can only be propagated from cuttings or divisions, for it is usually non-flowering.

(b) *Narrow-Leaved Sage.* For the production of a crop of sage for drying this is normally grown as an annual. The seeds are sown in April and the whole crop cut in September or October. This variety produces many blue flowers which are kept cut off as the plants are required for their leaves and not seeds.

To propagate from seed, the round black-brown seeds should be sown in humid soil and lightly covered with soil. Germination takes 10–14 days. The young plants can be transplanted 15–20 in. (40–45 cm.) apart in May.

WINTER PREPARATION The plants should be mulched with old manure or a dressing of old soot will help the plants through the winter. Before the plant shoots in the spring it may be found necessary to cut the woody stems back; this will help it to bush out.

WINDOW-BOX AND INDOOR GROWING Sage can easily be cultivated in the window-box or in a pot though it must be kept bushy and shaped by cutting back young shoots. The plants will probably have to be renewed fairly often. One or two varieties are particularly suitable: *pineapple sage*, with its lovely scarlet flowers and fruit scent, but it is not a hardy plant, and *dwarf garden sage* because of its compact structure.

Sage

How to Harvest and Dry Sage plants must be well established to allow a good harvest; second-year plants are usually richer in volatile oils than the first-year ones. The richest content is expected just before flowering, but as this does not happen with the broad-leaved sage a cut can be made in June and one in August. If this is done the bushes do not become too woody. The narrow-leaved sage is cut in September or October. Sage can be cut with scissors or a hook hand high above the ground. The leaves should then be dried in thin layers at a low temperature.

The drying of sage is more difficult than that of most other herbs, as the tough leaves require a much longer drying period and very easily discolour if the temperature is too high.

Uses

For medicinal purposes:

Sage Tea: Sage tea is an excellent tea, particularly if made of red sage, for gargling and for sore throats because of its astringent qualities. It is also one of the herbs to be used for a steam bath, which has not only cosmetic qualities but therapeutic qualities in the case of a severe head cold.

What Sage Can Do for Our Food Sage should be used sparingly as it has a strong flavour; it helps digestion when used with rich meats and rabbits fed on sage produce a particularly tasty meat. It lends itself to fish dishes and is an important ingredient in Hamburg Eel soup—a famous traditional German dish; and sage leaves wrapped around pieces of eel are a delicacy. Roasts can be wrapped in sage leaves or 'larded' with them, and 'Kebabs' are much improved by sage leaves between the various pieces of meat on the skewers. Sage is used in cheese-making, and herb butter and pickled cucumbers benefit by the addition of sage.

For culinary purposes:
Egg and cheese: In Cheddar or cream cheese spreads; cheese omelettes; sage fritters.
Soups, stews and sauces: Cream soups; fish chowders; beef, lamb, veal stews; in meat sauces.

Sage

Meat and fish: With all roast meats and their gravies; with liver; in meat puddings and loaves; in stuffings for pork and veal; in sausages. In water to boil fish; with eels and all fat fish; with other herbs as part of a *bouquet garni.*

Poultry and game: Rubbed on goose, turkey, duck and all game birds and in stuffings for them; hare, rabbit and roasted venison.

Vegetables: In water to boil spinach, onions, peas, with most tomato dishes and pulses.

Beverages: Summer fruit drinks, clear apple juice, in wine-making, in wine cups, cocktails; sage tea, served hot or iced, blends also with mint and lemon thyme.

EEL IN SAGE LEAVES

Ingredients:

2 medium-sized young fresh eels

$\frac{1}{4}$ cup lemon juice

$\frac{1}{2}$ cup vegetable oil

1 large finely chopped onion

Fresh chopped or green-dried parsley

Herb bouquet for fish dishes (green-dried)

Fresh chopped or green-dried sage

Bacon slices

Fresh or green-dried whole sage leaves

Method:

1 Skin eels and cut into pieces 2 in. or 3 in. long, according to thickness, and pour over the following marinade:

2 Mix well lemon juice, oil, onion and herbs and if there is not enough liquid to cover the pieces of eel in a bowl, add a little water or stock to the marinade.

3 Set aside to marinate for about 1 to 2 hours.

4 Wrap each piece of eel in a slice of bacon and then in sage leaves (crossways) and tie with thread.

5 Place wrapped pieces of eel in a flat fireproof dish and pour the marinade over them.

6 Bake in the oven uncovered for at least $\frac{1}{2}$ hour.

SALAD BURNET

(Sanguisorba minor)

Virtues Salad burnet is a perennial and almost an evergreen, though it sows itself every year and the young leaves are much more tender than those of the old plant. It has been used from time immemorial, but only since the sixteenth century has it been planted in this country. The leaves have a nutty flavour and a taste of cucumber; they contain among other things tannins and are particularly suitable in salads and with other herbs as a herb for soups. It is an excellent herb for flavouring drinks. Burnet is the last of the herbs to die back in winter and even pokes its head through a light fall of snow; it is a herb which provides in most climates green leaves all the year round. This herb is a perfect example of the claim that herb gardening is easy.

Description The decorative plant grows to a height of 12–15 in. (30–40 cm.). The leaves are pinnate with serrate leaflets and the flowers grow in small round heads first green then reddish. The plants flower from June to the end of August, pollinated by wind. The rosette of compounded leaves produces a most attractive little bush of greenery—during winter in an otherwise hibernating herb garden.

Growing Salad burnet has no special requirements but prefers chalky soil. It is advisable to sow it in rows 12 in. (30 cm.) apart. The seeds germinate best in the dark within 24 days. Salad burnet should be sown in April and the seeds be covered by less than 1 in. of soil. If it is allowed to go to seed it will self sow and the fact that the leaves stay green all winter, and even the broad leaves are always tender, helps the herb gardener. Salad burnet should not be transplanted but the weak seedlings can be pinched off at ground level.

Some people prefer to grow salad burnet as an annual. In this case it should be cut before the unattractive greenish red flowers can be formed.

WINDOW-BOX For the herb gardener who grows salad burnet in his garden there is no need to grow it in a flower-pot as the leaves will be available during winter; for the town-dweller it is particularly suitable to grow in flower-pots.

Harvesting When the first flower shoots appear, the first cut can be made. If well developed two or three cuttings can be made each year. As it grows in the same spot for many years, to prevent self-sowing and to keep plants from blooming all summer cut off the flower heads. For constant use and a supply of young leaves for salads cut it back to 4–5 in. high.

Uses Salad burnet brings the taste of cucumber to salads, herb mixtures, herb soups and sauces and particularly to claret wine cups and cocktails. It has also been used as a tonic and has, in fact, a reputation similar to borage. Its delicate-looking foliage is also an attractive decoration and adds to the appearance of iced drinks as well as to their flavour. All salads with French dressing or mayonnaise and asparagus, celery, bean and mushroom soups will benefit by it. The herb should be placed into soups at the beginning of cooking.

SAVORIES

SUMMER SAVORY (*Satureia hortensia*)
WINTER SAVORY (*Satureia montana*)

Virtues The savories, which belong to the *Labiatae* family consist of: an annual plant—summer savory, and a perennial plant—winter savory. Both savories seem to have originated in the eastern Mediterranean though winter savory is a 'mountain savory'. The name of the savories is supposed to come from the satyrs and the word *satureia* can often be found among Roman writings. This connection may explain that the plant was originally considered an aphrodisiac. The Romans brought savory to England during the time of the Caesars and it then became popular in Saxon cooking.

Savories are the herbs nearest to a seasoning or a spice. The main purpose of summer savory, however, is to flavour beans of all kinds and it is known as the 'bean-herb' (Bohnenkraut) in Germany. Without adding a different flavour, it strengthens the bean flavour; it will also give a piquant and pleasant flavour to many other foods.

Savories

Though summer savory has to be treated as an annual in this country and gives the herb gardener the trouble of sowing it each year, it does reward him with a much more delicate flavour not contained in winter savory. This small evergreen sub-shrub is stronger and coarser in flavour. It has to be used with great care and is also more restricted in its use, while only summer savory enhances all savory dishes.

Both savories have a strongly aromatic smell and there is a high content of volatile oil in the plants, the main constituent of which is carvacol; the savories, therefore, also serve medicinal purposes and have sometimes been infused as a digestive medicine.

Both savories are excellent bee plants and though they are some of the lesser known herbs in the English herb garden, summer savory is most useful and should be tried by every herb gardener. Not much need be sown of it because it grows quickly, and is so strong as a seasoning that only little is needed.

Appearance of the Plant Summer savory is a bushy, tender plant 12 in. (30 cm.) high with sparse leaves scattered along the stem. The root is widely branched and the stem is erect and strong, hairy, obtuse-quadrangular and becomes woody at the base. The dark green leaves are a little thick, narrow and without a clear stalk; they are $\frac{1}{2}$ in. in length and blunt-tipped; the leaves carry a number of glandular scales which, if held against the light, appear to be small points.

The whole plant appears to be purplish. The flowers are very short but definitely stalked; there are often five together—small, heliotrope, lilac, pink or whitish—at the axils of the leaves. The plants flower from July to September sometimes into October. The fruits are small nutlets, round to egg-shaped, approximately 1–1·5 mm., slightly three-cornered; they are dark brown to black with dark veins.

Winter Savory is a compact, hardy, perennial sub-shrub 6–16 in. (15–40 cm.) high with erect or ascending stems and stiff erect branches. It has a strong tap root of medium to dark brown colour which is sometimes slightly curved; the side roots are lighter and strongly branched, showing a rich fibrous growth. The stalk is obtuse-quadrangular and sometimes nearly round. It quickly becomes woody and is covered with a silky bark which can easily be removed. The greyish green, somewhat shiny leaves are almost lanceolate, sometimes leathery and prickly without a clear stalk. They have small glandular scales, similar to summer savory.

The flower is stalked and three to seven are together in the axil of the leaves. The crown of the flowers is white, pink or violet. They flower sometimes from June, definitely from July to October. The herb has a very long flowering period and the bees make the best of this.

There is an upright and a more creeping type. The stems are often so weak that they fall over and make the plants suitable for edges or to cover artificial boundaries; they are excellent for rock gardens.

Growing

(a) *Summer Savory* is best grown from seeds sown in a sunny position in fairly rich soil but not soil which contains fresh manure or compost. The seeds should be sown in rows 1 ft. (30 cm.) apart in April or May and subsequently thinned to one plant every 6 in. (15 cm.). From this sowing it is possible to obtain two cuts, the first and largest in August, followed by a much smaller harvest in October.

Summer savory can also be grown by raising plants early in March and April in a greenhouse for later hardening and planting out, but unless carefully transplanted the crop will not be as good as that produced from plants raised and grown from seed *in situ*.

Though summer savory has a great need for humidity during the actual sowing period, it is not sensitive to drought and can be sown from the end of March to the end of June, provided the soil is well worked beforehand. If sowing is done in May or June, the herb would be ready in time for French and runner beans. Germination usually takes place then in 10–14 days and one can usually rely on 70 per cent germinating. If too much soil falls on the seeds, which can easily happen with a light soil, the rows of seeds will show big gaps.

(b) *Winter Savory* requires poor, light, preferably chalky well-drained soil in full sun. It can be sown in August or the beginning of September.

When raised from seed in a frame or on a site the seeds should not be covered as it is a seed which germinates by light in 10–12 days; they should be sown in drills 12–15 in. (30–40 cm.) apart. Winter savory is slower growing than summer savory and it is easier there-

fore to propagate by cuttings in spring from side shoots or by layering. All plants may be divided and replanted in March. Winter
savory gives the least trouble and the plants thrive year after year in
the same plot.

In continental countries there are several varieties, one of which
is a creeping winter savory which needs a little more space in planting
(approximately 15 in. (40 cm.) than the upright variety. The creeping
type is called *Satureia montana* var. *subspicata*; the upright plant, var.
communis. Winter savory should be neatly trained and have the
appearance of a shrub.

WINTER PREPARATION Winter savory may be killed if the soil is too
damp or too rich. Though it is relatively hardy, a light covering may
be advisable to avoid losing parts of the plant by frost. It should be
well clipped before the winter starts, but after the winter the herb can
be cut back to 2–4 in. (6–10 cm.), after which it starts shooting and
the cutting may induce new growth.

WINDOW-BOX AND INDOOR GROWING The savories should be
planted in boxes or pots in August and these can be grown indoors
so that there is always some fresh savory available. Summer savory
grows well in pots if they are carefully transplanted and given a place
in the sun. The plants of winter savory should be trimmed back as
mentioned, and when the plants have recovered from this they
should be put in sandy soil, rich in humus, and gradually be adapted
to indoor growing.

How to Harvest and Dry

(a) *Summer Savory*. The young shoots can be collected as required
for use. The best time for cutting for drying is shortly before or just
after the beginning of flowering. Even when in flower the shoots can
be dried and rubbed and placed in air-tight glass jars. If summer
savory is well dried at the right moment it will keep its flavour for a
long time. The seeds should be harvested as soon as they start to
become brown as they easily fall out later.

Summer savory should be placed on frames, covered with a narrow
net and these be put in a dark cupboard with a low temperature—up
to 95° F.—and constant ventilation.

(b) *Winter Savory* may be cut from May onwards in the second year. If cut before flowering the content of volatile oil is at its highest peak and the stalks are not too woody. The whole herb is not harvested but individual shoots and tips are cut out of the plant.

As dried winter savory leaves become very hard, more so than summer savory, it is preferable to grow winter savory indoors during the winter and use it from there rather than dry it, unless some can be picked from the garden all through winter.

What the Savories Can Do for Our Food *Summer savory* is a delicious herb and provides a distinct and attractive flavour with a character all its own. Yet it is the one herb for which the advice 'start with a little and add with experience' is most apt. All herb mixtures intended to be used instead of salt or pepper or other hot spices should contain some summer savory, particularly when salt and pepper have to be replaced.

It has the digestive qualities which are noticeable when flavouring dishes difficult to digest. The traditional flavouring of beans with summer savory may have had its origin in the herb's help against flatulence. To the same category of food belong cucumber salad and lentils. Every kind of uncooked salad, in a raw food diet for instance, benefits by summer savory. A few leaves can be added to the water in which turnips, cabbage or brussels sprouts are cooked; this will reduce the strong odour of these vegetables in the kitchen.

Both savories give flavour to stuffings, pork pies and sausages and the fresh tops can be boiled with peas, broad beans and with beans of all kinds.

Winter savory is not as delicate as summer savory and should be used much less, mainly in conjunction with other herbs, for example in *bouquet-garni*; it can be used with most of the suggestions for summer savory but everywhere with the lightest possible touch, for people have been permanently discouraged by heavy-handed use of winter savory.

Culinary Uses

Hors-d'œuvre: In vegetable juices.
Salads: With tossed-green, tomato, cucumber and potato salads.
Eggs and cheese: In scrambled eggs, omelettes and devilled eggs; soft cheese dips.

Savories

Soups, stews and sauces: Cooked with bean, pea or lentil soups; fish chowders; in meat stews; in horseradish and barbecue sauces.

Meat and fish: Sprinkled over roast meats; with baked ham or smoked pork; in meat pies. Sprinkled over grilled or baked fish.

Poultry and game: In stuffings for chicken, duck or turkey; in fricassees and creamed chicken; with venison and rabbit.

Vegetables: In all bean dishes: broad beans, French and runner beans and—above all—for frozen and tinned beans. In water to cook peas, cabbage and tomatoes; in sauerkraut and mushroom dishes.

BEAN SOUP

Ingredients:

1 lb. approx. runner beans, sliced

¼ lb. potatoes

Stock (approx. 2 pints)

Flour for thickening (1 tablespoon)

1 tablespoon butter or oil (if wanted)

Fresh shoots or 2 teaspoons green-dried summer savory

Cup of sour cream, or 2–3 tablespoons if thick

Method:

1 Cook the beans and potatoes in the stock with the summer savory until tender.

2 Blend the mixture in a liquidizer (or if the beans are old and stringy pass through a sieve).

3 Thicken the soup with a little flour smoothed with cold stock, or sauté the flour in a little butter or oil and smooth with cold stock.

4 Add and allow to simmer for about 10 minutes.

5 Shortly before serving add sour cream and a little salt.

6 Add chopped or green-dried parsley and serve.

Note. To make it a main dish, small sausages, frankfurters, can be cooked in it.

SOLIDAGO
(*Solidago virgaurea*)
GOLDEN ROD

Virtues Golden rod has an old history of being an excellent wound herb—and a more modern history of being helpful in the case of kidney and bladder troubles. Its old Latin name was *Consolidae saraceniae*; this was originally translated into 'Heathen's Wound-Herb' in Germany and the Latin name seems to indicate that it originally came from the Middle East and was used by the Saracens during the crusades. In this country it had the same reputation and was applied externally or taken as a drink for internal wounds. In Tudor times it was considered an expensive herb as it had to be obtained from overseas; it is reported that at one time it was 2s. 6d. per oz. but then Gerard found that it even grows 'in Hamstead Wood . . . near a village called Kentish Towne' and it then became less precious.

Solidago contains volatile oil, tannins and saponine. It has a diuretic effect, is anti-inflammatory and speeds up the healing of wounds. It is reported to be helpful with every kind of trouble of kidney and bladder, and is even reputed to help with the dissolving of kidney and bladder stones; it is supposed to improve every kind of elimination through kidney and bladder.

Description Golden rod is a perennial which can be from 4–24 in. (10–60 cm.) high. The stem is usually glabrous below the flowers. The leaves are mostly lanceolate 1–4 in. (2½–10 cm.) long, sometimes slightly toothed, stalked and oblong at the base, narrow, more lanceolate and unstalked up the stem. The flower heads, in branched spikes, small, bright yellow, shortly rayed, are large 3–5 in. (8–12 cm.) across on ascending leafy branches. The leaf broadens towards the top and is smaller near the stem. The flowers have stalks of equal length and are arranged along a central stem, the lowest flower opening first. They are visited by various bees and insects and are self-pollinating.

Growing The plants grow and are widespread in dry woods, heath and hedge banks and on rocks. They can easily be cultivated, but the common golden rod, usually found in gardens, is *Solidago canadensis* and is different from *virgaurea*. The *Solidagos* are a genus with very many species of perennial herbs, most of which are hardy and grow well in any soil. They are rather coarse and apt to impoverish the soil. They are useful for planting in rough places and on the borders of shrub gardens. They are easily propagated by division in autumn or spring.

Harvesting The herb is harvested during its flowering period from July to October. The whole of the flowering herb is used without rootstock. They must be carefully dried to retain the colour of leaves and flowers. The dried herb is then broken up into relatively coarse pieces. The temperature in drying should not exceed 100° F.

Uses For Solidago Tea 1 teaspoon of the cut-up herb with flowers per cup should be boiled for 1 minute and steeped for 10 minutes before straining. It is used in cases of dropsy, inflammation of bladder and kidney, and is mildly diuretic. Two to three cups daily are suggested and the influence on the functions of the kidney and bladder should be noticed immediately. It would be interesting to experiment with the anti-inflammatory effect on hastening the healing of wounds which was its purpose in old times. In Switzerland it has also been used as a disinfectant and as an ointment.

SORREL (FRENCH SORREL)

(*Rumex acetosa*) (Buckler leaved—True French Sorrel)

Virtues Sorrel is known for the acidity of its herbage and French sorrel is particularly popular in France because of the excellent soup which can be made of the leaves. It can also be used as a slightly sour seasoning, but not too much should be used of it too regularly because part of the plants contain oxalic acid which can be damaging to health. The Greek and Roman doctors used sorrel leaves for medicinal purposes as it is supposed to be a diuretic plant, and has been particularly recommended for kidney stones. There was also a saying that it 'drives away the poison from the heart'. Sorrel is considered to have blood-cleansing and blood-improving qualities and is said to contain vitamin C.

Description The sorrels are perennial members of the *Polygoneae* family, of which there are quite a number of botanical varieties in cultivation. The broad-leaved French sorrel is the one most culti-vated and used. The leaves are oblong, slightly arrow shaped at the base and succulent. A slender, perennial plant about 2 ft. high (60 cm.) with juicy stems and leaves, and whorled spikes of reddish green flowers. It grows abundantly and can be easily cultivated. It flowers from May to July.

Growing The French broad-leaved kind is best propagated by divi-sion of the roots in spring or autumn. It should be planted out 15 in. (40 cm.) apart. It grows best in light rich soil and full sun. It can also be grown in the shade. A sheltered position is advisable if available. The flowering plant should be cut back to prevent it from going to seed and the leaves from becoming tough. At the end of March, sorrel can be sown like spinach in rows.

Harvesting Sorrel can be harvested three to four months after the plants have started to grow, particularly when the individual plant has formed four to five leaves. Sorrel leaves can be dried carefully in the same way as other herbs so that colour and flavour are preserved; they should be kept in the dark when drying and stored in air-tight jars in dark cupboards.

Uses French sorrel is excellent combined with other leaves or herbs as it is sometimes too bitter alone; for instance, a sorrel, lettuce, and herb salad, or sorrel and lettuce soups are excellent. Sorrel has to be used in moderation. The leaves are cooked in early spring as greens and featured in a cream soup. The delicious lemon-flavoured young leaves are best in salads or boiled like spinach or with spinach. Small quantities can be added to spinach but leaves can also be dried and used as a sour seasoning in small quantities.

SWEET CICELY

(*Myrrhis odorata*)

Virtues Sweet cicely is a tall beautiful plant and handsome enough to be in the herbaceous border. It is an important herb in the garden for it is the last one to die off in winter and the first to appear in spring as an ever-spreading perennial and it can be used as lavishly as it grows. The most English of herbs, it grows wild in the north of England and southern Scotland. It has a sweet aniseed flavour and this makes it popular with children particularly when they have to be tempted to eat such dishes as salads and fruit and vegetable juices. For an invalid, finely chopped sweet cicely leaves stimulate the appetite by tempting him to eat. Its use as a sugar-saver is described on p. 199.

Appearance of the Plant Sweet cicely is a perennial and remarkable for its sweet and highly aromatic foliage; it belongs to the *Umbelliferae* family. It grows from 2–3 ft. (60–90 cm.) high, but can take 8–10 years to reach 5 ft. (150 cm.) as an ultimate height. The stem is furrowed and hollow. The light green leaves are large, up to 1 ft. (30 cm.) long, thrice pinnate, cut and slightly downy. The flowers are white and grow in terminal downy umbels 2–4 in. (5–10 cm.) in diameter; the bracts are only partial, whitish and finely fringed. It flowers profusely in May and June. The fruit is large (about $\frac{1}{2}$ in. ($1\frac{1}{2}$ cm.) long); it is dark brown with sharp ribs and has the same concentrated flavour as the rest of the plant.

Growing Sweet cicely is a rampant-growing perennial, becoming bigger and better each year. Though slow in gaining height, particularly if the leaves are cut frequently, it spreads profusely once it is established. It may even be difficult to get rid of at certain times and in certain places, as the taproots can become very large, growing deeply, and it can appear where it is not wanted through self-sowing, in fact multiplying in several ways. It is therefore hardly ever necessary to divide and transplant, unless the plants have to go to another position.

It can be propagated by seed sown in March or April and grows best in medium-rich well-drained soil, and in partial shade. However it does succeed in any soil but if it has to be planted in full sun then it requires a fairly moist soil. The plants self-sow freely and can be transplanted readily even when several years old. The final spacing of plants should be about 18 in. (45 cm.).

Propagation by division of roots must be done with care for the plants are taprooted. When dividing, in spring or autumn, the long tapering parts should be cut off altogether before cutting the rest of the root into sections. Each section should have one 'eye' only and they should be planted 1 ft. (30 cm.) apart with the 'eye' about 2 ins. (5 cm.) below the soil.

WINTER PREPARATION Sweet cicely dies down late in autumn—November—but is already coming up again in February. There are only two months—December and January—when the herb gardener is without this herb. No special attention is needed as it is a very hardy plant. In February the rolled-up, fern-like leaves are pushing through the soil and soon a profusion of large leaves of an exquisite fresh, light-green colour appears, followed in May by equally profuse flowering.

How to Harvest and Dry The leaves can be picked as soon as they are fully developed and it does not matter in what quantity as there is always more than can be used. The flowers should be picked all the time—just before they open—if the leaves are wanted for flavouring.

The seeds however can be dried. These should be picked when ripe and spread out on a tray until thoroughly dry. Afterwards they should be pulverized as they are too hard to use whole.

Sweet cicely is a very difficult herb to dry because it droops as soon as it is brought indoors and has such large leaves.

What Sweet Cicely Can Do for Our Food Sweet cicely improves all *bouquets* or mixtures of herbs, it should be added to salad dressings, soups and especially root vegetables and cabbage. Nowadays it is usually the leaves which are used to give a delicate flavour to foods but the roots boiled and eaten with oil and lemon or in salads have an excellent taste.

Chopped sweet cicely can either be added to sugared strawberries or added as a green topping to the whipped cream. For trifles and other sweets the herb can be mixed in.

Sweet Cicely

Sweet cicely provides a pleasant way to reduce acidity in tart fruit and thus reduces the quantity of sugar needed in stewing them. This applies to rhubarb, unripe gooseberries, red or black currants, plums, etc. Several large fresh leaves and stalks or 2–4 teaspoons dried sweet cicely and some lemon balm added to the boiling water in which these fruits are stewed, adds a delightful flavour and helps to save sometimes almost half of the sugar needed. This saving is not only important for diabetics, but also for most other people, since sugar has fallen into disfavour for a number of reasons, and particularly for the figure watchers.

As this is one of the herbs used to flavour Chartreuse liqueur it can no doubt be used with success to flavour other drinks as well, both alcoholic and non-alcoholic.

CULINARY USES

Hors-d'œuvre: Fruit juice cocktails; raw vegetable juices; slimming cocktails.

Salads: In all salads and dressings; salad mixtures; all raw vegetables and green salads, especially for children.

Eggs and cheese: Omelettes and pancakes.

Soups, stews and sauces: Soups; stews; herb butter.

Meat and fish: Herb butter.

Vegetables: With root vegetables.

Sweets and beverages: Fruit salads; uncooked fruit and vegetable juices; summer and alcoholic drinks. Liqueurs—e.g. Chartreuse.

GOOSEBERRY TART WITH SWEET HERBS

Ingredients:

1 lb. unripe gooseberries

2–3 teaspoons sweet cicely (green-dried)

1 teaspoon lemon balm

2 oz. sugar

Pastry for lining tin

Cashew or breadcrumbs (milled)

Top:

2 oz. hazelnuts or almonds shredded in Mouli shredder (coarser)

1–2 oz. sugar

1 egg

3 tablespoons top of milk, Yoghourt, sour cream (mixed)

Tarragon

Method:

1 Line tin with pastry and allow for a good rim.
2 Sprinkle cashew nuts or crumbs over the pastry.
3 Boil gooseberries with herbs and sugar in water until tender but not mushy.
4 Take out gooseberries with perforated ladle (unless water is soaked up).
5 Fill pastry case with them.
6 Top: Mix all ingredients and spread over the gooseberries.
7 Bake for 1 hour in moderate oven.

TARRAGON

(*Artemisia dracunculus*)

Virtues Tarragon is probably the king of all culinary herbs and if culinary herbs were classified in guide-book fashion it would be a three-star item. It has a most distinguished career in *cuisine*, particularly in French cooking, but the exquisitely flavoured herb has not been used for medicinal purposes and there is little if any legend or folk-lore connected with it. The name tarragon comes from the French *estragon* meaning a little dragon and arose because it was believed to cure the bites and stings of venomous animals.

Known to connoisseurs the world over for its unusual and intriguing flavour, it figures in many of the traditional and sophisticated recipes of all countries. It has an aromatic flavour, sweet and slightly bitter at the same time, so for all its delicate fragrance there is a hidden tang; this will only be unpleasing though, if too much tarragon is used. Tarragon should therefore be used discriminately.

Appearance of the Plant Tarragon belongs to the *Artemisia* family but is a little darker than the other *Artemisias*; tarragon differs also in having an entire leaf, while southernwood and wormwood have a divided leaf. There are two varieties of tarragon—both perennials—which are often confused. French tarragon may attain up to 3 ft. (90 cm.) with slim stalks; Russian tarragon is the tougher one, growing up to a height of 5 ft. ($1\frac{1}{2}$ m.), hardier during winter, but has not as much flavour as French tarragon.

The French strain has very smooth, shinier and darker leaves though they are lighter underneath and have small visible oil glands. The slender dark green, graceful leaves are widely spread on the stems, which also carry clusters of greyish woolly flowers. In England the flowers never open properly, nor do the seeds mature; it must, therefore, be propagated by cuttings. Today, tarragon is widely cultivated in southern England and in the temperate zones of the United States, as well as throughout the colder New England.

Russian tarragon, with rougher leaves of a fresher green, has less flavour and is therefore inferior for first-class flavouring. It is supposed to become more aromatic if left to grow for a long time in one place, and this has certainly been borne out by experience, but it never reaches the excellence of French tarragon which, however, has a tendency to deteriorate with age. This may be due to reversion to the coarser Russian type, causing a loss of flavour and may happen after division or when growing in the same place for too long. It is therefore suggested that each year before cutting, the leaf should be rubbed to find out whether it really has the strong, yet subtle scent of French tarragon. What an odd situation; the excellent French tarragon may decline, while the poorer Russian tarragon may improve!

Growing Two plants of tarragon are sufficient for a family's herb garden. They should be planted 2 ft. apart after the last frost. Eventually they will develop a root structure occupying about 4 ft. Though it may appear a ridiculously large area for the young plants it should be allotted to them, as they like plenty of room, and will amply fill the space later on.

There is often a strong plea made for special drainage for tarragon, as a too-wet soil at the beginning of winter may be another reason for endangering the survival of tarragon plants during winter. If tarragon stands on slightly sloping, stony ground, well exposed to winds, no special drainage precautions need be taken. Where this is not so, little ditches leading away from the plant's root structure will help to avoid the danger of 'wet feet' for the plants. If these ditches can be channelled so that the excess water will flow towards the mint bed, it will be welcomed there.

Tarragon

French tarragon needs, above all, a dry and sunny position; the soil should be well-drained, light and fairly poor. If coddled, it makes too much succulent growth and the plant may then die during winter; therefore no manure, or very little should be used. French tarragon does very well in England: as it is perennial it will become better as a plant with each year of growth, but its flavour should be watched; and after four years it is advisable to transplant it to another piece of ground. March and September are possible times for planting or transplanting. Propagation can only be done by pulling apart the underground runners in March or April, and by cuttings in warm weather in spring or summer.

WINTER PROTECTION Though tarragon is fairly hardy it should be protected in very severe weather, unless it be in a sheltered position or in a southern county. However, when grown in exposed places it is advisable to have a mulching of leaf mould placed round the plants as the cold weather approaches. At the first frost pile leaves on the plants and—if necessary—the leaves can be covered with a very light open-weave basket, such as those in which berries are sold. The baskets should be weighed down so that winter winds do not blow them away. Great care should be taken in uncovering them in spring. The mulch should come off gradually and not entirely until the weather has settled down to a steady temperature. Also either straw or stable manure containing a lot of straw can be used for winter protection of the roots after the leaves have died down. They start appearing again in April.

WINDOW-BOX AND INDOOR GROWING Tarragon is not a plant which is very suitable for restricted places and therefore not one of the best herbs for growing in a window-box or as an indoor plant, but—for those whose garden *has* to be a window-box and who would not like to miss the few sprigs of fresh tarragon, and want these during winter in addition to the green-dried tarragon—both are worth trying. The success will depend on the situation of the window-box discussed on p. 37 and p. 40 and what indoor conditions can be provided. Tarragon does not want rich soil, and the extra feeding of the soil which is usually suggested for window-boxes and indoor growing should be avoided. As such indoor plants exhaust the soil quicker and more completely, it is advisable to provide richer soil than in the garden. A good mixture of soil, therefore, as suggested for indoor growing p. 39, is recommended. Drainage, however, is most important indoors, as well as in the window-box and therefore all the suggestions *re* drainage given in the chapter on window-box and indoor growing, p. 39, should be followed.

Tarragon may be grown in a window-box by starting a new plant from a division of the parent plant root in March, or a new small plant should be bought. All the foliage growth of the plant should be cut back to 2 in. (5 cm.) above soil level. If tarragon is kept as a compact bushy plant it will provide more volatile oils and aroma than a leggy plant which is more vulnerable.

If, in September, two of the tarragon plants are transplanted into small pots, they should later be transferred to larger containers when the roots can be seen growing through the drainage hole. More than with any other plant, 'wet feet' will be the death of indoor tarragon; the soil in the pot should be barely moist, and if the pots are set in containers of pebbles the tarragon need not be watered more than once a week.

In order to bring the plants indoors by stages, first tarragon should be transplanted from the garden into a small pot; be kept outdoors during daylight and brought in at night. The foliage growth should be cut back to the 2 in. (5 cm.) above soil level, otherwise tarragon will shed its leaves completely before sending out new shoots, and so delay its recovery.

Another way to provide fresh tarragon leaves during winter: a few plants can be lifted and be replanted in a frame or greenhouse.

For many all this may be too much work, and they may feel it is not worth the trouble as the flavour can be achieved from the green-dried tarragon which, for the purpose of flavouring, provides almost the full aroma. For the vinegar enthusiasts, to whom a warning finger is raised on p. 23, the occasional sprig in their tarragon or herb vinegar may seem worth the trouble.

How to Harvest and Dry Fresh leaves of tarragon can be used all the time during the growing period, in fact, from the end of June to

Tarragon

September, but they have the highest concentration of flavour at the beginning of their flowering period.

For drying, plants can be cut just above the ground at the beginning of flowering, at the end of June or beginning of July. Tarragon can be cut several times during the season, and if it is safely established even three cuts can be achieved. It is difficult to cut tarragon without bruising; the leaves have to be handled very carefully and gently, as each bruising means loss of valuable volatile oils and aroma. Bruising also causes discolouring and the tarragon can become brown even before being dried. If tarragon is to be dried it has to be done at a very low temperature under 100° F. in the dark, for the aroma is easily lost.

What Tarragon Can Do for Our Food Tarragon can be used freely chopped in salad dressings, sprinkled over salads and main dishes such as steaks and fish, and on all vegetables. It figures prominently in all French cookery and is first-class with all sauces.

Melted butter with chopped tarragon leaves and sauces using tarragon are most excellent accompaniments to delicate vegetables such as mushroom, asparagus, and courgettes, as well as to steaks, fried fish, etc. Tarragon has a subtle flavouring effect on marinades, stuffings for fish and poultry, lobster and other shell-fish.

CULINARY USES

Hors-d'œuvre: Tomato juice cocktail; fish cocktail. Tarragon butter for canapés and biscuits; shell-fish, lobster. Sandwich fillings; aspics; crab; shrimps. Advocado pear filling.

Salads: Green salad; all other salads. Pickled cucumbers. Chicken salad—pinch in sour cream dressing; in tarragon vinegar. Specially good with asparagus and bean salads.

Eggs and cheese: In all egg dishes if used lightly; omelettes; scrambled eggs.

Soups, stews and sauces: Clear broth; chicken, mushroom, tomato, turtle soups, fish soups and chowders. Sauces: béarnaise, hollandaise, mousseline, mayonnaise; herb sauce, tarragon sauce; in melted butter; herb butter.

Thyme

Meat and fish: Steaks, sirloin, veal, sweetbread; Yorkshire pudding; chopped liver. All fish and shell-fish baked or grilled in wine marinades.

Poultry and game: Chicken, duck, hare, rabbit; in stuffings; chicken livers with cream.

Vegetables: Spinach, courgettes (baby marrow or squash). In melted butter for artichokes, mushrooms, asparagus. In *fines herbes*; sauerkraut, salsify, celeriac.

TARRAGON CHICKEN IN CASSEROLE

Ingredients:

1 quarter of chicken per person

1 tin of concentrated Cream of Chicken Soup and ½ this tin filled with stock

½ lemon with peel (whole)

Oil or butter to brush

Tarragon (freshly chopped or green-dried)

Bouquet for poultry and game

½ glass sherry

Method:

1 Brush quarters with oil or butter.
2 Rub with tarragon.
3 Empty soup and ½ tin of stock into casserole.
4 Add lemon and 1 tablespoon tarragon and/or poultry mixture.
5 Add prepared quarters.
6 Cover with well-fitting lid.
7 Leave for 1½ hours in the oven (375°–400°).
8 Allow to brown for ½ hour either without lid in the oven or under the grill.
9 Serve in casserole, add ½ glass sherry before serving.

THYME

(*Thymus vulgaris*)

LEMON THYME (*Thymus citriodorus*)

Virtues The thymes, superior in strength and flavour to many other herbs, have been used since time immemorial for medicinal purposes and culinary seasoning. Thyme is a native of the Mediterranean and was extensively used by the ancient Greeks. It came to England with the Romans where it soon became an important herb; in the Middle Ages it was an emblem of courage, probably from its uses as a source of strength, and thyme soup was, in 1663, considered a cure for shyness!

A strongly aromatic herb, it helps to digest all food and stimulates the appetite. Thyme contains tannins and resins and the volatile oil of thymol which has a strong antiseptic effect, both internally and externally. It is effective against mucous in the bronchial organs and the stomach, and a tisane sweetened with honey is very good for catarrh and for coughs. Thymol has been used to medicate gauze for surgical dressings and has a great germicidal action. Oil of thyme, distilled from thyme, can be used for liniments, also as an addition to baths, and is used in toothpaste and mouth-washes.

Lemon thyme is mainly used for flavouring and perfumery, but like the other thymes is a good bee plant and gives honey a most delicious flavour; but bees will only collect the nectar on warm days.

Appearance of the Plant There are a number of ornamental thymes with pleasant scents but the two main culinary thymes are common garden thyme and lemon thyme.

Garden thyme is a perennial belonging to the *Labiatae* family. A low evergreen bush, it grows about 4–12 in. (10–30 cm.), with pale mauve flowers in heads or whorls in the axils of the leaves; they flower throughout June. The leaves are small, only $\frac{2}{5}$ in. (1 cm.) long and narrow, though there is a broad-leaved cultivated thyme, but the flavour is not so strong.

Lemon thyme is also a perennial and is similar in growth to the common garden thyme, reaching a maximum height of about 12 in. (30 cm.) in favourable conditions. It can be distinguished from the common thyme by its distinct lemon scent and by its leaves which are much broader in comparison.

There is also a golden lemon thyme which has golden-green leaves, is of creeping growth and reaches a maximum height of about 6 in. (15 cm.). It is a good ground cover; the leaves have a lovely aromatic lemony scent; they flower in July.

There is also a wild thyme which can be found in dry heathy places.

Thymes

Growing Thyme likes a dry, well-drained, sunny position and thrives best on chalky but fertile soil. It is a most suitable plant for rock gardens where it can climb over rocks and down slopes. The garden thymes seed themselves and these can be planted out 2 in. (5 cm.) apart. If plants are raised from seed they should be sown ¼ in. deep in drills 2 ft. (60 cm.) apart.

Thymes can be propagated either by division of the old plant or by cuttings taken in April or May. Side shoots can also be layered in March or April. The rooted cuttings or layers can then be transplanted 12–18 in. (30–45 cm.) apart in rows 2 ft. (60 cm.) apart. A thyme bed should be replaced every 3 or 4 years as the plants become straggly and woody. Lemon thyme can be increased by cuttings. The thyme beds should be kept well watered and free from weeds.

WINTER PREPARATION In the autumn the soil around the plants should have a light dressing of compost and in a very exposed position should be protected by a light covering of straw during severe weather conditions. Before the winter they should be cut back, though not too much. In some parts of the country the plants need further protection and should be covered with earth.

Lemon thyme is not so hardy as the common thyme, and winter protection with straw or leaf mould is recommended in exposed positions.

WINDOW-BOX AND INDOOR GROWING For indoor growing the plants should be trimmed back to about one-third of their original size. After the plants have recovered from their trimming they can be placed in pots containing a mixture of compost and sand and gradually adapted to indoors where they can be used throughout the winter.

If thyme is grown in a window-box it is advisable to plant it in a pot within the window-box so that it will not spread too rapidly. The soil in the window-box should be fairly rich and the plants kept well watered in the summer, for they need greater humidity in a window-box or when indoors.

How to Harvest and Dry When harvesting and drying thyme the flowers can be put in with the leaves so that the time to cut is during the flowering period, usually July, or just before flowering in June. They must be harvested before the flowering is over. In the first year only one cutting should be made but from the second year onwards two cuttings can be made. The first in June and the second not later than the end of August, as the plant—being an evergreen—should have sufficient growing time left after the second cut to re-establish itself to withstand the winter weather. Plants harvested in September or October will not normally survive the winter. Thyme does not thrive when the stems are cut from the base of the plant; if a third of the stem is cut here and there the growth will not be disturbed. Shoots about 6 in. (15 cm.) long should be cut and spread out on a tray and dried in the dark at a temperature of not more than 100° so that they retain the colour and aroma. When dry thyme can be rubbed through a coarse sieve and stored in air-tight glass jars in the dark.

What Thyme Can Do for Our Food Thyme has a warm, clove-like flavour which is pungent and can overpower more delicate herbs if used too liberally. As it aids the digestion of fats it will always be used with mutton or pork, with eels and all shell-fish. It is one of the many herbs in Benedictine liqueur.

Thyme tea, excellent for coughs and colds is made by pouring two cups of boiling water over 2–3 teaspoons of dry thyme. It should be allowed to draw 5–10 minutes and then drunk in small quantities during the day.

Cottage and cream cheeses will have a delicious flavour if ½ teaspoon of thyme is added to ¼ lb. of cheese and allowed to permeate. Thyme soup, a dish from France, is made with hot light beer, a great deal of thyme and small quantities of other herbs—this is the soup to cure shyness!

Lastly, thyme is an important part of the *bouquet garni* which is added in so many versions to so many dishes.

CULINARY USES

Hors-d'œuvre: Tomato juice; fish and sea food cocktails; sauerkraut juice; mixed raw vegetable juice. Crab; mussels; tomato aspic.

Valerian

Salads: All raw vegetable (in moderation).

Eggs and cheese: Scrambled and baked eggs (cautiously). Pancakes; cheese sauce for eggs. Cream cheese spread; with strong cheeses.

Soups, stews and sauces: In thick soups and stews; tomato soup, minestrone, split pea soup, bean soup, tomato sauce, herb sauce.

Meat and fish: Rub beef, lamb, mutton, fat pork, veal lightly before boiling, braising or roasting; gravies; sausages; lean and fat baked and grilled fish, eel.

Poultry and game: Chicken; turkey. Stuffings for chicken, goose, turkey, veal, venison; rabbit stew; jugged hare; vol-au-vent; pies, ragouts.

Vegetables: Mushrooms and fungi; beans, beet, carrots, aubergines; sauté with vegetables or blend herb with melted butter and pour over vegetables. Potatoes.

Sweets and beverages: Lemon thyme in custards. In Benedictine liqueur.

LIVER IN ORANGE SAUCE

Ingredients:

1 lb. sliced liver	2 teaspoons thyme
2 oz. flour	Seasoning
¼ pint orange juice	Oil for sautéing

Method:

1 Mix flour with thyme and seasoning.
2 Coat the liver pieces with the mixture.
3 Sauté the liver quickly in oil.
4 Add orange juice to saucepan.
5 Cover and simmer 3–5 minutes.
6 Serve with orange juice spooned over liver.

VALERIAN

(*Valeriana officinalis*)

Virtues Valerian is an old, highly valued, Nordic medicinal plant. At the time of Hippocrates in the fifth and fourth centuries B.C. valerian was used extensively in medical practice, and only more recently was it used for medicinal purposes again. The word occurs in Anglo-

Valerian

Saxon recipes of the eleventh century. The mediaeval name of valerian comes from *valere*, to be healthy, because of its powerful medicinal qualities. The plant contains a strong volatile oil and its derivatives have been used as a sedative. Valerian tea, made of the dried roots, is one of the strongest sedative drinks made from a plant. It is not only soporific but also has a calming effect on the whole of the nervous system.

It contains, apart from the volatile oil, a glycoside and valerian acid. It is an excellent tranquillizer, particularly valuable against insomnia, but as the nervous system may get used to it it should not be used uninterruptedly for a lengthy period. In all nervous troubles which arise suddenly an infusion of valerian root can be used with success. Strangely enough valerian was used as a spice and even as a perfume in the sixteenth century and was laid amongst clothes.

The strong-smelling plant has at all times and in most countries played a large part in keeping away evil spirits. The roots of the plant have a strong and strange fascination over cats, causing an ecstasy when the animals are brought into contact with them. They love to roll in it. The same effect is noticed in rats, which dig up the roots; and the Pied Piper of Hamelin has always been considered to have carried valerian roots on his body. The same attraction can be noticed in the case of earthworms.

Description The plants of *Valeriana officinalis* reach a height of 3–5 ft. (100–150 cm.) and are a variable, usually unbranched, perennial, high, hairy in parts, with pinnate leaves, the lower stalked, the leaflets toothed. The numerous flowers, small, very pale pink, darker in bud, stand in close terminal umbel-like clusters, the calyx forms a pappus in fruit. It flowers from June to August. The root is an upright rhizome, short and thick. The roots grow out like a head of hair and runners grow to about 5 in. (12 cm.) in length; they can be pulled away.

Growing Valerian can be found wild in ditches and damp places but also in dry and stony mountainous regions. Though many of the different species are used in gardens for decorative purposes and the dwarf species are good rock plants, *only* the *officinalis* has medicinal qualities. Almost every kind of soil is useful for valerian provided that it is not too heavy for the plant to form a good root. Medium to damp positions are preferable even exposed positions are still suitable. Propagation can be done by seed or by division of root. The germination power of the seed is, in most cases, only up to about 50 per cent. As the seeds are slow in germination it is advisable to sow a marker crop with them.

The seeds need only be pressed down carefully, but not covered with soil because they germinate in the light. The distance of planting should be 1 × 1 ft. (30 × 30 cm.). The spacing can also be 2 ft. (60 cm.) in order to allow sufficient space for the plant to develop. If they are planted at a distance of 12 in. (30 cm.) the rows should be 2–3 ft. apart (60–100 cm.). It is better for the development of the rhizomes if the flower tops are cut out during growing, but many young plants do not flower the first year.

Harvesting In the late autumn of the second year the roots should be dug up. The fine fibrous rootlets should be combed out and not used. If the roots come from a heavy soil they must be well washed and brushed under running water, or a hose could be used as it is very difficult to get all the soil out. The roots can be split into quarters, otherwise they take very long to dry and afterwards they must be broken up into small particles. They should be really dry all through in order not to absorb moisture again from the air. As with all herbs, they have to be kept in the dark during drying and stored in airtight sealed containers.

Uses The root of the valerian is the part used for making tea. The tea is best made in the cold way without boiling it. One level teaspoon of the broken-up roots should be soaked in one cup of cold water, covered and kept in a cool place for 12–24 hours. It should be strained and drunk approximately 1 hour before retiring. If it is too strong, half of it can be used and water added to the remainder; this can be used next day. This tea taken an hour before going to sleep, particularly over a number of days, is often better than any sleeping pill or tranquillizer, but it has to be used over some time as the effect may not be noticeable after the first cup. Though its flavour is not

Verbascum

'everyone's cup of tea' it will have a general soothing effect on the nervous system and induce good sleep, especially in the case of strain and overtiredness.

VERBASCUM

(*Verbascum thapsiforme*)
COMMON MULLEIN, and (*Verbascum thapsus*)

Virtues *Verbascum* or mullein is not only a medicinal plant of great value but one of our most beautiful decorative plants in the garden. There are many different varieties but the one which is mentioned here is the large mullein, *Verbascum thapsiforme*, also called 'Flannel Plant'. The bright yellow flowers, either freshly picked or carefully dried so that they retain their beautiful colour unimpaired, are extremely helpful in the case of difficulties caused by surplus mucus in any part of the body; they are used as an expectorant and will help to get rid of mucus in the bronchial tract; they will also help to counteract inflammation of mouth, throat or bronchial parts. Only the freshest or brightest yellow flowers will be useful because the healing is connected with the colouring matter, and if the slightest discoloration takes place during wilting or drying the flowers are either less effective or become completely useless.

The plant contains saponine, mucilage and traces of volatile oil; saponine and volatile oil have the expectorant effect, the mucilage is soothing for a cough. The flowers also contain some sugar and bitter principles. The mucilage, in conjunction with the saponine, is responsible for the anti-inflammatory effects.

Verbascum in its tall beauty has been given many names. Its name 'Aaron's Rod' came from the Bible because it 'was budded and brought forth buds and bloomed blossom' (Numbers xvii. 8). The name was also connected with fairies and the devil. It has at one time been used as a candle because the stalks were dipped in suet or pitch to burn at funerals and other solemn occasions, hence the name 'King's Candle' (Königskerze).

In German-speaking Catholic countries it was often used as the centre-piece of a 'Blessed Herb Posy' which has been and still is taken by children on the day of St. Mary's Ascension to the church to be blessed; it was then taken home and hung in the attic for drying. Throughout the year this herb posy was used for all the family's and animals' medicinal needs. Apart from being so useful for human coughs verbascum had also been used for consumption in cattle.

Description The tall erect biennial plant of the *Scrophulariaceae* family becomes 4 ft. (120 cm.) high, but may grow up to 8 ft. tall; the leaves are in a rosette and alternate up the unbranched stem. They are covered with thick white wool and are flannelly, broad, lanceolate; their base runs down as wings on the round stem. The flowers are rather large, and yellow. They stand in dense spikes, the corolla is flat with a short tube and five petal-like lobes, the calyx is five-lobed and has five stamens. They are hardly stalked, nearly 1 in. across. The fruits are egg-shaped, hardly exceeding the calyx.

Growing Verbascum is a plant making few demands on the soil, it will even grow on sandy or marshy soil, but the plants thrive on a well-drained chalky soil. It is best to choose a sunny position, sheltered from wind, as the plants become so tall. They can be started in a frame or nursery bed for which a specially fine tilth has to be prepared. They must be planted out on to the site from *August to September* and will then produce flowers in the following year. Verbascum can only produce small flowers and will not provide much harvest if the plants are planted out in spring. The distance from plant to plant should be 20–24 in. (50–60 cm.). The plants will seed themselves out if the ground is undisturbed, but they should always be given the right distance.

Harvesting The plant flowers from June to August and during this time the flowers should be picked almost daily on dry days, because they open one after the other and then may easily fall out. As the fallen flowers cannot be used any more, they should be picked when they are fully open, yet still on the plant. The easiest way is to take a fully opened flower between thumb and index finger, because this prevents the flower closing again. They should be picked and used immediately when required for verbascum tea, or early on a dry morning as soon as the dew has dried off in order to be dry when going into the drying cupboard; picking should possibly be finished by 11 o'clock as the flowers then start to wilt. While there is a strong wind, picking is difficult because it can start irritation of hands and arms; if the fine hairs get into the eyes these can become inflamed, and in this case it would be advisable to wear goggles. The flowers should not be crushed during picking, heaped up or pressed down (like chamomile flowers) and put carefully in one layer on frames covered with nylon net. The drying should be done immediately after picking and the temperature should not exceed 95–100° F. (35–40° C.). They should come out of the drying looking as colourfully yellow as when freshly picked, and be kept in air-tight containers in a very dry place away from the light.

Uses When making the tea 1 teaspoon should be used per cup, allowed to stand for at least 5 minutes and then be well strained; two cups per day can be drunk over long periods if a cough should persist. Sometimes it is advisable to put a piece of muslin into the strainer because the pollen of the flowers may stimulate further coughing with those who are already troubled with it. Verbascum tea is also useful when hoarse, when losing the voice, particularly for those who have to speak or sing, or when having difficulties in breathing. It can be used for children and old people to help with their respiratory troubles. It is also helpful in the case of an intestinal catarrh.

VERBENAS, THE

Vervain (*Verbena officinalis*)

Lemon Verbena (*Lippia citriodora*)

A great deal of confusion has been caused by the two verbenas and as they are completely different plants they should be described separately. What is normally called 'verbena' is the vervain which has been known in this country from olden days because it was a famous plant of the Druids, and which is now known as a slightly bitter

tisane for medicinal purposes, and is also used a great deal in France
as a digestive.

Lemon Verbena, however, is a scented, not native, plant which is
used for flavouring, also drunk as a scented tea in Spain.

VERVAIN (*Verbena officinalis*)

Virtues Vervain, which the Druids considered to be as sacred as
mistletoe, tastes slightly better, but has a soothing effect and is also a
good digestive. Vervain is the only wild verbena in England and its
great reputation is connected with legends as well as with witchcraft.
It was also called *herba veneris* and this suggests that it was once used
as an aphrodisiac. It has been said to cure jaundice and dysentery as
well as diseases of the eye and the throat. It is very difficult to know
how much of the medicinal reputation was caused by legends and
superstition, but it is still considered to be a good nerve tonic with
febrifuge properties and is used as a tea in insomnia and nervous exhaustion. It contains tannins, saponine, mucilage and a glycoside
verbenalin as well as an unknown bitter principle. It is also considered to be diuretic and stimulates perspiration, and as an anti-
spasmodic has been known to be helpful in persistent headaches.

Description Vervain, or verbena, is a rough, hairy, scentless perennial with stiff square stems, 1–2 ft. (30–60 cm.) high. It has pinnate,
lobed, toothed opposite leaves, the upper lanceolate, unstalked; and
long slender spikes of small lilac, more or less two-lipped, flowers—
an attractive plant.

Growing Vervain is readily raised from seed sown in early spring or
from cuttings and shoots which have no flowers. As a hardy perennial
the species may also be raised by division of rootstock. Verbena requires a well-drained, rich soil and a sunny position and may be
planted in the open border during summer from the middle or end of
May.

Harvesting Vervain, or verbena, is harvested with side branches and
leaves. It should be collected in June before the flowers are really
open, but also the flowering herb can be used. It should be dried very
carefully because the glycoside verbenalin may disappear.

Uses The tea made of vervain, or verbena, is sedative, mucolytic and stimulating production of bile. Its qualities are discussed in virtues, but for nervous exhaustion and as a sedative tea, as well as a digestive, this tea is very popular in France. It is slightly bitter and soothing. The tea is made of 1 teaspoon verbena per cup; whole or freshly crushed verbena leaves should be placed into a warm, but dry, cup or teapot. The tea must be allowed to steep for 3–5 minutes only, strained and taken sweetened with honey or without. There has been an old, but persistent, reputation that verbena clears the eyes and the sight.

LEMON VERBENA (*Lippia citriodora*)

Virtues Lemon verbena originally came from Chile and was introduced into this country in 1784. In some books the old botanical synonym *Aloysia citriodora* is still used. The leaves smell and taste of lemon and its fragrant tea has a more interesting flavour than verbena tea. It will also flavour fruit drinks, jams and jellies and can be added to potpourri because all parts of the herb, including the flowers, have the same delicate scent. Lemon verbena tea is also reputed to have a peculiar sedative effect on the mucuous membrane of the bronchial and nasal regions.

Description Lemon verbena is a member of the *Verbenaceae* family. The leaves are mostly in three's, lanceolate, 3–4 in. (8–10 cm.) long, and are a yellowish green colour, the upper side of the leaves is shiny, the lower rough and dull. The flowers are pale lavender or pale purple, small, in slender terminal downy panicles, 3–5 in. (8–12 cm.) long.

Growing Lemon verbena should have a poor soil with some humus, but no manure, as it should not make too much soft growth; it should also be kept as dry as possible. Like most tender plants it seems to be hardy in mild climates if given a sheltered position.

WINTER PREPARATION The roots of lemon verbena should be covered with wood-ash or leaf mould during winter, and it should have the kind of protection suggested for the more tender herbs.

INDOOR GROWING Lemon verbena has long been enjoyed as a house plant. It is best to start it as a house plant from green or soft wood cuttings. It may be successfully brought indoors in ample time for the plant to get accustomed to indoor environment. The plant should be cut back after it is potted to about two-thirds of its original size.

Harvesting Lemon verbena flowers in August, all parts of the herb should be dried.

Uses The delicious lemon-scented young leaves should be used in fruit drinks and salads, cooked with jellies, and they are most refreshing in summer. They can be cooked with lemon rind in sauces for fish or veal. Some lemon verbena leaves in the bottom of a finger-bowl add a delicate fragrance to it in the same way as rose geranium. In fact, most of the suggestions for rose geranium for using leaves at the bottom of a home-made ice-cream, trifle or jelly would apply in the same way to lemon verbena. Lemon verbena tea makes use of the whole fresh or green-dried leaves; it should be infused in boiling water and allowed to draw for a few minutes like ordinary tea. It is also blended with mint, served hot or iced; it is popular in Spain.

WOODRUFF

(Galium odoratum or *Asperula odorata)*

Virtues Woodruff is one of the sweetest-smelling herbs, but the scent, which is connected with one of the constituents of woodruff—cumarin—will only become noticeable after the herb is slightly dry. This famous woodruff scent, which provides an excellent flavouring for a wine cup, can only be used when the plant has slightly wilted or been half-dried. The scent is reminiscent of freshly mown hay and was used in potpourri and linen cupboards. In the fifteenth century it was cultivated in English gardens and its lovely scent of new-mown hay was utilized by making garlands and bundles hung up in houses and churches; 'Bunches hung up in the house in the summer doth . . . make fresh the place to the delight and comfort of ɔuch as are there in' (Gerard). It was used as a strewing herb; was stuffed into beds amongst the linen and into chests and cupboards to impart its perfume and to keep the moths away.

Growing wild along the banks of the Rhine sprigs of woodruff—called in German 'Master of the Woods'—have always been gathered and steeped in dry white wines to impart their flavour to the wine. The French use the herb with champagne, the Swiss serve Benedictine and cognac impregnated with woodruff. The Americans in their 'May Wine Punch' use a variety of wines as well as Benedictine and brandy and enjoy—as the height of luxury—to have sweet woodruff growing in their herb garden for use with many drinks, from hock to vodka. It is also delicious if used with fruit drinks and a clear apple juice flavoured with woodruff is one of the best fruit drinks. No wonder that it became famous as the herb for the spring drink, the 'Maitrank', the May cup or 'Mai Bowle'.

Like borage, only more stimulating, woodruff has the reputation of relaxing tension while uplifting the spirits; taken as a tea it relieves headache and migraine and is supposed to dispel accompanying melancholy.

In the Highlands of Scotland, where it grows up to 2,100 ft., and in France, woodruff tea has been appreciated for increasing perspiration to ward off colds. It is diuretic, tonic, and it helps the functions of gall-bladder and liver, and the spring function of cleansing the blood; the length and depth of sleep will also be improved.

Description Woodruff is a wild plant of the *Rubiaceae* family. It can become as high as 6–12 in. (15–30 cm.). It is a wild-growing native plant and found in shady beech copses or woods. It is an almost hairless, erect, carpeting perennial with slightly shiny leaves, edged with minute forward-pointing prickles, standing in whorls of 6–8 up the unbranched stem. Woodruff is easily recognizable by its white star-shaped flowers rising out of the dark-green whorls of its rather rigid leaves. The whorls of leaves stand like a rosette round the stem and have given the plant its 'ruff' name.

Growing It is essential for woodruff to grow in a habitat similar to the wild one. It is advisable to use a position under trees, in a copse

Woodruff

or spinney to give it its natural habitat, but it is very difficult to get any woodruff growing from seed and therefore it is advisable to buy plants. Heavy dry soils which are likely to form a crust are unsuitable, but a mixture can perhaps be provided in which leaf mould is mixed with wood-ash and sand; possibly a soil on which heath has grown can be provided.

The germination of seed takes sometimes a year. Woodruff can be propagated by pulling off rooted pieces of its creeping rootstock in spring, and these can be set 4 in. (10 cm.) apart. Good deep soakings will set the plant up; they will then self-sow, spread and become a hardy ground cover if grass is not allowed to encroach. Propagation can be done through the division of the roots of the older plants. The distance from plant to plant should be at least 8 in. (20 cm.).

WINTER PREPARATION In autumn the plants can be covered with leaf mould or moss if they live in a bleak climate.

INDOOR GROWING Woodruff can also be grown in pots.

Harvesting The plants flower from April to June; they have their highest content of cumarin in spring, but as they only develop their full scent when the plant is picked and starts to dry it is advisable to pick them in spring, either shortly before flowering or during flowering and dry them. They must be dried at a very low temperature so that they retain their green colour and do not become darker. Packed loosely but whole (leaves on their stalks) in hard air-tight containers such as jars or cardboard containers, they should look almost exactly as when fresh. They should have retained their scent and can be used throughout the year for flavouring of wine or for making tea, or as addition (a few leaves) to ordinary tea.

Uses The main use for woodruff is to impart an outstanding flavour to drinks, and therefore it should be used in May for the May cup or throughout the year for a woodruff cup. Any kind of drink, however, will be improved in flavour, scent and immediate effect by woodruff, dried or half-dried and steeped into a clear drink, such as hock or apple juice.

Woodruff

Woodruff tea is made either by infusing and steeping the leaves, which have all the qualities explained in 'virtues', or by adding a sprig of the dried herb to China tea. If green-dried leaves are used it simplifies the making of tea, and this is delicious either hot or iced and will prove very helpful. A small addition of woodruff, for instance to an early cup of tea, can make a difference to the mood of a person for the whole day, because woodruff is not only stimulating and invigorating, but has proved to drive a melancholic mood away and make people happy.

Woodruff cups or drinks, or cider cups to which woodruff has been added, will add a sparkle to the dullest party, without using more alcohol. Woodruff cups benefit much from the combination of woodruff leaves with peaches or strawberries, and are therefore the ideal summer drinks.

WOODRUFF CUP

Ingredients:

1 bottle of white wine	Sugar
Lemon juice and grated rind	Sparkling water
Strawberries and peaches	or, According to
Bunch of fresh woodruff (dried for two days in well-covered china bowl) or green-dried whole woodruff leaves	better still, taste champagne

Method:

1 Add ⅓ bottle wine to the woodruff leaves.
2 Allow to steep for 1 hour.
3 Then filter and add more wine.
  Flavour with lemon juice and rind.
5 Add strawberries or peaches.
6 Add sugar and sparkling water or champagne, according to taste.

GROWING CHART

Giving information on:

YEARLY CYCLE
HEIGHT OF PLANTS
SOIL
POSITION
PROPAGATION
DISTANCE
FLOWERING PERIOD
SEASON FOR USE
HARVESTING TIME FOR DRYING
PARTS TO USE

Herb	Perennial Biennial Annual	Height	Soil	Position	Prop Sowing
ANGELICA	Biennial	8 ft.	Rich but not too heavy; medium damp	Shady spot	In drills 1 in. deep when seeds ripe—Aug.
BASIL	Annual	2 ft.	Well-drained; moist; heavy —lightened by sand	Sunny, sheltered	Seed, thinly in May after frosts
BASIL, Bush	Annual	6 in.	Grown in pots	Sunny, sheltered	March, indoors
BAY LEAVES	Evergreen perennial tree	Up to 30 ft.	Moderate quality	Full sunshine; sheltered	—
BERGAMOT	Perennial	18 to 35 in.	Rich, moist	Sunny	—
BORAGE	Annual	1½ to 3 ft.	Loamy or sandy; chalky; moist; well-drained	Sunny	Shallow drills in March, April, July
CELERY	Biennial	2 ft.	Light; moist; rich; well-composted	Sheltered	Mid-March to mid-April in boxes under glass
CELERIAC	Biennial	2 ft.	Deeply dug; well-composted	Damp and shady	March
CHAMOMILE	Annual	18 in.	Moist during germination	Sunny	Early spring and autumn. Seeds mixed with sand or woodash
CHAMOMILE, Roman	Perennial	9 in.	Dry	Sunny	—
CHERVIL	Hardy biennial	12 to 20 in.	Well-drained, light, sandy	Half shade in summer; full sun winter	Best late summer for crop in spring. Any time

...ation	Distance for		Flowering	Season for use	Harvesting for drying	Parts to use
Planting	Rows	Plants				
Transplant seedlings autumn	3 ft.	3 ft.	Normally second year	April to May	Leaves before flowering. All summer; Roots dig in autumn first year	Flowering stalks; leaf stalks and roots
Avoid transplanting	1 ft.	8 in.	Late summer	July to September	Before flowering, late summer	Leaves for flavouring
—	—	—	—	—	—	—
Cuttings in autumn	—	—	—	All year round	All year round	Leaves
Division late summer and spring	2 ft.	2 ft.	July to September	Summer	Before flowering	Leaves and flowers apart
—	1 to 2 ft.	1 ft.	July until heavy frosts	All summer	Only young leaves at any time	Young leaves and flowers apart
Seedlings planted out when large enough to handle	2 ft.	1 ft.	—	Late summer	Before lifting	Leaves only
May to June	2 ft.	1 ft.	—	Late summer	Before lifting	Leaves only
—	2 ft.	1 ft.	May to October. Eight weeks after sowing	Summer; mainly dried	Flowers all summer	Flowers and small stalks
Division and cuttings April	—	4 in.	May to October	All summer; mainly dried	Flowers all summer	Flowers only
—	1 ft.	9 in.	May to June second year	Before flowering	Before flowering	Leaves only

Herb	Perennial Biennial Annual	Height	Soil	Position	Pro
					Sowing
CHIVES	Perennial	6–16 in.	Light, medium, rich, damp, sandy, loamy or chalky	Warm and half shade	Spring
DANDELION	Perennial	2–12 in.	Any garden soil	Anywhere up to full shade	Spring
DILL	Annual	3 ft.	Not too light; no stagnant humidity; well-drained; fine tilth	Sunny	April to June
ELDER	Perennial	9–30 ft.	Fertile, damp	Sunny	—
FENNEL	Hardy perennial	20–50 in.	Deeply dug, rich and chalky, not too humid	Warm	Drills— April to Ma
FENNEL, Florence or Sweet	Grown as annual	2 ft.	Rich in compost	Warm, sunny	After frost April to May
GARLIC	Hardy perennial	12–40 in.	Rich soil	Sunny, damp	—
HORSERADISH	Perennial	2 ft.	Rich; moist	Damp	Early sprin
HORSETAIL	Perennial	4–12 in.	Loamy; sandy	Waste grounds; dry	Not recom mended

‑ion	Distance for		Flowering	Season for use	Harvesting for drying	Parts to use
Planting	Rows	Plants				
oot ‑ivision ‑ring to ‑utumn	10–15 in.	10–15 in.	Flowers should be nipped off	May to September	When normal height reached	Leaves only
—	1 ft.	1 ft.	April to autumn, flowers to be nipped off	April to September	April to September, young leaves only and roots	Young leaves only and roots
—	20 in.	Thin to 9 in. if wanted for seed	July to August	6 weeks to 2 months after sowing. Seed head when 10–12 in.	Before flowering or beginning of flower bud	Leaves; seed heads partly in flower. Seeds
‑uttings in ‑utumn. ‑oot ‑ivision	—	—	June to July	Flowers: June to July. Berries: September to October	Flowers: June to July. Berries: autumn	Flower heads and berries
‑ivision of ‑ootstock; ‑pring	18 in.	18 in.	July to September	Leaves June to end October or dried. Seed heads mid-July onwards. Roots March to end April	June to end of October. Roots March to end of April	Leaves, seeds and roots
—	18 in.	9 in.	—	Earthed when size of egg; harvested 2 weeks later	Used as vegetable when ready	Swollen base of stalk
‑arch or ‑ctober	12 in.	8 in.	Flowers to be nipped off	All year— bulbs lifted when leaves dead	Before winter	Bulbs
‑pring and ‑utumn	1–2 ft.	1–2 ft.	—	9 months after planting	Dig up roots 9 months after planting	Roots
—	—	—	—	May onward but best in late summer	June and July; late summer	Green barren shoots

Herb	Perennial Biennial Annual	Height	Soil	Position	Pro. Sowing
HYSSOP	Evergreen hardy shrub	2–4 ft.	Light	Sunny Spring	¼ in. drill; spring
JUNIPER	Evergreen shrub	4–12 ft.	Limestone; chalky	Sunny	—
LADY'S MANTLE	Perennial	4–6 in.	Normal garden soil	Sunny	Spring
LEMON BALM	Perennial	2–3½ ft.	Fairly rich; warm; moist	Sunny sheltered	March to April
LEMON THYME (see THYME)	—	—	—	—	—
LEMON VER-BENA (see VERBENA)	—	—	—	—	—
LIME	Deciduous large trees	80–100 ft.	—	—	—
LOVAGE	Perennial	8 ft.	Any soil—rich, moist, preferable; well-composted, deeply dug	Damp	Spring or autumn
MARIGOLD	Annual	20 in.	Any soil—preferably loamy	Full sun	March and April; seed *in situ*
MARJORAM, Sweet	Grown as annual	8–10 in.	Medium rich	Warm and light spot	End of April and in May
MARJORAM, Pot	Perennial	2 ft.	Dry, light	Warm spot	April in drills
MARJORAM, Wild	Perennial	2 ft.	Chalky; gravelly	Dry and warm	April

tion	Distance for		Flowering	Season for use	Harvesting for drying	Parts to use
Planting	Rows	Plants				
pring and utumn	2 ft.	1 ft.	June and August	When flowering starts	Before flowers or with flowers. Second cut possible	Flower and tops
Male and emale trees	—	—	April to May	Autumn	Autumn	Berries only when blue/black from female trees only. Green shoots
Division n spring	2 ft.	9 in.	July	May to September	July	Whole herb
Division pring and utumn	2 ft.	1 ft.	August	June to October	June to September	Whole leaves for tea; rubbed for flavour
—	—	—	—	—	—	—
—	—	—	—	—	—	—
Autumn	—	—	June to July	Dried all year round	June to July	Flowers and bracts
Division pring and utumn	24 in.	24 in.	July to August	All summer; roots in spring and October	May to September; several cuts	Leaves and stalks for flavouring; as vegetable; roots; seeds and stalks for candying
—	18 in.–2 ft.	18 in.–2 ft.	June to November	Summer	While flowering	Petals for flavouring
—	10–12 in.	Thin to 6–10 in.	July to September	When knots break and after	When knots break. 2 cuts; last September to October	Leaves, buds flowers for flavouring
Division n spring or utumn	2 ft. drills 8–9 in.	1–2 ft.	,,	July to September	July to September	Leaves and flowers
—	Up to 20 in.	—	,,	,,	,,	,,

Herb	Perennial Biennial Annual	Height	Soil	Position	Pr	Sowing
MINT, Spearmint	Perennial	18 in.	Moist; rich	Partial shade		—
MINT, Bowles	,,	2–4 ft.	,,	,,		—
MINT, Apple	,,	12–18 in.	,,	,,		—
MINT, Curly	,,	2–2½ ft.	,,	,,		—
MINT, Eau-de-Cologne	,,	—	—	—		—
MINT, Pineapple	,,	,,	,,	,,		—
MINT, Peppermint (Black) and (White)	,,	18 in.	,,	,,		—
MINT, Water	,,	6–36 in.	,,	,,		—
MINT, Pennyroyal	—	—	—	—		—
MUGWORT	Perennial	2–4 ft.	Any soil	Often wild in waste places		—
NASTURTIUM	Annual climber or dwarf	Dwarf 12 in. Climber up to 6 ft.	Sandy, rich, wet for leaves Poor dry for flowers	Sunny		March to April
NETTLE, Stinging	Perennial	2–4 ft.	Rich in organic material	Everywhere		—
ONION GREEN	Hardy perennial	12 in.	Rich, well-drained soil	Sunny		April and September
PARSLEY, Curly	Biennial	6–8 in.	Rich; well-worked, moderately humid; fine tilth	Sunny or partial shade		Feb., May and July

| tion | Distance for | | Flowering | Season for use | Harvesting for drying | Parts to use |
Planting	Rows	Plants				
New shoots in spring or roots in autumn	1 ft. apart	6–9 in. apart	August	June to October; dried all year	Beginning of flowering while in bud to end of August. 2nd cut in September	Leaves rubbed for flavouring; whole for tea
,,	,,	,,	,,	,,	,,	Leaves for Mint Sauce
,,	—	—	,,	,,	,,	Leaves
,,	—	—	,,	,,	,,	,,
—	—	—	,,	,,	,,	,,
,,	—	—	—	,,	—	,,
,,	12 in. apart	6–12 in.	,,	—	1. cut first year. 2. later	Whole leaves for tea; rubbed for flavouring
—	—	—	,,	—	—	Leaves
—	—	—	,,	—	—	,,
Division	2 ft.	2 ft.	July to September	July to September	When buds developed before opening. Top shoot 5–6 in.	Buds only
—	2 ft.	1 ft.	From July onwards	All summer	Leaves before and after flowering	Leaves, flowers, seeds
—	—	—	—	Young shoots, best in spring, or all year	Spring	Young shoots only
Division in spring or autumn	1 ft.	1 ft.	Rarely—nip off	All year round	May to October	Green leaves
—	8–12 in.	6 in.	2nd year	All summer	Best summer and autumn	Green leaves

Herb	Perennial Biennial Annual	Height	Soil	Position	Pro Sowing
PARSLEY, Hamburg	,,	24 in.	Deeply worked	,,	March
ROSE GERANIUM	Perennial, not hardy	3 ft.	Light, sandy, well-composted	Warm; sheltered	—
ROSE HIP	Shrub	4–10 ft.	Clay soil	Sunny or partial shade	—
ROSE HIP, Sweet-briar	,,	,,	Clay or chalky	,,	—
ROSEMARY	Perennial, evergreen shrub	5 ft.	Light; sandy; dry; fairly chalky	Sheltered position; south aspect; best against wall	April
SAGE	Perennial	2 ft.	Light; dry; chalky	Sunny; dry	April
SALAD BURNET	Perennial	12–15 in.	Chalky	Sunny	April
SAVORY, Summer	Annual	12 in.	Rich; humid	Sunny	March to May
SAVORY, Winter	Perennial	6–16 in.	Poor; light; chalky; well-drained	Full sun	August to September
SOLIDAGO	Perennial	4–24 in.	Any garden soil	Sunny	—
SORREL	Perennial	2 ft.	Light; rich; moist	Sheltered; full sun or shade	March

| on Planting | Distance for | | Flowering | Season for use | Harvesting for drying | Parts to use |
	Rows	Plants				
in to n.	12–18 in.	,,	6 ins.	Dig roots when leaves die. Lift in October	Lift before flowering	Green leaves and vertical taproots
tumn	3 ft.	3 ft. for hedges	From June	Dried all year	From October after touched by frost	Fruit: Rose hips
,,	,,	,,	,,	,,	,,	,,
ttings in ugust	2 ft.	2 ft.	June to September	Summer. Dried all year	August	Leaves
ttings division May	6 in.– 3 ft.	1st 6 in. then 3 ft.	May to June	All year round	From 2nd year; any time up to August. After full flowering	Leaves for tea. Leaves and flowers for flavouring
vision, ttings in ay	2 ft.	2 ft.	No flowers from broad leaf sage. Narrow leaf sage flowers in July	June to October	1st cut June. 2nd cut August: broad leaf. 1 cut Oct.: narrow leaf	Whole leaves for tea; rubbed for flavouring
in to n.	12 in.	6 in.	June to August	All year round	When flower shoots appear	Leaves
vision tumn or ing	2 ft.	1 ft.	July to October	July to October; dried all year	During flowering	Whole of flowering herb
vision ing or umn	2 ft.	15 in.	May to July	Before flowering and later	After 4–5 leaves formed	Leaves
—	1 ft.	Thinned to 6 in.	July to August and October	Summer	2 cuts; August and October after beginning flowering	Whole herb
ttings in ing. vision rch	12–15 in.	12 in.	June to July	From May of 2nd year	Before flowering	Shoots and tips

Herb	Perennial Biennial Annual	Height	Soil	Position	Pr Sowing
SWEET CICELY	Perennial	3–5 ft.	Medium rich; well-drained	Partial shade, full sun if in moist soil	March to April self-sows freely
TARRAGON, French	Perennial	3 ft.	Well-drained; light and fairly poor	Dry and sunny	—
TARRAGON, Russian	,,	5 ft.	,,	,,	—
THYME, Garden	Perennial evergreen bush	4–12 in.	Chalky; dry; well-drained	Dry; sunny	Spring
THYME, Lemon	,,	12 in.	,,	,,	,,
VALERIAN	Perennial	3–5 ft.	Medium to damp	Dry and damp. Wild in sunny soil	Self-germinati
VERBASCUM	Biennial	4 ft. (up to 8 ft.)	Any; best chalky, well-drained	Sunny, sheltered	August
VERBENA, Vervain	Hardy perennial	1–2 ft.	Well-drained; rich	Sunny	Early spr
VERBENA, Lemon	Perennial (Tender)	2 ft.	Poor; some compost	Under glass most of year	—
WOODRUFF	Perennial	6–12 in.	Near to woodland and heath soil	Grows in shady beechwoods under trees	Self-sowing

tion	Distance for		Flowering	Season for use	Harvesting for drying	Parts to use
Planting	Rows	Plants				
Division of roots in spring and autumn	2 ft.	2 ft.	In May	February to November	Before flowering or after flowers pinched off	Leaves
Division spring and autumn	2 ft.	2 ft.	July	June to September	June to October, several cuttings	Leaves
,,	3 ft.	3 ft.	,,	,,	,,	,,
Division or cuttings April to May. Side shoots layered in March or April	2 ft.	12 in.	June	From June onwards	Before and during flowering period	Leaves and flowers
,,	,,	,,	July	June to September and October	2nd year; 2 cuts June to August	Leaves and flowers
Division of root	2–3 ft.	1–2 ft.	June to August	All year-dry roots	Late autumn second year	Roots (dried)
Transplant in October	2 ft.	20–24 in.	2nd year June to August	June to August; all year dried	June to August	Flowers dried for tea
May	2 ft.	1 ft.	July	Summer	June before flowers open also flowering herb	Herb with side branches and leaves
Division in spring	Mostly in pots	—	August	,,	August onwards	All parts of herb
Rooted pieces; creeping rootstock in spring	—	8 in.	April to June	Spring and later	Spring and after flowering	Leaves and flower on stems

CHART FOR USING HERBS

The uses of individual herbs have been discussed with each individual herb in this book; a general view of the wide use to which herbs can be put is what is offered here. When the herbs in this book are grown in one's own garden, at least there should be no complaints that they cannot be fully used! For practical reasons the herbs are divided in this chart according to where they are most likely to be used:

1 *In the Kitchen:*

Though no doubt cookery has probably the widest use for herbs, still it is only one part of their enormous usefulness.

2 *At the Table:*

The second method of using herbs is the way in which they can be added not to the cooking, but at the table for individual flavouring and seasoning. These last-minute additions some people like to do at the table, because the concoction of an interesting salad dressing or a bouquet of herbs, made at the table usually adds to the interest in the food and to the reputation of the hostess.

3 *In the Living-room*

There we take all the herbs which help to entertain our friends, by offering them aperitifs before or digestifs after a meal, after-dinner drinks, coffee substitutes, cordials, wine and fruit cups, drinks with snacks, biscuits and eventually night-caps. All the various herb liqueurs were—at one time—only used as digestives, similar to the herb teas suggested here. To think that the monks used 130 herbs to make Chartreuse, the famous liqueur which is still made today and is one of the best of all liqueurs, though drunk for pleasure.

4 *In the Bathroom:*

When looking at the medicinal and cosmetic uses we retire to the bathroom where we examine the herbs in our medicine chest suggested by old and modern experience of many countries. The trouble needed to prepare them is small compared to their harmlessness and usefulness if properly applied, Hardly more trouble than just walking to the nearest chemist's shop, buying preparations about which little is known.

Chart for Using Herbs

Herb	In the Kitchen	At the Table	In the Living-room	In the Bathroom
ANGELICA	Candied leaf stalks used for decorating cakes and pastry. Tips and flower stalks used for flavouring and making jams, and roots and stems cooked with rhubarb, or any other tart fruit to remove tartness and add a delicate flavour		Leaves used in potpourri	Used as a bath addition for stimulating the skin. Used as blood cleansing, diuretic tea
BASIL	A noble herb, excellent when used sparingly with tomatoes, also with mushrooms, in egg, cheese and fish dishes. Imparts delicious flavour to insipid vegetables, spaghetti and rice.	Can be sprinkled on tomato sandwiches	The crushed leaves of basil have been used as a snuff for people who suffer from headaches. Leaves allowed to permeate wine, make a digestive tonic after meals	Mixed with salad oil is good for constipation
BAY LEAF	Often used as part of *bouquet garni*; used in marinades to flavour and tenderize meat; improves flavour of court bouillon, vegetables, smoked tongue and ham (when cooking them) and many other dishes		Crushed leaves used in potpourri	
BERGAMOT			Leaves can be added to wine or cocktails, or to India Tea; a soothing tea as a nightcap before retiring; induces sleep	A real sleep-inducing and relaxing tea before going to bed
BORAGE	Can be used for cooking with cabbage, in soups such as pea and bean and also in stews	Flowers, as well as leaves, add to flavour and beauty of salads. Leaves also sprinkled on vegetables or potato salads	Exhilarating when added to claret cups and Pimms No. 1; when mixed with lemon or sugar in wine and water it makes a lovely drink; the candied flowers are a sweet and colourful decoration	
CELERY LEAVES CELERIAC LEAVES	Increase the strength of soups, sauces, stews and stuffings; they are really the bi-product of two vegetables: celery and celeriac, grown in the garden	Can be added last to soups, stews and clear broth; can be added at the table		

235

Herb	In the Kitchen	At the Table	In the Living-room	In the Bathroom
CHAMOMILE FLOWERS			One or two cups per day are drunk in France, dealing with digestive disturbances or taken after a heavy meal to help settle it down. Flowers used in potpourri	Valued in facial steams as it improves the skin, and for heavy colds and digestive upsets. As a tea against heavy colds. As an eye-bath in the case of inflamed eyelids. As a hair rinse for blonde hair; for nose rinses, for mouthwashes, for sore mouths after tooth extraction; for compresses. Little bags of chamomile flowers can be placed externally on painful places to reduce pain in the case of toothache or earache. An infusion can be used for enemas
CHERVIL	So delicate; it can and needs to be used generously in most dishes. Best of all in Chervil Soup or Sauce. Important part of Green Spring Sauce and Soup	Enhances salads of any kind; also can be used sprinkled over soups and in herb butter		
CHIVES	Can be used for any dish where mild onion flavour is required, particularly in broth, with omelettes and cream cheese	Can be sprinkled on salads, soups, broth and over hors-d'œuvres		
DANDELION	Can be sprinkled over food; made into purée or added to spinach purée; used for health reasons	Should be sprinkled on a salad or eaten on sandwiches and sprinkled over food in general	The root can be made into coffee or the leaves used to make a stout, often mixed with burdock. A wine made from leaves and flowers is good for the digestion after meals	
DILL	Pungent, aromatic, slightly sweet; accompanies fish and flavours bland vegetables; is used in pickling cucumbers and for cucumber sauce	Sprinkled on cucumber sandwiches, as well as on salads		Has blood cleansing and diuretic qualities; finely chopped and warmed it can be applied to bruises and painful joints

For DILL in the Bathroom: A tisane is good for hiccoughs or vomiting; against flatulence; baby's gripe water; seeds boiled in wine can be taken for insomnia

236

Herb	In the Kitchen	At the Table	In the Living-room	In the Bathroom
ELDER FLOWERS	Flowers make excellent fritters —a delicate sweet		Make a refreshing drink in summer, also Indian and China tea can be flavoured with them and they can be made into wine. Used in potpourri	As a tisane promotes perspiration in cases of colds and is sleep inducing. Elderflower water can be used as an eye or skin lotion; is good as a bath addition. Excellent for facial steam bath as it has cosmetic qualities. Berries have a reputation for cleansing the blood and their juice is good for chills and for people who suffer from sciatica
FENNEL	Sweeter than dill, delicious in all fish dishes when used wisely; can also be added to egg dishes, creamed chicken	Added to salad dressing for beetroot and carrot salads	Gives a fresh flavour to vegetable cocktails and freshly expressed vegetable juices; the seeds are used in cordials and liqueurs	Made into a tisane for digestive upsets; is good for slimming purposes. It is also made into a facial pack as it is good against wrinkles. Eye-baths and compresses
GARLIC	Cooking utensils in which 'fondue' is cooked are rubbed with garlic. Pounded with salt it can be used to season rice, beans, soups, salads, vegetables and meat dishes. The famous Italian Aioli Sauce it is a special dish for those who do not mind a lot of garlic. For others just rubbing the salad bowl may be quite enough. Flavours vegetable and meat casseroles and many other dishes			
HORSE-RADISH	The hot and harsh, but delicious root, used in connection with apple and cream to go with fish, such as trout, carp or cod; together with other herbs makes an excellent filling for Avocado Pear. Goes well with boiled and roast beef, smoked meats	Finely grated or minced it is an excellent condiment and provides a 'dip' for fish and shell-fish		

Herb	In the Kitchen	At the Table	In the Living-room	In the Bathroom
HORSETAIL				As an infusion helps to stimulate the passing of water. It can be used for brittle nails, and healing wounds. Useful for strengthening and toning the skin because of its astringent and antiseptic qualities
HYSSOP	Goes well with fat fish, eel, game, kidney, lamb stew, soups, but even apricot or peach pie can have a little sprinkled over the fruit before covering it with a crust	Young leaves, finely chopped give the salad a minty flavour		
JUNIPER BERRIES	From a tree which grows well in the herb garden; can be used to flavour game, meat, stews, poultry, sauerkraut, pickles		Is added to fruit cocktails, e.g. made with cranberries; they can be flavoured with one or two leaves in the bottom of a serving dish	Chewed berries cleanse the blood, and the digestive organs; increase perspiration. As a diuretic helpful for gout and rheumatism. Good for liver and kidney conditions. In fact—a universal medicine chest. The branches and berries can be burned to prevent infection and sweeten the air in an invalid's room
LADY'S MANTLE				A tea important to all women, helpful during pregnancy, regulating monthly cycle and for easing the change. Also recommended for obesity and against diarrhoea. There are many more uses for this 'woman's best friend'
LEMON BALM	Flavours custards, jellies; is a substitute for grated lemon peel, if added to soups and stews with lamb and fish. Helps to reduce sugar in tart fruit together with sweet cicely	Sprinkled on melon, fruit juices salads and mayonnaise	Provides the famous Melissa tea, a refreshing drink to be taken in the evening for relaxing and improving sleep; also added to claret cups, wine cups, sherbet and milk shakes	As a morning drink this tisane has calming relaxing effects and yet is invigorating. Good for palpitations, nervous pains migraine or at the start of a headache. Washing in Melissa tea is good for all skin conditions

Herb	In the Kitchen	At the Table	In the Living-room	In the Bathroom
LIME			Flowers are drunk as a tea sweetened with honey after meals (Tilleul). Used in pot-pourri	Tea, if taken hot last thing at night, promotes perspiration in cases of colds and is good against skin troubles
LOVAGE	Excellent in soups, casseroles and stocks; in fact for all dishes which need strength; it replaces meat stock; use economically. An important flavouring for vegetarians for its yeast-like flavour	Sprinkled on salads, used in cheese biscuits flavoured with lovage	A cordial, used to be made of seeds as a comforting and warming drink; was at one time sold in pubs	For a deodorant: taken as a tea, and an infusion, used as a bath addition. Tea also stimulates milk production in nursing mothers
MARIGOLD	Replaces saffron, and added to fish, venison, chicken broth and particularly rice (instead of saffron rice) provides not only colour but flavour; marigold buns and bread baked with milk, in which petals are soaked	Added last to salads to provide flavour and decoration		Used externally in oils and ointments in the treatment of old wounds and scars and other skin disturbances; also for tired feet
MARJORAM	A meat herb—especially good with sausages, but goes well with all tomato and mushroom dishes, with pulses and potatoes	Is used in salads with cream cheese or sprinkled over sauces	Also used as snuff	In oil is used for sprains and bruises; an infusion is used for gargling and for drinking as a help against hay-fever
MINTS	Are used in meat cookery for Mint Sauce, mint fritters, omelettes and peppermint in all kinds of sweets		Mint or Peppermint tea after meals is good for the digestion and as a pick-me-up when tired, especially Peppermint tea is a favourite in many countries. Peppermint milk as a nightcap; if added to ordinary tea it makes a stimulating drink. Spearmint is used in the famous Mint Julep, also in fruit and wine punches; hot Mint tea also in chocolate and iced drinks. Eau-de-Cologne Mint, dried leaves are used for pot-pourri	Cool Peppermint tea is a good mouthwash for an inflamed or sore mouth. It also cures offensive breath. Leaves can be taken into the bath for strengthening; used in tooth-paste; rubbed on the forehead. Good for headaches, also neuralgic pains. An infusion of mint is helpful for skin troubles and for bathing the face

Herb	In the Kitchen	At the Table	In the Living-room	In the Bathroom
MUGWORT	Once added to beer, it is now a flavouring and seasoning for meat, fish, goose, duck and eel and has a digestive effect, apart from its flavouring	An addition to a raw vegetable salad; recommended as a seasoning for diabetics		Helpful for chronic diarrhoea
NASTURTIUM		Can be added cautiously to cream cheese at the last minute, but cheese becomes bitter if allowed to stand. As it is an antibiotic it is suggested to be eaten on sandwiches and salads; gives a peppery flavour to all dishes where this is liked		
NETTLE	Young shoots can be used in the same way as dandelion, mixed with lettuce spinach or sorrel; or used as a vegetable in spring. Used for health reasons	Sprinkled over food for health reasons		
ONION GREEN	Where stronger onion flavour is wanted; with most vegetable dishes and stews			
PARSLEY	Can be used with practically any dish and is also used as a garnish to tempt the eater	The roots can be used grated for raw salad and the leaves sprinkled over salads		Parsley water is supposed to remove freckles and moles. Parsley tea is a remedy for rheumatism and also an anti-flatulent, diuretic herb
ROSE HIPS	Apart from making tea, excellent as sweet purée or sauce		Both pods and pips are made into a daily tea of great value (vitamin C)	Tea helpful for kidney and bladder
ROSE GERANIUM	Scented fresh or dried leaves give a delicate rose flavour to custards, baked fruits, ice-creams, jams, jellies or cakes	A scented leaf to be placed in the bottom of finger bowls	Leaves can be added to China tea, their fragrance makes fruit cups or lemonade attractive; used for garnishing wine cups. Tea of the leaves can also be blended with mint and served hot or cold. Leaves used in potpourri	

Chart for Using Herbs

Herb	In the Kitchen	At the Table	In the Living-room	In the Bathroom
ROSEMARY	Strong but subtle flavour; add lightly to meat, poultry, egg and vegetable dishes as well as to turtle soup, strong game and many fish dishes	Flavours, jams, jellies, vinegars and herb honeys, but is also added to shortbread biscuits	Can be added to wine, cider and claret cup, to fruit cups as a refreshing digestive. Added to potpourri	Externally rosemary stimulates the circulation. It can also be made into rosemary wine, which stimulates the heart. As a tea acts on a weak digestion and is good for flatulence and neuralgic pains. Oil of rosemary is good for bruises, gout; rosemary water for washing and improving the skin. An infusion as a hair rinse, especially for dark hair, improves the growth of hair
SAGE	Used in rich meats, and fish dishes, with roasts and in cheese making, in herb butter and pickled cucumbers	Can be added to cream cheese	Is used in wine cups, cocktails and summer fruit drinks and with clear apple juice	Tea is generally refreshing; also used for gargling for sore throats, and an infusion is used in steam baths
SALAD BURNET	The best winter stand-by with its luscious green; can be used for herb soups and sauces, salad dressing, mayonnaise, in fact everywhere where its cucumber flavour and its green are welcome; should be added at the start of cooking		Brings a cucumber taste to claret, wine cups and cocktails and decorates iced drinks, even during winter	
SAVORY, Summer	The 'Bean Herb', a traditional flavourer of all beans, but also flavours stuffings, pork pies, sausages and is an excellent substitute for pepper	Is added to all uncooked salads, helpful to those on a raw food diet and as pepper substitute		
SAVORY, Winter	Much stronger than summer savory; should be used most carefully for similar foods			
SOLIDAGO				Can be used for inflammation of bladder and kidney and dropsy; is mildly diuretic

241

Herb	In the Kitchen	At the Table	In the Living-room	In the Bathroom
SORREL, French	Use in moderation with spinach and lettuce, improves these green vegetables, particularly the special Sorrel Soup which the French adore and which, mixed with cooked lettuce, is an excellent dish	Can be added in small quantities to salads		
SWEET CICELY	Added to tart fruit, as it reduces the sugar needed; used in bouquets for salads and soups and added to root vegetables and cabbage when cooking	Added to sugared strawberries and other fruit as a topping on whipped cream. It is also sprinkled on soups, salads and in salad dressing	Used in summer in fruit and vegetable juices, alcoholic drinks and in liqueurs	Has been used as a perfume
TARRAGON	Sweet, yet slightly bitter; delicious and aromatic when used judiciously in sauces, for delicate vegetables, in marinades and stuffings, for famous Bearrmaise and Hollandaise Sauce, for fish and poultry, lobster and shellfish; Avocado pear filling	Added to melted butter for a sauce or sprinkled over salads, steaks, fish, asparagus and added to salad dressing	Leaves used in potpourri	
THYME	Twin to marjoram, used with sausages, mutton and pork, eels and all shell-fish; gives a delicous flavour to cottage and cream cheese; use with care	Can be sprinkled over raw salads in moderation because it is fairly strong	Used in Benedictine liqueur	Can be used as aromatic baths. Tea is used as a sedative; useful for bronchitis; also a deodorant and a disinfectant; used as a gargle
THYME, Lemon	Can be used in stews with rich meat and poultry		Used in potpourri	
VALERIAN			Not everyone's cup of tea; not suitable for living-room; strong smell	The tea, taken one hour before retiring, promotes sleep better than any other herb; has a general soothing effect on the nervous system in the case of strain; is a tranquilizer and sleeping draught in one
VERBASCUM FLOWERS			Used in potpourri for colour; if well dried only	Used for cases of persistent coughs and bronchial colds, particularly during winter; is a great help

Chart for Using Herbs

Herbs	In the Kitchen	At the Table	In the Living-room	In the Bathroom
VERBENA, Vervain				Is used as a sedative tea; good for nervous exhaustion and indigestion
VERBENA, Lemon	If cooked with jellies and added to sauces for fish or veal is most refreshing	Can be added to salads and a leaf can be put in the bottom of a finger-bowl, as suggested for rose geranium	Leaves used for potpourri. Is drunk as a fragrant tea and served hot or iced	
WOODRUFF			Exhilarating and scented; flavours wine cups made from hock, can be added to apple juice, to cider cups, to wine and fruit cups made with peaches or strawberries. Exhilarating also as a tisane	Can also be used as a tea in the morning as it is stimulating and invigorating. Used as a moth repellent and to perfume cloths and linen

INDEX

Index

Index

Index

Index

Index

Soothing (demulcent): red bergamot tea, 62; chamomile, 70;
valerian, 212; ~ a cough, verbascum, 212

Soporific: dill, 90; lime flowers, 124

Sorrel (French sorrel): 195–6; for
window-boxes, 40; growing
chart, 230; chart for using, 242

Spasms: allaying ~, lime flowers,
124

Spices: 22; in potpourri, 25

Stakes: for window-boxes, 40

Stems: in drying, 46

Stimulating: ~ appetite, bay leaves,
61; chives, 79; dill, 90; fennel,
99; horseradish, 109; juniper
berries, 114; sweet cicely, 197;
thyme, 206; ~ digestion, garlic, 108; parsley, 162; horseradish, 109; ~ bile, dandelion,
88; ~ glandular system, elderflower tea, 97; ~ the heart,
lemon balm, 119; ~ mind and
spirit, borage, 63; ~ pancreas,
dandelion, 88; ~ kidneys, juniper berries, 114; lovage, 127;
~ perspiration, mint and peppermint, 145; vervain, 215;
borage, 64; chamomile tea, 72;
chervil juice, 73; elderflower
tea, 97, 98; juniper berries, 114,
116; lime flowers, 125, 126;
woodruff, 218; ~ growth of
hair, rosemary, 177; ~ properties, wild marjoram, 134; ~
drink, peppermint tea, 154

Storing herbs, 48–9

Sugar: ~ and herbs, 22, 23; ~ and
sweet cicely, 22, 199

Sweetbriar (see rose hips), 173–6

Sweet cicely: 197–200; ~ and sugar,
22, 199; hibernation, 33; ~
with rhubarb, 54; ~ recipe,
199; growing chart, 232; chart
for using, 242

Tarragon: 200–5; in a herb garden,
28; in winter, 34, 202; in pots,
38, 202, 203; indoor harvesting, 40, 202; in frozen bouquets, 50; ~ recipe, 205; growing chart, 232; chart for using,
242

Tea(s): see herb teas; tea of chamomile and peppermint for vomiting, 72

Teeth: ~ sugar, 23

Temperature: for drying herbs, 44–8

Temperatures and fevers: ~ reducing, borage, 64; lime flowers,
124

Thermometer: in drying, 47

Thyme and lemon thyme: 205–9;
thyme and pepper and salt, 22;
in potpourri, 25; in a herb garden, 27, 28; in winter, 34, 207;
as pot plant, 38, 207; in frozen
bouquets, 50; in bread stuffing,
86; ~ recipe, 209; growing
chart, 232; chart for using, 242

Thymus vulgaris, thyme, 205

Thymus citriodorus, lemon thyme,
205

Tilia europaea, common lime, 124

Tilia cordata, small leaved lime, 124

Tilia platyphyllos, large leaved lime,
124

Tilleul (see lime flower tea), 24,
125–6

Tisane(s) (see herb teas)

Tissue: astringent effect on ~,
horsetail, 111

Tomatoes: with basil, 17; ~ recipe,
60

Tonic: never a ~, chamomile, 70;
elderflowers, 99; salad burnet,
188; nerve ~, vervain, 215;
woodruff tea, 218

Tooth: ~ ache, chamomile, 72; ~
paste, oil of thyme, 206

Transplanting: herbs to indoors, 38

Tropaeolum majus and *minus*, nasturtium, 158

Ulcers, 22

Urtica dioica, nettle, 160

Index